MEXICO
AND THE OLD SOUTHWEST

KENNIKAT PRESS

NATIONAL UNIVERSITY PUBLICATIONS

SERIES IN AMERICAN STUDIES

Under the General Editorial Supervision of
JAMES P. SHENTON
Professor of History, Columbia University

HALDEEN BRADDY

MEXICO AND THE
OLD SOUTHWEST

PEOPLE • PALAVER • PLACES

NATIONAL UNIVERSITY PUBLICATIONS
KENNIKAT PRESS
Port Washington, N.Y. // London

To

Tom Mahoney

Richard O'Connor

Dale Walker

Acknowledgments

Mexico and the Old Southwest, a miscellany of folktale and myth, represents a selection of my published papers assembled over a period of thirty-five years in the U. S. A.-Mexico Southwest. A considerable number of other long or brief pieces have been omitted, as have any excerpts from related book-length studies, which are either now available or being made again available soon.

These longer works comprise *Cock of the Walk, Legend of Pancho Villa* (1955; reissued by Kennikat Press, Inc., 1970); *Pancho Villa at Columbus (Southwestern Studies,* III (1965), 3-43; Texas Western Press, El Paso, Texas); *Pershing's Mission in Mexico* (El Paso, Texas Western Press, 1966); and *Pancho Villa Rides Again* (El Paso, Texas, Paisano Press, 1967).

Acknowledgment for permission to reprint the present selections may be here gratefully expressed to the periodicals which first issued them. These media are indicated by short or standard abbreviations like those in *PMLA (Publications of the Modern Language Association).*

PEOPLE—1. *Singers and Storytellers* (Texas Folklore Society, No. XXX (1961), pp. 98-106.—2. *SFQ,* XXVI (1962), 107-21.—3.*WF,* XI (1952), 93-99.—4. *Western Review,* I (Spring, 1964), 50-53.—5. *Texas Parade,* XII (April, 1952), 43-44.—6. *American N & Q,* I (1941), 5-6.—7. *JAF,* LXIX (1956), 62.—8. *SFQ,* XXVII (1963), 180-95.—9. *New*

Mexico Folklore Record, XI (1963-64), 23-26.—10. *Western Review,* I (Fall, 1964), 37-41.

PALAVER—1. *Dialect Notes,* VI (1937), 617-21.—2. *AS,* XXXI (1956), 96-101.—3. *AS,* XV (1940), 220-22.—4. *AS,* XXX (1955), 84-90.—5. *AS,* XXXV (1960), 79-80.— 6. *SFQ,* XXV (1961), 167-77.—7. *SFQ,* XXVI (1960), 225-71.—8. *Texas Parade,* XIV (July, 1955), 40-41.

PLACES—1. *JAF,* LIV (1941), 60-67.—2. *NMQ,* XI (1941), 97-99.—3. *California Folklore Society,* IV (1945), 359-63.—4. *SFQ,* IV (1945), 187-89.—5. *JAF,* LIX (1946), 317-19.—6. *SFQ,* XVIII (1954), 222.—7. *SFQ,* XXV (1961), 101-12.—8. *Guns,* VII (January, 1962), 38-39, 60. —9. *Texas Parade,* XVI (January, 1956), 17-19.—10. *Montana, The Magazine of Western History,* XIX (Autumn, 1969), 32-45.

For writing materials, typing, and specialized services, particularly the part-time editorial survey of both Technical Assistants Richard-Félicien Escontrías and Fannalou Guggisberg as well as the part-time secretarial aid of Student Assistant Corrine Peschka, I am under obligation to the Institute of Organized Research of The University of Texas at El Paso. The dedication is to Messrs. Tom Mahoney, Richard O'Connor, and Dale Walker—three Irish-Americans who have encouraged me to continue my research in Mexican and Old Southwestern myths and folklore.

Haldeen Braddy

The University of Texas
at El Paso
El Paso, Texas 79999

Preface

Few labors compare in tediousness and seriousness with writing or compiling a book. To produce a meaningful, unified story out of research gleanings and oral testimonials (covering virtually a lifetime of inquiry) obviously necessitates rephrasings of key passages, rearrangements of pertinent materials, and cleaving above all else to one worthy purpose. The passage of time brings irrevocable changes. The institution referred to in this volume as Texas Western College became in 1967 The University of Texas at El Paso. Recent worthwhile improvements in the guise of central shopping centers, interstate highways, and international airports exhibit a rock-scarred terrain being transformed into a New Southwest. An equally revolutionary upswing has occurred in Mexico. The conventionalized portrait of the average Mexican depicts a peon in cheap sandals, in a white cotton coat and trousers, and a big straw sombrero, who simply does not exist today. That shadowy figure of the past has been replaced in a modern *Republica* by the skilled worker, the trained mechanic, and the educated office clerk.

Mexico and the Old Southwest offers an answer to "hate books." It treats both Southwesterner and Mexican impartially; it rejects odious comparisons damaging to either the Anglo-American or the Latin-American. Beautification of the region does not involve racism or the exclusion of one people or another because of creed or color. All these prejudices and superstitions belong to yesterday; in this book they never count as among the vanished glories. Early in my researches into vice and narcotics I caught a point of view from one of my most brilliant students, namely the late Reuben Salazar, from Los Angeles. In the fifties

Mr. Salazar, who visited my home, convinced me from his wide experiences that every wickedness in Mexico had a counterpart on the American side of the Rio Grande. Reuben Salazar, a peerless news detective, spoke the tongue of truth: vice is no respecter of national boundaries.

Had space afforded, I might have expanded my account of the Mexican Revolution. Among informants who spoke to me knowingly on that tragedy, I here may name Rodolpho Benavides (Juarez), Ing. Horacio Fernandez (Parral), Ira Lerner (Mexico City), Edgar Cohen Penick (Durango), and Ford Rackley (El Paso). For the reader interested in a longer and definitive historical discussion, I recommend a recent study by a Londoner friend of mine; that is, Mr. Ronald Atkin's *Revolution! Mexico 1910-20* (New York, 1970), pp. 354. It would have pleased me to say more of Ambrose Bierce except for the fact that I regard the subject as already having been handled authoritatively by Richard O'Connor in his biography of Bierce (1967) Other American authors whose writings on Mexico I have consulted include Arthur L. Campa, Tom Mahoney, Philip Dorrough Ortego, Ramon Villalobos, and Dale Walker. The fascinating miracles of Santa Teresa, an Indian maiden reared in Arizona by the Yaquis, will soon be told by Professor Howard McCord, of Washington State University, Pullman. He shortly plans to return to his native Southwest to investigate the marvels surrounding Teresa, the Yaqui Jeanne d'Arc. Exploits of *perdidas* (the lost ones) in border brothels comprise another activity which I have rather neglected. But a recent paper by Dr. Lurline Coltharp, "Invitation to the Dance: Spanish in the El Paso Underworld", centers on prostitution at the Pass of the North and also contains a bibliography pertinent to that subject (Glenn G. Gilbert (ed.), *Texas Studies in Bilingualism* (Berlin, 1970), pp. 7-17).

To be honest, my book touches on several topics but omits others. I submit no excuse for this; I hardly think an excuse is called for. Let one point, however, be made. The expansive geographical region which forms the setting of *Mexico and the Old Southwest* is of course roomy enough for everybody—*gabacho* and saint, *chicano* and sinner, *tinto y blanco*. As a land abounding in legend, this frontier country indubitably will continue to draw scholars down Borderland way to explore a culture rich and multifarious.

Contents

MEXICO
AND THE OLD SOUTHWEST

Introduction

Shortly after graduating from high school in Commerce, Texas, I made a trip with my father to the Western part of the state. There, at an impressionable age, I first heard of the exploits of Pecos Bill, on whom years later I wrote an article. Stories and legends of the Old Southwest thus fired my imagination as long ago as 1925. My initial interest in Mexico came in 1929, when I completed a Master's thesis on Ambrose Bierce at The University of Texas at Austin. Bierce, a Californian writer and journalist, disappeared about 1915 and evidently died soon afterward somewhere in the Mexican Republic, possibly perishing at the hands of the noted revolutionary Francisco (Pancho) Villa, or a Villista sympathizer. I have never ceased looking for traces of Don Ambrosio Bierce, though so far I have been unable to unearth the obscure circumstances of his death.

In 1935 I moved from New York, where I had been teaching, to West Texas, settling briefly in Alpine. That area bears a sobriquet, the Big Bend. Before the admission of Alaska as a state, Alpine prided itself on being the biggest city in the biggest county in the biggest state in the U. S. A.

The Big Bend Country and its stalwart residents remain today frontier earth and frontier people. It is one of the few places where the Old Southwest lives on: cowboy lore and lingo still serve those wide-open spaces as a rich source of oral literature yet largely unexplored. On the southern borders of this region, across the Rio Grande, one may enter Mexico and go into

3

either Chihuahua state or Coahuila state. In those times I often motored down to Ojinaga, Chihuahua, to see the *vaqueros* and *rancheros* and to hear of the epic deeds of Don Pancho and his Villistas. My first sojourn in Alpine, "Out Where the West Is," lasted only a year (1935-36); but, after returning to New York, I could never get the tempo of that Texas frontier out of my blood. I therefore went back to Alpine in 1939 for a short stay. Now I continue irregularly to visit the area. Several of my writings on cowboy diction, lost mines, southwestern myths, and witches' spells as well as my yarns about Pecos Bill, Ambrose Bierce, and Pancho Villa resulted directly from my experiences in the Big Bend.

Folklore has always been more or less a hobby with me. I never formally studied the subject in an academic institution for as much as a day in my life; I did, however, teach a course in Southwestern Literature at the University of New Mexico, Albuquerque, in the summer of 1949. At learned gatherings of three prestigious societies, namely the American, New Mexico, and Texas Folklore Societies, I met in some twenty years most of the eminent folklorists of my generation, scholars like J. Frank Dobie, Richard Dorson, Archer Taylor, and Stith Thompson. I also taught in Texas or New Mexico with such equal celebrities as Americo Paredes, T. M. Pearce, C. L. Sonnichsen, and John O. West. I hope a little of their brilliance rubbed off on me; at any rate, they paid me the high compliment of accepting me as one of their own brand and saw fit more than once to appoint me to significant offices governing the procedures of their associations. During my terms of office I saw all three of these learned societies hold their annual conventions at the Pass of the North.

Recently, so many professors over the land have written me about my publications that I decided to compose this volume, *Mexico and the Old Southwest*. May it prove useful to the large body of readers now delving into frontier culture and to the numerous institutions today offering courses in folklore and Latin-American letters or history.

For the past twenty-four years I have lived in El Paso, Texas —at the Pass of the North. Here and in neighboring Mexico and New Mexico I have found practically every form of excitement that a writer could dream of or desire. Whatever I may have missed locally, I surely must have encountered in my repeated junkets to all the major cities in the Republic of Mexico. I have often been in the homes of Luz Corral de Villa and Soledad Seañez de Villa; I have enjoyed friendships with agents of the Customs, Border Patrol, and Bureau of Narcotics; I have known personally the beautiful *toreras* of the Juarez bullring; I have even interviewed La Nacha through the courtesy of her attorney, the celebrated criminal lawyer, the Hon. Joe Rey, Sr.

El Paso-Juarez—"The International City"—comprised the deepest influence on my work. In El Paso I knew many of the automobile drivers, professionals and amateurs, who took part in the Pan-American Road Races on "The Road of Death." In El Paso I garnered information from all kinds of people—from lawmen and preachers, from outlaws and *pachucos,* from sociologists, welfare workers, taxi drivers, and private investigators. In Juarez I conferred with physicians and jail-keepers, with bartenders and musicians. In Juarez I had a look at police round-ups, cock pits, and gaming tables. In El Paso I had the rare privilege of conversing with American veterans of Pershing's campaign in Chihuahua in 1916; and in Juarez, with Villistas who accompanied Villa on his attack on Columbus, New Mexico, and during his escape from Pershing. In other words, I listened to both parties, the pursuers and the pursued. In 1969 during Project Intercept, an inspection procedure adopted to forestall the smuggling of narcotics and marijuana, I have waited hours in my car on the International Bridge before passing through the Customs. The investigations that I made from 1935 to 1970 enabled me to set down with some degree of realism the actual words and behavior of the human beings whom I observed.

Lore of the folk comes through oral transmission; therefore an investigator must learn to speak and hear, to look and listen, to remember and record. This is what *Mexico and the Old Southwest* endeavors to do.

I

PEOPLE

1

Champion Cockers and Feathered Duelists

Out in the Paso del Norte country you might cuss a man and get by with it, but you would not get by with cussing his chickens, not his big red rooster.

This healthy westerner, close to the earth and in love with living, takes more pride in his fighting cocks than he does in his livestock. Something hot and vigorous in his blood makes him admire a rowdy rooster. He enjoys calf roping, bullfighting, and horse racing, to be sure; but his chest really expands with pride when he keeps fighting chickens. Owning a flock of champion cocks advertises to his neighbors that he has wealth enough to partake of the sweets of life. The cocker is the prince among sporting men.

Cockers who gather on the Texas-Mexico Border to pit their battling roosters bring these entries from far and near. Many come from Old Mexico; others fly the airways to El Paso from New Mexico, Oklahoma, and distant points of Texas. Still others live at the Pass itself, native *Paseños* who claim that the sun and wind of Borderland breed the finest brand of fighting cocks alive today. In the dust-laden air of the gusty Southwest all of the roosters, no matter where they come from, soon develop gravel in their craws, so that championship contests always feature ferocious but evenly matched roosters. Their brilliant plumage, gleaming brightly as a choker of rubies in the ruff along the neck, derives, not from the soiling wind, but from rich feeding and the radiant sunshine of the southwestern winter. The cockers of El Paso walk with a strut. They believe in the prowess of their cocks and will back them with plenty of betting money.

For seven months, from early December to the Fourth of July, cockers live but for one purpose—to pit their cock on a Saturday night in a battle to the death. The cockfighting season opens at a period when outdoor sports have closed for the winter. Spectators throng to the heated indoor enclosures during the cold months of the year, surrounding the fighting pits in a circle of closely packed bodies. More imposing pits have circular rows of grandstand seats. At these places bettors walk the rim of the pits flourishing fists full of greenbacks. Spectators comprise both men and women. All of them are intent, serious, well-behaved. Drinking, with its attendant merrymaking, is forbidden, because it would be dangerous to stumble into the pit. Cursing and loud talking also come under the ban, for the crowd wants to hear the referee announce the owners of the chickens and the cockmasters who handle the roosters in the respite between rounds. The best way to spend a cold winter evening on the Border is to see a cockfight in a warmly heated arena.

Until recently, thrilling cockfights occurred in Juarez, Mexico. Now those days may be forever gone, because Juarez has banned the sport and closed its famous Pan-American Cocking Arena. On February 8, 1956, Ponciano Humberto Solorzano, a federal district attorney, went himself to the doors of this arena and personally shut them. He placed government seals on the locks. Then he ordered the manager, Abel Soto, arrested. This Mexican closure disappointed many cockers, as both American and Mexicans had frequented the Pan-American pit.

Immediately the enthusiasts turned their attention to the north banks of the Rio Grande, to the New Mexico pits adjoining El Paso. Here cockers brought their families, the women and children. Youngsters displayed zest for the sport, rallying the roosters with loud outcries. "Stick him in the heart!" some of them yelled, while others, more at home in Spanish, said, *"Picale en el corazon!"* All the time, the bettors kept shouting their odds in a pitch louder than the children. *"Ocho a cinco!"* (eight to five) announced one gamester, holding his money above his head as he walked about the ring. Somebody took that bet. Then the bettor became fevered with the gambling lust, for he saw his chicken beating its opponent. *"Dos a uno! Dos a uno!"* (two to one) he repeated frenziedly. This time there were no takers. The one-sided fight had suddenly ended. The bettor's chicken had sliced the throat of its adversary.

The appeal of novelty has nothing to do with the popularity of cockpitting. Border enthusiasts had their counterparts in the long ago. As old as civilized mankind, the sport entertained the Athenians of ancient Greece. Prince and populace attended the fights throughout that land. Soon enthusiasm for the sport spread in various directions, to Asia Minor, to the island of Sicily, and to cities like Alexandria, Delos, Rhodes, and Tanagra. The Romans at first pretended to despise this Greek diversion but in the end adopted it enthusiastically. They boosted cock-fights as morale builders for their far-roaming legions. As they roamed northward, they introduced the pastime to other European races. Rooster fighting thus attracted devotees in all the major countries of Europe—in England, Germany, the Low Countries, and Spain.

Cockfighting probably entered the British Isles with Caesar's invasions in 55 B.C. and 54 B.C. or when Britain became a province under Agricola in 80 A.D. At first only the conquerors indulged in the sport; later the natives adopted it along with other Roman pastimes. In the English language the word "cocking" (fighting) was current *circa* 1230. The anonymous author of *How Goode Wyfe* (about 1450), in the Ashmole MS of the British Museum, warned his readers to stay away from the fights. "Ne go thou not to no wrastlynge," he said, and added, "Ne yet to no coke fyghtynge." Other moral writers and church dignitaries railed against the sport. Nonetheless fights occurred annually in early Britain on the school grounds under the supervision of the Masters. At the finish, the dead birds went to the schoolmasters, as noted about 1565 by N. Carlisle: "The said Schoolmaster shall . . . have use and take the profits of all such cock-fights . . . as are commonly used in Schools." By 1684 Charles II had a Royal Cock-Pit at Windsor. Kings like Henry VIII, James I, and both Charles I and II had royal cockmasters who presided over the pits at Whitehall.

Cocking entered America with the early British settlers,

although New England always frowned on it. Today the United States has long had a prohibition against the sport, but it continues to be popular down South. Portable pits have been invented to avoid police raids. Since its founding by Richard Martin in 1824, the Society for the Prevention of Cruelty to Animals has vigorously opposed cockpitting. Its illegality has not stopped the cockers. Their vulgar colloquialism, "to beat cockfighting," has come to mean "to surpass everything else."

A fact not generally known in the United States is that cockfighting, not bullfighting, is the national sport of the Republic of Mexico. Mexican devotees include *peones* working on isolated ranches where staging a battle of roosters is much easier, much less expensive than fighting the bulls. Throughout South America cockfighting is a pastime of the people, not of the Latin aristocrats who have vigorously opposed it. In Argentina it gained serious criticism and recently was pronounced unlawful. Paraguay has prohibited it also. But the cocks have their partisans in spirited Puerto Rico, where it is the favorite pastime of poor and wealthy alike. Cuba also has recognized the strength of folk opinion by legalizing the sport and putting its operations within municipal approval.

At the Pass of the North, where two cultures meet, cockfighting has long been an established custom. At the end of the nineteenth century the notorious Juan Nepomuceno Cortina, King of Cattle Thieves, who had robbed Texas Border ranchers blind, was everywhere touted for being addicted to gambling and cockfighting. Probably no place in the world offers such a variety of breeding stocks and cockfighting skills as the twin cities of Juarez and El Paso. Here congregate the fowl-fanciers, *peones* from below the Rio Bravo, oilmen from Oklahoma, or foremen from the farspread King Ranch of South Texas. Here the gamblers and promoters flourish. Here the chicken trainers play and toil.

Al Pandelides, or "Lefty," is one of the really superior trainers on the Border. To put his cocks in fettle, he wraps miniature boxing gloves around their spurs, encouraging them in the art of sparring. So protected, the birds do not damage each other but get needed exercise in the fundamentals of cockfighting. The single largest factor in "Lefty's" success with the fowls derives from his own knowledge of the prize ring. For two years, 1954 and 1955, he held the title of middleweight boxing champion of Mexico.

There are plenty of Border men who "have taken the feather," or succumbed to the spell of cockpitting. Salvador Fierro, of Sahuarita, Arizona, has long been a devotee. So has Pablo Viramontes, of Las Cruces, New Mexico. So also has Chico Chavez, once the sheriff of Juarez, Mexico. Max Slade, of Tulsa, Oklahoma, has likewise won renown with his flocks. A frequent winner in Border derbies is M. L. Davis, of Alpine, Texas. Equally renowned cockers, who nomadically travel to mains from Arizona or Oklahoma to New Mexico, are Buckheister, Cunningham, Garcia, Kelly, O'Neale, Prichard, Royster, and Sanders. Their signatures on the pit blackboards become familiar names to cockfighting fans. George Simpson and "Bull" Adams, two of the wisest chicken men in El Paso, have trailed the sport for years. They travel to Oklahoma and various southern states to see champion roosters fight. Mr. Simpson and Mr. Adams know well the lingo of the pit and have bred many champion fighting fowls.

Beginning breeders choose their favorite color and select a family of chickens that will breed true. A farm or a few acres in the country will provide the necessary facilities. Fowls need a place to fly and to range; they also require access to water. Gamecocks ordinarily enter their first mains when between one and two years of age. Before they go into the pit, they undergo intensive training.

The most important experience of the young stag commences when his trainer moves him from his solitary cage and places him in a hennery. There he bosses his harem of hens, living and learning the meaning of his cockhood. Later, when the trainer takes him away from the pullets, the cockerel turns into a bird of Mars. Now he has a lust to fight, his lust arising from his strong sex drive. For no other creature displays as much jealousy as the gamecock. In Shakespeare's *As You Like It,* Rosalind says to Orlando, "I will be more jealous of thee than a Barbary cock-pigeon over his hen." Jealousy and an instinct to fight are synonymous with the gamecock.

Pedigreed roosters cost a lot of money. A fine untrained cockerel may bring as much as fifty dollars. A trained cock, one who has graduated from muffs to lethally-pointed steel gaffs or long and razor-edged Mexican slashers, will sell in the hundreds. Few "Rocky Marcianos" survive repeated settings in a cocking main, where a "K. O." means curtains for the losers. Even when victorious, fowls often lose parts of their combs and one of their eyes. Birds who have won five or more fights may sell for $15,000. Usually a proved champion retires from the pit in order to become a brood cock in a hennery. Cock fanciers eagerly gather eggs from a breeding cock's hens. Then the gatherers pay "high" to farmers to hatch these prize eggs for them.

Ordinarily a gamecock needs no encouragement to fight. The folklore of fowls, however, contains ignoble instances to the contrary. When a beaten gamebird decides to withdraw from the battle, he lifts his hackle, showing to the spectators the white feathers underlying his ruff. This act gave rise to the famous expression, "showing the white feather," which symbolizes cowardice. When a rooster refuses to continue the fight, his handler places him breast-to-breast with the other chicken. Sometimes, to stimulate him, handlers force pellets of marihuana down his throat. If he still will not fight, it is ruled that he has forfeited the contest, and therefore his adversary wins.

Professional cockfighting is not for the poor man or the piker. Tall tales never appear in the legends of its gamblers; the plain truth is enough. In the big mains, wagers sometimes go as high as $5,000 on a single match and $10,000 on the main itself. The novice had better keep his eyes open and stay alert. An experienced fan never pays his bet until the birds are carried out, because a cock supine on his back may give a vicious slash and kill his opponent, or a bird that looks like a winner may awkwardly slice his own throat when threshing his feet about.

Cockfighting has no rival for excitement. It can forge men's nerves into steel. The primal release of pent emotions at the moment of the kill, springing from dark recesses of mental frustration, floods the spectator with a needed sense of relief. And so Chanticleer must die. Man's fascination with the kill goes deep; his passion for it, steady and abiding, is the same as that of ancient man. The average sportsman, who relishes a fight by creatures born for that purpose, hates to see the cockfighting season end.

Before Juarez banned cockfighting, an outstanding battle occurred across the Rio Grande. This contest may serve to explain how an actual fight takes place. It caused a lot of excitement among Border gamblers. The bout pitted the inexperienced but much-heralded cock *El Negro* against the veteran rooster *El Blanco*. Scheduled at three o'clock on a Sunday afternoon, the bout was to determine who was champion of the Juarez chicken pens.

El Negro, proudly owned by Juan Carlos Lopez, tipped the scales at five and a half pounds, which is heavy for a fighting bird. His feathers gleamed black as jet. His whole appearance, from the bristling ruff about his neck to the belligerent stance of his strong gray feet, was so similar to that of a bird of carrion he might with full reason have borne some such name as "The Vulture."

El Blanco, the prize rooster of Seymour Miller's pen, had won many fights, enough to establish himself as a ruler of the roost and the chicken to defeat before any other could be named the champion. Spotlessly white in color, *El Blanco* weighed about the same as his opponent. He looked strong and durable but not so fierce of mien as *El Negro.*

Both roosters wore Mexican gaffs on their spurs—that is, double-edged, razor-like blades nearly three inches long. The two owners handled the birds soothingly, awaiting the signal from the cockmaster that would start the contest.

All at once came the word, "Pit!" The cockers immediately turned the birds loose at each other. Their beaks were keen as sabers; their combs stood erect. The small knives fixed on their spurs tore their flesh as cruelly as lances. Soon both cocks bled freely. Early in the test, gore accumulated on *El Blanco's* white feathers, turning them a vivid red. Between rounds, the owners patched up the wounds on their birds as best they could. Once or twice the men pursed their lips and blew hard on the feathers above the rumps of the birds. The hot, moist air served to stimulate the whole blood stream of the cock when the handlers blew strongly on this vital area. The men also applied their mouths to the injured necks of the birds, sometimes "creasing" them as they ran their lips up and down the necks. At other times they accepted the cock's head into their mouths to massage the wounded areas. After these procedures, both cocks re-entered the fray with quickened fervor, training their bright eyes fixedly on each other.

Midway of the fifth pitting, *El Blanco* tottered to the ground with a gaping hole in his head where the black one's spur had sunk. Groveling in the gravel, he shook spasmodically once or twice, and then he died. Digging his tired talons firmly in the hard earth, *El Negro* upreared himself, swelling his lungs with air, and let out a shaky clarion of victory. Exhausted as he was, he had grasped the fact that he was the winner and new champion.

2

Queens of the Bullring

In Borderland (El Paso, Texas, and Juarez, Mexico) the melding of two cultures, Anglo-American and Spanish, had produced at mid-century a new folk custom, lady bullfighting in the *Plaza de Toros*. There, amid isolated boos and general cheering, a modern figure stepped into an ancient pastime of facing a maddened bull—the slender figure of an adolescent girl.

Though oldsters complained that the new sport ridiculed traditional bullfighting, Texan fans in ever increasing numbers crossed into Mexico over the International Bridge. By taxi, in sports car or private automobile, and on foot, they went to see the latest Border spectacle, a brave girl *versus* a goring bull. A Mexican poet, Alberto de la Rosa, overcome with enthusiasm, wrote

> *Olé,* your feminine figure,
> *Olé,* of elegant distinction,
> Is magnified before the bull,
> And exclamations arise
> Of astonishment and admiration.

Joy Blair, a native of Burkburnett, Texas, aged twenty-two, illustrated the flaming degree to which the feminine fever for the bullring attained. Undeterred by her five-foot stature, Joy more than once pitted her strength in the blood and sand. But she never relinquished her amateur standing. Her explanation of the

17

newest Border sport, uninfluenced by professional considerations, had a ring of truth to it.

Women first became *toro*-minded, Joy said, in response to the great literary publicity given to male tauromachians. They read writers like Hemingway, but especially Barnaby Conrad's article on a renowned fighter, "The Death of Manolete," in *Reader's Digest* (April, 1951) and his exciting novel, *Matador* (1952). Another book which promoted the boom was *Lady Bullfighter* (1954), by the well-known *torera* Pat McCormick, who as a "cute blonde" co-ed once attended Texas Western College. She subsequently taught bullfighting to the late actor, James Dean. Pat at first had only successes with no setbacks or gorings, so that all the girls, tomboys and lady-like debutantes, too, wanted to become Pat McCormicks. The single most important early factor to create enthusiasm, however, was the popularity of the movie version of *The Brave Bulls* (1949), by the native El Pasoan, Tom Lea.

What attracted American girls, Texans in particular, to the sport was its pageantry. They liked, Joy said, the noise and the color, the sound of *"Olé! Olé!"* ringing in their ears, together with the bright flashing to and fro of the crimson cape before the angered bull. They liked the costumes which they wore, the clutching grip of embroidered pants tight on the soft roundness of their buttocks, the short buttoned coat around their frilled shirts, and especially the flat black hat, or *Córdoba,* atop their knotted-up hair. They liked the money, too. But they loved the notoriety, the newspaper editorials, the magazine articles, the encomiums over the radio, and their pictures full and live on television. Grandma helped to carve western culture from a frontier, mama voted women's benefits into the federal constitution, and daughter simply could not take the comforts of civilization. Modern girls wanted something different. They wanted it as rugged as possible; therefore something masculine. They had created a stir by wearing shorts, a furor by wearing jeans; had startled the sports world by appearing as wrestlers; and had raced motorcycles, automobiles, and airplanes in cross-country derbies. Still these activities lacked danger, wanted death and blood. Nothing would satisfy them except that ancient gory custom born in the Old World—bullfighting.

The International Club at Texas Western College, Joy continued, served to quicken the interest of young women who had not yet come directly in contact with Spanish culture in its unadulterated, raw state. They heard about bullfighting and decided to see it; they saw it and decided to try it. Enthusiasm for the sport spread everywhere. Professor Ray Past, of Texas Western, even lectured on the technique of the sport at the Unitarian Church.

Long before this, novices had sprung up all about the campus: Petite Pat Hayes, from out of town, became one of the first Texas Western co-eds to start training and to take lessons from the experts. Julie Williams, an El Paso girl, began at the same time. Hitherto Julie had distinguished herself at the college as a brilliant student and a talented poetess. Now this promising member of the intelligentsia changed into a burning enthusiast for bullfighting. Quite some time before Pat McCormick came upon the scene to capture fame and win for herself a satisfying income as a professional *torera,* Julie Williams commenced publicizing the subject until it became the campus rage. She sought to draw the backing of people far and near, trying once to interest *Mademoiselle,* the magazine for young ladies, in what was occurring in the border country. At that time nobody outside of El Paso appeared to share the enthusiasm of the Texas *toreras.* Chagrined, Julie threw away her book and pen, got married, and later moved to New York, to remove herself from a scene that quickly attracted the spotlight of international attention.

On the border Señor Alejandro del Hierro first taught the art of bullfighting to girls in Juarez, Mexico. Himself a masterly technician, Señor Hierro gave the girls excellent instruction, introducing them to a strict regimen of conduct and insisting on the significance of rigid training. He tried and succeeded in getting down to basic principles with them, teaching in recent years such celebrated *toreras* as Pat McCormick and Joy Marie Price. He gained his success by sticking to business, by keeping his eyes off the girls and on their performances, by drilling them in the fundamentals of passing the cape and thrusting the sword. For his reward, he had young *toreras* who sparkled with bounding health, who owned quick flashing eyes and vigorous alert minds—who epitomized poise. As one result of his success, other schools for girls began to open. Today the new profession of being *maestro* to tauromachians has moved far south of the Rio

Grande, down to the capital at Mexico City. There one recently opened near the central airport. It had a tiny ring but considerable atmosphere. Adjoining it stood a bullfight museum and a typically Mexican restaurant. Classes met on Mondays, Wednesdays, and Fridays; the *novillada* fights took place on Sundays at 5:30 p.m. (4:30 p.m., El Paso time). Señor Hierro started something when he first placed his female protegées in the arena of blood and sand.

What psychological factors lie behind women's love for the world's most dangerous game? Joy Blair, known under the *alias* Julia Burnett in the arena, said that it was not a love interest, though many people thought that perhaps the girls experienced some deep yearning for the *matadors,* the *picadors,* or the *toreros.* She stated further that the girls disliked being hurt, none of them deriving any kind of inner gratification from the masochistic experience of being knocked down in the dirt by a bull or being gored by one of his horns. Nor did the death motive figure as the paramount factor. Joy admitted that women have a secret knowledge of death, since nature has conditioned them to pass within its shadow when they bear children; but she pointed out that most ranch women early condition themselves to handling domestic animals, to throwing them down and branding them, and to seeing them die.

Joy had ready answers for a series of questions about the girls, pointing out that men and women fighters differed somewhat. She said that a girl group from Argentina who came to Juarez seemed particularly concerned about their toilette, about their powder and lipstick.

"What about a girl's hair?"

"None of them cut their hair to fight better. They are all concerned with their appearance, but the hair is nothing to worry about. You pin it back in a pony tail, put on your hat, and there you are," she said.

"How did you feel in the ring?"

"O.K. I was all right. When I got knocked down, I was not worried about being stepped on. I was worried about getting dirty. It is hot and dusty out there, and the dirt sticks to you."

"Do the girls get tired of the same costumes?"

"No, not much. Bette Ford came out in the Juarez ring in a

pink suit. It was breaking tradition, for standard colors are black, brown or gray. The *aficionados* didn't like it."

"But they like women bullfighters?"

"Yes, they do," Joy replied. "A long time ago old folks objected to women's polished fingernails, to wearing earrings, and to having bobbed hair; but they got used to it."

"Do male and female fighters wear the same suits?"

"No. Women avoid wearing heavy *traje de luces,* or the suit of lights, because it makes their hips look broad. They wear a short coat, or *traje de corto,* and tightly fitting Spanish pants."

"What do women dislike most about bullfighting?"

"Few of them like the kill," Joy said. "All of them get a definite physical thrill or sexual gratification out of it. They are drawn to death. Some of them draw artistic satisfaction from fighting, but these are few. I don't like the kill. I have never killed a bull. I can do all of it except kill the bull."

"What kind of sublimated experience do they have?"

"Maybe they all don't have it. I knew one nymphomaniac; her conscience drove her to punish herself, possibly to kill herself, because she had a guilt complex. Some are cold, cool, calculating. They want the money and have no emotional reactions. All of them have to be gymnastic. They are all tremendously body conscious."

"What can a woman gain from bullfighting?"

"It has more than fad value," Joy said. "At first girls are awkward; then they gain balance. The equipment weighs like lead and at first is only a burden. Later it seems one half as heavy. At first girls drag the equipment; later they wield it gracefully. Bullfighters make graceful dancers. The sport is good for the health and fine for the figure. A girl must avoid getting fat and stay mentally alert. It is exhilarating to be always in the open air and sunshine."

"Do girls mimic the men?"

"No, indeed. All of them must stay feminine; none of them become Lesbians; in fact, femininity is emphasized. A woman is perfect for the sport because she is so aware of her body. The proximity of a goring horn to tear their flesh makes them full of physical awareness."

"Do they have a sense of physical triumph?"

"Yes," Joy answered. "Their primitive sense of victory is as strong as a man's. But hardly any of them have a sense of blood lust. Most *toreras* regard a bloody, messy fight with disgust and nausea. Their reaction to a victory is one of sheer physical exhaustion."

"Do they compare themselves with men?"

"They do not equate themselves with men. A woman thinks she can do what a man can do but doesn't talk about it. A woman has as much courage as a man. Maybe she lusts more for audience approval. She knows that most of her audience is male and knows that she will get more attention than a masculine bullfighter. To tell the truth, the women usually get the little bulls. Some cheating and burlesquing in bullfighting is possible for the *torera;* but probably not as much as with the men. Men have longer training periods and learn to fake with more skill."

"Why do girls surpass *toreros* in popularity?"

"Feminine pulchritude," Joy said. "The male audience focuses its eyes on the girl, not on the animal."

Night club performers and strip-teasers, according to Joy Blair, have their fans all right, but not nearly so many as the *toreras.* Highlights in the bullfighting careers of two or three of them may show why they have stolen the spotlight from other female border entertainers.

The quest for adventure, the longing for diversion, emotions which animated the majority of the border dwellers, had brought a new sport to the Rio Grande. Border women were strong and capable enough to compete with the men. To understand these people, it was necessary to recognize that the women had physical stamina in abundance and that they had originality enough to make a fresh approach to a sport traditionally cultivated for men only.

A young lady who in 1951 played second bassoon with the far-famed El Paso Symphony sought, in 1954, to achieve individual renown as a *novillera.* Gifted Patricia Hayes, born in Des Moines, Iowa, calls San Angelo, Texas, her home town. Her brother, Bill C. Hayes, lives in El Paso, where after his school days he learned to fence from Francis A. Ehmann and later won one of Texas's fencing championships. Patricia, folks say, got her bull-ring sword talent from her brother Bill. A border beauty, Patricia made a big splash during the fifties in the Latin-American world of *la fiesta brava.*

Unlike most other Texas *toreras,* Patricia Hayes has fought, not in the border towns from Tijuana to Reynosa, but within the interior of Mexico itself, before native crowds. Her first *corrida* came, it is true, at Villa Acuña, a few miles below Del Rio, Texas, where she whacked an ear from her bull as a reward for her victory. Her main fights have occurred in the state of Jalisco, at the resort city of Acapulco, and in Irapuato, near Mexico City.

Her triumphant appearance in Jalisco brought her the praise of Raul Zubieta, director of the weekly bullfight magazine *Ecos.* At Acapulco she received repeated ovations for her strategy, winning plaudits for being the only girl bullfighter to set the *banderillas* (barbed hooks) into her animal's shoulders before making the kill. That smoldering Sunday afternoon in Acapulco the bull knocked her down in the dirt. Patricia arose, refused to be taken from the ring, and fought on with grim determination to win. A few weeks later she appeared at Acapulco once more. In this *corrida* the bull struck her down six times, gored her in the leg, and reduced her almost to hysterics. But again, as before, Patricia refused to yield in the terrifying battle for survival, staying on to conquer the bull—and cheat death. Yet later, at Irapuato, the blonde *Norteamericana* established herself in the minds of *aficionados* as the daring damsel who never cries quit.

In her first year as a *torera* Patricia Hayes made a dozen public fighting appearances and killed fifteen *toros*. South of the border, the Lone Star charmer enjoys a reputation for bravery second to no other *novillera,* having more than once reentered the ring with bandaged wounds to finish the contest and dispatch her animal. In the dance macabre of *toro y torera,* Patricia has gained the respect of such trainers as Carlos Suarez and Raul Muñoz, such performers as *matador* Luis Procuna and *novillera* Rosa Berta Martinez, and such *empressarios* as Don Neto and Dr. Alfonso Gaona.

Patricia Hayes became interested in facing *el toro* in much the same way as the other girls. She was mainly influenced by reading books and seeing movies. She read the novels of Barnaby Conrad, Ernest Hemingway, and Tom Lea. As for the movies, she said: "I saw *Blood and Sand* at least four times, and of course *The Brave Bulls* and *The Bullfighter and the Lady.*"

By 1960 Patricia had achieved worldwide renown, having visited the capitals of Europe, fought in North Africa, and displayed her talents in Spain and Portugal.

The perfect symbol of feminine pulchritude at Texas Western

College a few years ago was lissome, petite Joy Marie Price. Another blonde, Joy Marie came to the Pass from Odessa, Texas. Before she came to college, she had never seen a bullfight. She told a reporter from the *Herald-Post* that "A friend of mine took me to my first *corrida* and introduced me to some of the *novilleros*. I knew then that I wanted to fight bulls—as soon as I could."

Joy Marie Price became the third co-ed bullfighter on the border, Pat McCormick, of San Angelo, being the first and Joy Blair, of El Paso, the second. Although a major in journalism at Texas Western, literature played no major role in her decision to enter the arena. The determining factor with her, as with many subsequent novices, was the scene of combat itself. Her favorable reaction to the spectacle of blood, sweat, and bulls bellowing in agony looms remarkable in view of her stature and daintiness.

About one-tenth the size of her four-footed opponents, the tiny *torera* (five feet, five inches tall) weighs only ninety-seven pounds, whereas most bulls opposing women load the scales at from 600 to 800 pounds. Blue-eyed, yellow-headed Joy Marie Price in 1955 owned the distinction in bullfighting annals of being the *novillera* lightest of weight. They breed them bold way out West! Joy Marie yields a weight advantage to her competitors, but none of them outmatch her in ambition, determination, or raw courage. Seeing only her attractive face and not her fighting heart, one might hold that she belonged, not to the bullring, but to her former college dormitory organization, the Bell Hall Belles.

Joy Marie took bullfighting lessons from the best trainers on the border. Famous Alejandro del Hierro, the first schoolmaster to Texas *toreras,* initiated her into bullfighting society. Señor José Antonio Luna, a *novillero,* became her second teacher. When last heard of, she was still making an occasional ring appearance and still taking lessons from experienced tutors. According to reports, the name of her third manager was Jimmy Corbett, of Chicago. Her newest manager is Don Francisco Gutiérrez, Empresa of the Jimínez arena.

Of late years she has had several fights, one unlucky appearance being at Phoenix, Arizona, in 1954. Then she failed to conquer her animal, and American law prohibits the bull to be killed. "He knew just what to expect," she said afterward. "He stayed away from the *muleta* (red rag attached to a short stick) and aimed for me. He picked me up and threw me down. Then he walked on me. I was just bruised. They got me out of the ring before anything worse happened." Since that date, her experiences have been memorable. She won two exciting combats in the interior of Mexico at Durango and Canatlan. Yet later, she fought in Mexico at Parral, winning out over the bull and cutting from him the winner's trophy, a blood-stained black ear.

Joy Marie has the qualities of the enthusiast. "There are," she said, "those who believe women should not fight. We will prove to them that we can become artists just as men do. We want to show the world that women bullfighters are more than novelties."

In the history of bullfighting Joy Marie Price has already secured a place for herself. She long will be remembered as one of the tiniest *toreras* ever to enter the bullring. She may later achieve greatness, as her erstwhile teachers predict, for everybody reports her an apt pupil.

Living at the westernmost tip of Texas, *Paseños* represent West Texans in the superlative degree. The fabulous Georgiana Knowles might well be called the most novel of the Texas *toreras*. She alone proudly sports the unique title of *"Rejoneadora,"* lady bullfighter on horseback.

Long an El Pasoan, she came to the border from Tucson, Arizona, where she was born. Reared and educated at the Pass, Georgiana exhibits in her person, her inventiveness, and her in-bred daring the native lady *torera* at her flamboyant best. When recently interviewed, her mother, Mrs. Mary I. Knowles, said that Georgiana rode horses at two and a half years of age and that as the child grew older, she showed increasingly a distinct taste for all things Mexican. In her last year in high school Georgiana saw the movie of *The Brave Bulls* and decided there and then to enter the bullring. From the start, the citizens of Mexico liked the *simpatico* Texas girl, with her pretty face and large green eyes. Deriving from many racial stocks, American Indian, English, Irish, Italian, and Spanish, she proved a natural attraction on the International Border, where people of varied lineage felt they had strong claim on at least some of her unusually fiery spirit.

Being seriously burned on her back when a child, Georgiana endured hardships in her girlhood and triumphed over adversity. Uncowed by her accidental burning, she developed into a fearless young woman with a firm will and much determination. She lived mainly out of doors and waxed strong in the El Paso sunshine. Of sturdy physical construction when she reached twenty-one, Georgiana outstripped most other girls in athletic prowess. It required strength and agility to wield a heavy *rejon* (javelin) while riding bareback, for in the arena she appeared *montado en pelo,* with only a leather strap to hold herself in place astride the horse. Throughout her training period her actions bespoke those of a champion.

What she first learned to do included manipulations of the heavy cape from atop her *toro*-trained steed and placement of two *banderillas* (fancy barbs) in the shoulders of the bull while both bull and horse were in rapid motion. Sometimes the horse slipped, fell, and received a goring. More than once the bull's charge against her horse jostled her to the ground. On all occasions she rose to resume the struggle, until finally her healthy body and steel nerves carried her to graduation: she now stood ready for the fight for keeps.

Riding a white horse which she uses only for the *paseo* (opening parade), Georgiana cut a fine figure as she entered the arena. The first figure sighted by the spectators, she introduced the bullfighting pageantry of the afternoon. As the air filled with parade music and the rhythmic beat of drums, Georgiana sparkled with excitement, her impressive white horse prancing majestically about for all the world to see. A born equestrienne, the talented *torera* put on a show second to none in sheer grace and exotic beauty. Afterwards, in *la fiesta brava* itself, Georgiana changed to her famous horse "Tony," a handsome palomino which she and her favorite tutor, the celebrated David *"Tabaquito"* Siqueiros, acquired from the fabulous King Ranch of South Texas. Then, when the contest started, her adroitness in handling a horse under pressure came fully into play. She vibrated with excitement in the foreknowledge of her role, for she knew that she must either kill or be killed. So far, she has ever emerged victor, amid the inspiring cries of cheering, riotous throngs.

Georgiana has fought all over the Mexican Border, virtually its entire length from Matamoros to Tijuana. She began fighting at Juarez under the tutelage of sage Siqueiros, described in sporting circles as "one of the brainiest, most dependable men in bullfighting today." Her successes there carried her to further glories in her appearances at Nogales, Nuevo Laredo, Piedras

Negras, Matamoras, Mexicali, Mexico City, and Villa Acuña. Easy to look at, vivacious Georgiana, whom the Mexicans call "Georgina," created a sensation when she killed her first bull from horseback. She thereby wrote a spectacular page in the history of border bullfighting that will be long remembered.

Her sterling performances have brought Georgiana Knowles deservedly excellent publicity. At the Pass, where the art dates from early times, a girl really has to show something to draw an encomium from the newspapers. On July 4, 1955, the El Paso *Herald-Post* had this to say about "Georgina":

> She has made history as the only American girl to fight on horseback.

> She is the first American girl to fight in the Plaza in Mexico City, the first to do capework atop a horse, and the first and only fighter to place *banderillas* from horseback with both hands.

About the same time a wide public was converted to bull-fighting by her local appearance on television, where she displayed her proficiency in using Spanish and flashing her all-conquering smile. She is *muy simpatico,* and the Latins cannot resist her.

For a little Texas girl, Georgiana Knowles has golden prospects, a ceiling unlimited.

The round of ovations given Texas girl bullfighters on the border and in the interior of Mexico soon brought a bevy of young feminine devotees from all parts of the United States to the Pass of the North. One of the first *toreras* to take bullfighting lessons locally came from Phoenix, Arizona, and bore the attractive name, Colleen Davis. She quickly mixed in with the bullfighting crowd, trained industriously, and made such a splendid debut in the Juarez ring that she decided to remain on the border to culti-vate her hobby. Another *torera,* Ruth Massey, came to the Pass from Anaheim, California. She took lessons from the masterly Señor Hierro and made a fine showing in her public exhibitions in Juarez. She has continued to devote much of her time to the sport and now rates high in the esteem of her instructor as well as in the eyes of local spectators. Ruth Massey has a heavier physique for fighting than Colleen Davis but not so much arm reach. Another bright newcomer, Gloria Clark, traveled to the border from afar, from the city of San Francisco. She has not yet established herself among local fans, but her admirers swear

by her talents. Brighter still, Carla Lee, an Arizonan from
Phoenix, won attention in history at Juarez in May, 1956, when
she appeared in the traditional suit of lights *(traje de luces),* the
costume usually worn by male bullfighters only. All four of
these pretty *tauromachians* remain enthusiastic about the ring.
They have notably promising futures for girls of college age.
None of the beauteous bevy ever before showed an athletic
inclination. It took the stimulation of bullfighting to awaken their
latent talents, and the sport is still pulling them into the ring,
sometimes from even such bewitching places as Hollywood.
Actresses there have cultivated the sport, not to promote films,
but for their own enjoyment.

Much favorable publicity centered on the local custom of pitting beauties against bulls when starlet Connie Moore, of Wichita,
Kansas, manifested an ambition to become a lady bullfighter.
Like other girls before her, Connie caught the bug from reading
a lot of books about bullfighting. Living in Hollywood at the plush
Studio Club, Connie one day startled the other starlets by re-
hearsing the bullfighter's actions with a bathrobe. She explained
then that she first became involved in bullfighting after her graduation from high school in Wichita when her uncle took her to
Juarez, where she met a retired *matador.* It was this *matador*
who arranged for her to work out with calves in Mexico. A year
later she moved to Hollywood, so she could be near the fights at
Tijuana. Recently she quit her job as a secretary in order to
devote all her time to *tauromachy,* arranging for lessons from
Budd Boetticker, film director, who used to fight bulls. She told
Aline Mosby, United Press Correspondent, that she hoped to
realize an ambition by staging a fight in Mexico City. With
Connie, the arena has become a deep-seated obsession. "I'll hate
to kill the bulls," she said. "But it's something I have to accom-
plish. It's a fight within yourself."

The appeal of the ring has reached yet more distant regions.
One of the newest *toreras* hailed from Detroit, Michigan. Her
name was Virginia A. Romain. On January 6, 1956, she wrote a
letter in the editorial columns of *Colliers,* saying that she had
made three trips in the past three years to Mexico City and that
she planned to make a debut in the spring at La Plaza Mexico.
According to her, some of the border beauties "are making a
ridicule of a sacred and traditional art." Virginia will be entering

fast company when she starts competing with the established band of bullfighting beauties. Her letter, however, has a spirited chord in it; and spirit galore is precisely what it takes for a girl to face the ferocious charge of a maddened bull.

Meanwhile, the sultry *señoritas* down in Mexico have not been exactly standing still. For a long, long time Conchita Cintrón has been fighting the bulls. Conchita, born in Chile of parents from the United States diplomatic corps, lays claim to being the first woman bullfighter in history. Another beauty from below the Rio Grande, Juanita Aparicio, a native of Mexico, has recently won top acclaim in Latin America. A *señorita muy linda,* Juanita de Los Reyes, of Guadalajara, has fought six or eight times in Mexico. She appeared once with the American girl, Joy Marie Price, in an international contest at Delicias. Bullfighting fever has affected both Mexican and *gringa* lovelies.

The current favorite among American newcomers on the border, Bette Ford (born Betty Dingdeldein, in McKeesport, Pennsylvania) creates a din of applause, mingled with wolf-whistles, when her graceful figure strides majestically into the ring. She has all the poise of a ballet dancer, an attribute probably deriving from her earlier experience as a fashion model. Her endowment includes a natural and self-confident bearing, much of her aplomb resulting from her dramatic roles on television and in Broadway plays. All these qualities, together with a warm personality, have made Bette Ford the sensation of the southern border.

From the first, Bette displayed a native bent for bullfighting. Though petite, she possessed unusual strength. Healthy to the core, she glowed with physical exuberance even in her first public appearances, when she rocked the spectators on their ears with her parade of skill and courage. In her third contest, at Juarez, she competed with two male performers, Ramón Tirado and Paco Sanchez. That day Sanchez narrowly missed death when he stumbled and missed on the thrust, landing before the bull, face down in the dirt; and Ramón Tirado fared still worse, receiving ten inches of goring which hospitalized him for thirty days. Bette, on the other hand, outfought her rivals by killing her two bulls. The second bull tossed her three times into the air and almost gored her, but after each fall she rose in response to the cries of her fans: "Get him, Bette. Kill him." Showing unparalleled determination, she went on to dispatch the bull with two thrusts of her sword. Then she accepted an ear and made *una vuelta,* a ceremonial strut about the ring, amid the roars of the crowd.

After that, Juarez belonged to her. The spectators threw hats and flowers at her feet. Autograph seekers mobbed her before she could leave the ring. At the *cantinas* that evening the topic on the lips of everybody was the daring of that paragon of female fighters, the non-pareil Bette Ford.

Celebrity reached Bette the hard way, after disappointment. Early in her career she took a mauling and heard for the first time the crushing clarion of boos amid the cheers. That Sunday in Juarez the manager pitted her against a black animal named *"Modista."* Twice she lost her cape and stood there *desarmada* (disarmed). Then she missed several passes, to hit the dust, to feel the heavy hooves of the bull bruising her flesh. Scrambling to her feet for the *suerte suprema* (death stroke), Bette was knocked flat again but, like a true-born wrangler, clung to the bull's nose in a protective move to come up unscathed. After that, she killed the bull but remembered him as a bad one.

In one of her top Juarez fights, Bette drew *"Rafaelillo"* (Raphael), a large animal with what the Mexicans term a *bizco* (cross-eye), a horn crumpled over one eye. Experts labelled him dangerous because of his deformity. As she made her first *veronica* (switch of the cape), *"Rafaelillo"* hooked to the right and lifted her into the air. Bette landed on her feet to resume battling. With an angry series of *derechazos* (right moves), such high and low passes as *manoletinas* and *pasos por alto,* she maneuvered the bull for the kill. From all sides she heard the urging of the crowd: "Make love to *el toro,* Bette. Kill him, honey!" In her first effort she connected with the *suerte suprema.* Once more the spectators cried, *"Vuelta! Vuelta!"* Again as ago, Bette, with a bull's bloodstained ear, pranced triumphantly, her gladiatorial heart shining in her face, about the ring's wide circumference.

Creating a perfect uproar every time she steps into the arena, Bette would be a full show all by herself. Away from work, this winsome girl epitomizes modesty. Her surprising humility stems from sincere emotion. "I'm a ham," she often says. But Bette the charmer stands for a great deal more than that. She has so much of the genius required that she converts everybody who sees her into a bullfighting fanatic. A really stupendous spectacle, featuring beauteous Bette at the focus, would overflow the stands, with or without the bull. Nobody showed surprise, therefore, when Bette Ford married a few years ago.

All of her objectives, before her marriage, lay within the ring. Nothing sham ever attached itself to Bette Ford, and she left a mark in the history of bullfighting. The only American girl who ever fought afoot in the Plaza de Toros in Mexico City, the largest in the world, Bette inoculated the border blood stream with a permanent serum, heightening the ever-burning pulse of a sports-loving populace.

"I'm determined," she said a few years back, "to be the best woman bullfighter in the world, no matter how many years it takes."

According to her backers, Bette succeeded in doing just that before she left the arena forever.

> *¡Olé tu femenina figura!*
> *¡Olé! de elegante distinción*
> *Ante el toro se agiganta*
> *Y exclamaciones levanta*
> *De asombra y admiración*

The custom of lady bullfighting, meanwhile, had established itself on the border. This new institution recently has attracted more and more female performers. Younger devotees included the pert Dixie Lee. At Nogales, Arizona, on August 16, 1959, this pint-sized girl gave the customers an exciting afternoon by her display of courage in fighting and killing her bull. Dixie Lee fought on after being twice tossed to the ground by the hooking animal and once gored in the fleshy part of the hand below the thumb. And the fiery *Sorena,* Rosita Barrios, hailed from Los Angeles, California. Rosita, who trained under the famous Patricia McCormick's handler, Alejandro, fought in ten formal *corridas.* Miss Barrios maintained that bullfighting is not a sport, but an art and a spectacle. All her interests focused in the bullring. Beautiful though she is, Rosita claimed that she had rather kill bulls than date men. An El Paso girl, Patricia Chagra, would like to inherit the cape of the noted Conchita Cintrón, who retired at the age of thirty-one. Miss Chagra admired the "Portuguese style" of opposing the bull with the fighter mounted on horseback, a style preferred by Conchita Cintrón. These three youngsters, Misses Lee, Barrios, and Chagra, afforded proof of the continuing fascination of the new border pastime.

As time goes by, other young girls also will turn their backs on the feminine tasks of the world as they seek to take their places as skillful beauties of the bullring.

3

The Faces of Pancho Villa

Who was the real Pancho Villa? Historians picture him as a courageous rebel leader fighting for the freedom of his country, as a lowly peon who rose to the magnificence of a giant. Novelists characterize him as a romantic soldier, at times a sneaking coward, at others a brazen murderer. Poets sing of his glorious victories, their descriptions bristling with examples of his matchless heroism. Biographers, thinking of social reform, celebrate him as the Robin Hood of Mexico, a relentless scourge of the rich and a faithful provider of the poor. Full of contradictions, changeable as a chameleon, Pancho Villa was a man of many faces.

In 1910 Pancho Villa blazed a name in Mexican history as the ferocious leader of the Madero Revolution. He was marvelously successful at guerrilla warfare. Sometimes he lurked in the hills threateningly. Sometimes he routed the enemy in a midnight rush. Killing soldiers, pillaging supplies, stealing horses, pilfering valuables, destroying communications, murdering guards, converting scouts, Pancho Villa turned the federal encampments into a shambles. Then this wraith of the desert and mountains disappeared, dropped from human sight into the vast reaches of the Sierra Madre. At his zenith he dominated the republic; at his nadir, he eluded the clutches of the entire Pershing Expeditionary Force. And then in 1923 he fell, the victim at Parral of the frenzied fusillades of assassins.

33

The most tantalizing figure of the chaotic revolution was born in 1872, a peon. His first face was that of a feudal slave, an ignorant country boy, a pitiful *leñero* who sold bundles of wood. He was named Villa, perhaps because he lived away from the city among *peones* who traditionally give their children no surnames. Perhaps he was the son of a poor farmer, Augustín Arango. According to legend, he grew up with this family and had a favorite sister, Mariana. After the death of Augustín, he was often in trouble and had a hard time making a living for both himself and the Arango family. He went to work for a neighboring *ranchero,* and later on he drove a freight wagon between Guenacevi and Chihuahua. It was then that his feudal lord chased him down as a fugitive. Doroteo (or Dorotello), as he was first called, was beaten unmercifully and kept for a term in prison. Much of Pancho's abiding hatred for the Spanish aristocrats came from his early tragic experiences as Villa the *Peon.*

It was about this time that his mother wrote him a letter telling him that his favorite sister had been raped by Leonardo Negrete, the son of the ranch owner. Doroteo, then working in Chihuahua, was enraged to the point of murder. Through a chilly night he rode home as fast as he could and early the next morning sought out the scoundrel. Although Leonardo denied that he had raped the girl, angry words led to a gunfight, and Doroteo killed him on the spot. In the outcry that followed, the *peones* justified Doroteo, since to them he was the protector of his family, the avenger of his sister's lost honor. Thus did the face of Villa the *Peon* add the mask of the Avenger.

From that day forth, Doroteo was branded an outlaw. He fled quickly away to the hills for cover, there joining the outcast band of the famous Ignacio Parra. Folklore has it that once upon a time, in an earlier epoch, there lived an old outlaw named Pancho Villa and that Doroteo Arango now simply adopted this name as his own. At any rate, he told Parra that he was Pancho Villa. Parra laughed at this until Doroteo is said to have explained that he was the oldster's namesake. Under the tutelage of Ignacio Parra, he learned the ways of outlawry and won the friendship of the band. When Parra was later killed, the bandits naturally looked upon him as their rightful *jefe.*

Pancho Villa never wore any face quite so naturally as that of Bandit Chief. The man behind the big *poncho* (belly) was a desperado at heart. He was impatient, unrestrained, an enemy of order and regulation, a daredevil who acted in the flush of excitement, a violent creature who exhausted his nervous energies in one explosive moment and then, by sleeping the clock around, rebuilt them doubly strong. He slept, recharging the battery of his mind with plots, mysteries, and plans, with everything and nothing, with remorse and vengeance. He awoke to waste days and days, or to sleep again. But always he finally bestirred himself to do a thousand dangerous deeds: to rob a train, to halt a lonely coach and pillage it, to dismantle a store, to destroy a town, to run the good beeves off the ranches of Terrazas, to borrow a woman for a night, to intercept a messenger loaded with gold, to kidnap a rich *gringo,* and to steal the mining companies blind. Silent or shouting at the top of their lungs, Pancho and his band were the marauders of Northern Mexico, leaving behind them destruction, disorder, death, or maybe an "I.O.U." all written out after a style he had learned from the *Americanos.*

Pancho Villa was a bandit by necessity and by fate, but, more than anything else, by instinct alone. He played so well the role of Bandit Chief that he thereafter was hardly anything else, not even when he was a lover, a Robin Hood, a great soldier—not even in that quiet period of peaceful retirement as a general *muy magnífico.* People still remembered his banditry in those last seemingly endless days before the hot, blinding moment when the air exploded about him, spouting his blood, fat, and flesh all over his Dodge automobile.

The face one sees depends somewhat upon the beholder. To the *peones,* the Bandit Chief was but another mask, and behind the camouflage they perceived the warm and smiling visage of Mexico's own Robin Hood with his Will Scarlet and Little John in the persons of his trusted Martin López and Tomas Urbina, with his Maid Marian in the handsome figure of Luz Corral. Here was the man all right, reckless, improvident—a staunch leader of his faithful *compañeros,* a big brotherly outlaw, a lover of children, and, best of all, a *bandido* bold who robbed the rich for the poor. Even the most woeful *peon*—sick, irresolute, reduced to hopelessness—warmed finally to the stories of this impossible man. Villa scattered his money about him everywhere. He crammed *dinero* into the pockets of decrepit old beggars, creased with coins the outstretched palms of small boys, or filled the empty lap of a bereaved mother of a dead Villista soldier with piles of shining silver.

In his heyday the *cantinas* flung wide their doors to Villa the Gay *Caballero*. His generosity was large and spontaneous. He drove his men hard but rewarded them lavishly, for stolen money came easy and went the same way. Yet he was a different kind of spender. For him, a clear head was a necessity; and wine, the witchery of the cup, was for others, not for him. For his pastime, he sang with a strong full voice the stirring battle hymns of the revolution—the one-step "Tierra Blanca" composed in honor of one of his victories, or the better-known "La Cucaracha," a favorite with the rebels. Or, after the Latin style, he made love. He had, it is reported, four legal wives, at least two of whom survived him, Señora Eustre Berta and Señora Luz Corral. The names of his other women are less certain. Often anonymous partners of a brief encounter, their identities are seldom preserved in either legend or song. There is, however, a *canción* about Adelita, which Villa's singer Ochoa sometimes sang for him.

> Adelita is the name of the young one
> Whom I love and cannot forget.
> In the world I have a rose,
> And with time, I shall pluck her.

Yet Villa as a *caballero* was probably a rather conventional and harmless type for revolutionary days. The principal evidence —other than that supplied by his friends and enemies—is the testimony of the Mormon colonists in Chihuahua, and their records contain nothing to discredit him.

The mirror which reveals Pancho as a Heartless Bluebeard reflects a false face. The story of his vengeance upon a woman who had borne him a son in Santa Rosalía is sheer fiction. It asserts that after a long absence Villa returned to the town and found that his *señora* had married again. The first thing he did was to hang her husband. Everybody thought he then would carry away the mother and child for his own. Instead, he took them to a stake and burned them. A similar tale has its setting in Parral, where Pancho met a young woman named Petra

Espinosa. When unable to obtain her honorably, he scandalously raped her, forcing her to live with him until he got tired of her. There is no doubt, of course, that Villa could be as rough as they come, but it is unlikely that he ever resorted to such strong-arm tactics simply to get a woman. Women in revolutionary Mexico were there for the asking, eager and willing at the mention of his magic name.

The darker shades in Villa's portrait show more unmistakably in his banditry, particularly in his determination to destroy the powerful *ranchero,* Don Luis Terrazas. Legend claims that he once unsuccessfully tortured Juan Terrazas, the son of Don Luis, in hopes of making him disclose the hiding place of a fabulous buried treasure. Villa's band strung up Juan by his thumbs and whipped him with their quirts, but he refused to divulge the hiding place. Whatever the truth of this fiendish incident, it is certain that Pancho for over a decade preyed upon the cattle of Terrazas, scattering and dwindling the valuable herds. In the beginning Don Luis was the richest cattleman in Chihuahua; at his end he was ruined and broken. The friends of Terrazas say that he swore on his deathbed he would appear before God on Judgment Day to denounce his enemy as "Villa the Villain."

Was Pancho, the so-called Terror of Terrazas, actually a villain? Don Luis paid his *peones* twenty-five *centavos* per day and lodged them in hovels, allowing them to stupefy in poverty and ignorance. These *peons* were the people whom Villa sought to awaken, to aid, and eventually to free. How justified is one, then, in calling Pancho a common cattle thief? From earliest times, history relates, huge herds of unbranded cattle roved the ranges of Chihuahua. Everybody regarded them as the free cattle of a public domain and so fed upon them after the custom of the country. President Benito Juárez introduced a hateful feudalism when he deeded these cattle lands to Don Luis Terrazas. The attitude of Villa, though not his actions, was approved by others, including Abraham (or Abran) Gonzales, the governor of Chihuahua. In *Vida y Hazañas de Pancho Villa,* Villa's reactions were recorded by his friend Elías Torres, to whom he said:

What do you think, Señor Torres? Do you think that I should have regarded the animals born in the wild as belonging to Terrazas when he did not know of their existence nor take care of them? My little brothers and I had the same right to the wild creatures as Terrazas. Do you think it was only the right of the old rich men to brand them and call them their property?

Under the circumstances, Villa's behavior was hardly as wicked as Don Luis let on. There were thus two views of his conduct. When people either cursed him as a criminal or praised him as a redeemer, he wore two faces at once. Don Luis saw Villa the Villain; the *peons* saw Villa the Vindicator.

In November, 1910, Governor Abraham Gonzales decided to join Madero in the war against Díaz. After making out his last will and testament in El Paso, Gonzales returned to Chihuahua and began to recruit a rebel army to send against the federalists. About this time Pancho, via a messenger, volunteered his services to the cause of the revolution. Governor Gonzales accepted the offer enthusiastically and at once sent him a military answer which said: "I appoint you, by the authority vested in me, a Captain in the Revolutionary Army." Villa and his band were ordered to report near Casas Grandes to the commander of the rebel forces, General Pascual Orozco. From the start, they made a bad impression, being dirty from travel and roughly clothed. The first night at camp Pancho stole a horse from a nearby *rancho,* and the next day General Orozco was so angry that he bawled him out and put him under arrest. Thus did the man whom the *peones* described as "Savior and Defender of the Poor" enter upon the first stage of the revolution as Captain Villa the Horse Thief.

In later days, after the murder of Madero in 1913, Pancho Villa became the main figure of the Mexican Revolution. The legend of Villa the Strategist arises in this era. He and his rugged band, now grown to an army of hypnotized followers, overran the Northern States. Frequently they demolished the enemy from front, center, and rear in little nameless towns or in great places like Parral and Torreón. Twice they held the important border city of Juárez. The *peon* leader rapidly advanced from captain to colonel and then to general. He marched on Mexico City and for a brief while controlled it. His unkempt followers were now transformed by uniforms with reams and reams of gold braid into the fantastic *Dorados,* "The Golden Ones of Villa." For

a day, hardly longer, the world of Mexico was his. He could
have been, they say, president of the republic. The citizens wined
and feted him. He bared his dark head, kinky as a Negro's, to
repeated ovations. Usually his face with its buck teeth looked
adenoidal, but now it was wreathed with the smile of a conqueror. The cunning of the mountain outlaw had brought him
to the top, though behind him there lay the debris of a country
torn asunder. He had—by ambush, by cold-blooded murder, by
counterfeited orders, by planted spies, by mass attacks, and by
pretended retreats—at last destroyed the enemy or else driven
him mad. A magnificent guerrilla fighter inhaled the incense of
victory and was drunk with it.

The saga should end here, and it would, had Villa acted wisely.
Had he been a natural strategist, as claimed, he would have
coöperated with Carranza and awaited a propitious time to strike
down the rebounding federalists under General Huerta. Instead,
he became increasingly reckless and heeded no one. He disre-
garded the advice of Colonel Felipe Angeles, who warned against
an immediate attack, and so lost the crucial battle of Celaya.
He turned against all foreigners and was known for a *gringo*
hater. For nothing, in utter bravado or as a somber whim, he
murdered the Englishman William S. Benton. As he bestrode
its crest, the structure of his fame collapsed. He rallied briefly,
launched a new attack, and was soundly trounced anew. This
defeat occurred at Agua Prieta, near the Arizona line, where
Huerta contacted him after a journey from El Paso over a
United States railroad. From the ever narrowing field of his
now desperate operations, he loosed in 1916 a retaliatory surprise attack on Columbus, New Mexico. Needing to replenish
his supplies and believing that the Americans had aided Huerta,
Villa the Invader struck a blow that reverberated around the
world.

Shortly afterward General Pershing, leader of the American
Expeditionary Force, began his epic pursuit of Villa. John J.
Pershing had once been Pancho's friend, and photographs were
taken of the two in smiling poses. These men, who had earlier
hunted together, now were the hunter and the hunted.

In Mexico ten thousand troops of General Pershing saw everything—everything except Villa. They saw in particular the *peons*
enrich themselves on their coin, for the Americans paid for

what they used. They saw their prey appear when they retreated but vanish when they approached. The spoor grew alternately hot and cold, and at whatever place they paused Villa had been there yesterday or was expected in a day or two. But nobody so much as glimpsed the elusive Pancho. A myth arose in which he became the Wraith of the Desert. As they chased his unseen human figure, he changed into a coyote and barked at their heels. For nearly a year, eleven long months, the *gringos* chased him high and low. Their frustration must have been maddening, especially since misinforming the *Americanos* became the national pastime of the *peones*. Pershing's scouts questioned the Mexicans, who said, vaguely, that they had heard of the fellow. Colonel Tompkins, who chased Villa hard, ferreted out a lead. Pancho Villa, the colonel learned, was a man named "Dorotelo [*sic*] Arango," or something like that, and Carranzas said that he was a bastard. So it went, almost exactly. The Americans maneuvered, used for the first time in conflict overhead machine-gun fire, and experimented with dropping supplies to stranded soldiers from the air. What the Villistas did nobody really knows. Perhaps they were dispersed, as Colonel Tompkins claims in *Chasing Villa* (1934), or perhaps they only pretended they were. Villa was, in any case, still very much alive when General Pershing's army left Mexico at the end of April, 1917.

During the year 1918, when the attention of the New World shifted to Germany, Villa meditated a triumphal return to power. On June 10, 1919, he sought to realize his dream of new conquest by taking Juárez. A surprise, however, was due him, for he had not been forgotten in the United States. The rumor had gone that Villa's raid on Columbus had been inspired by German agents, so that the Americans were seriously incensed at him. When he attacked, the army of Carranza, aided by two thousand colored soldiers from Fort Bliss at El Paso, routed him completely. The defeat marked the end of Villa's career as a fighter. After conferring with his friend Elías Torres, he accepted retirement from the Mexican government on the grounds that his continued fighting would embroil his country in war with the United States. In the cast of the mighty Mexican drama, General Villa struggled for the role of hero to the last.

Villa lived peacefully after being retired near Parral at El Rancho del Canutillo until his assassination in 1923. In his book *One American* (1938) Frazier Hunt recalls a visit he once paid Villa at this *hacienda*. Villa's foreman at Canutillo, Jimmie Caldwell, now of Santa Fe, New Mexico, sometimes reminisces about the happenings of that past era of stirring adventure. Perhaps at the last, Villa, as his assassins charged, was planning a fresh coup, a final attempt to regain his old prestige.

The spirit of the conqueror which animated Villa was certainly deathless. Three years ago in Phoenix, Arizona, an old-timer was anxious to revisit the familiar places he once knew so well as an American soldier-of-fortune who had fought for him. His resurgent spirit is celebrated throughout the Mexican Republic. In 1949 a movie theater in Mexico City crowded its seats to capacity with spellbound spectators who applauded the film "Pancho Villa Vuelve," "Pancho Villa Returns."

Today a ghost roams Mexico. A shadowy figure, who walks the rock-fenced countryside of Parral, comes by midnight to lift a lowly *peon* and urge him to rise. Men have seen the ghost, and there is cause for their tales. Who knows Villa's final resting place? What of his head, which, they say, was severed from his body? How much of him remains in the Parral grave? Why is the splendid mausoleum at Chihuahua an empty tomb? In legend the symbol of Villa the Unconquerable persists, so that the past does not contain him fully. Today the unquiet ghost of Villa, who haunts the little people of Mexico, steps into the future with the big-legged stride of a folk hero.

Across the passing scene of Mexico's romantic history, the unpredictable rise and quick fall of Pancho Villa flashed briefly. Out of the multitude of his faces, which was the actual Villa? For a moment one of them may appear to crystallize—that of a patriot who triumphed over everything—but then the face blurs into villain or hero and shifts from giant to *peon* again. Carl Sandburg, in a passing reference, catches Villa in a luminous phrase, "a rock of the people." But the truth, alas, is a mirage. In the tales of love and bloodshed, of glory and death, Villa is a human enigma, the *hombre* of many faces.

4

Dr. Husk on Pancho Villa

Among the Pershing Papers (Box 372) in the Division of Manuscripts of the Library of Congress, Washington, D.C., there appears a short biographical sketch of Pancho Villa (1879-1923), fierce Mexican revolutionist, written by an American physician, Dr. Carlos E. Husk, then a resident of Santa Barbara, Chihuahua. Dr. Husk dated his manuscript March 15, 1914, and shortly sent it to John J. Pershing, Fort Bliss, Texas. On the following September 14, Pershing acknowledged receipt of the material and remarked: "My impression of the general corresponds to your own. I think he will yet do great things for his beloved Mexico." The future did loom radiantly for Villa at that stage of the Revolution, but in the next year (1915) his enemy, Alvaro Obregon, extinguished his bright prospects by defeating him in a series of crucial battles. These defeats, followed by American recognition of the government of his enemies, helped to precipitate Pancho's vengeful raid on Columbus, New Mexico, on March 9, 1916.

Dr. Husk's sketch possesses rare value because the physician personally interviewed the bandit leader before composing it. He thus correctly reports Pancho's native state as Durango. More significantly, he helpfully explains that the patronymic Villa, about whose origin there has been much speculation, was the name borne by his real father. He similarly records as fact, not legend, the attempted rape of the bandit's sister. Furthermore, current tall tales of Pancho's extraordinary horsemanship evidently had some basis in reality, as is seen in the incidents related by Dr. Husk. Finally, one may note, the wife Villa lived with in El Paso, unnamed in the sketch, was Señora Maria Luz Corral de Villa, now of Chihuahua City and honorary New Mexican citizen of Columbus.

Grateful acknowledgment for permission to publish this hitherto unprinted vignette goes to General Pershing's son, Mr. Francis Warren Pershing, of New York City, and to Dr. Husk's sister, Mrs. F. P. Smith, of Batavia, Illinois. According to Mrs. Smith, Dr. Husk died of "typhus" fever in March, 1916, as a "martyr to medicine." He graduated as Charles Ellsworth Husk from what is today the Medical College of the University of Illinois, became the president of the National Medical Society of Mexico, and ever remained a loyal friend of Pancho Villa. In the text that follows, the student of history now has available an eyewitness estimate of the most controversial patriot of the Mexican Revolution.

Francisco Villa was born on a small ranch in the State of Durango about thirty-five years ago. Of his parentage but little is known, except that his mother, a rather remarkable Mexican woman of Indian blood, was of the middle class, and his father, a man of lesser ability, was of the Spanish-American blood. Several children were born of this couple, born out of wedlock, as their parents were not married, a status common among Mexicans of this class.

After the death of his father his mother then married, the children assuming the name of her new husband. Pancho was a hard worker on their rented ranch and at the age of fourteen he, with his brothers and sisters, on learning their true parentage, discarded the family name by which they were known up to that time and adopted the name of Villa, the true name of their real father. This clears up reports that Villa is not his true name. . . .

FIRST KILLING

At the age of sixteen, in company with a younger brother, engaged in plowing corn in a field near their ranch house, he noticed two horses standing for some time near their door, and out of boyish curiosity left his work team and started out to make an investigation. On nearing the house he was surprised to see that one of the horses belonged to the son of the ranch owner, the other to his private mozo. The door was shut, and on approaching he heard the sound of his mother's voice screaming and pleading with someone inside, begging them to save her daughter's honor. Breaking open the door, Pancho saw this ranch owner's son almost in the act of raping his fifteen-year-old sister, who was noted among her ranch friends as being a very comely, pretty, well-developed girl. He, as he expressed it, went crazy; rushed across the street to his cousin's house, grabbed a rifle and shot his sister's would-be seducer, breaking his leg, but he managed to get on his horse and, with his mozo's assistance, made his escape.

That night a body of rurales sent by the father of the wounded man came to the house and took Pancho a prisoner to the ranch headquarters, for he had committed the unpardonable crime of trying to defend his family from a dissolute son of a rich father. The next morning he was started out with a guard of rurales toward Durango City, but being now thoroughly terrorized at his probable fate, for undoubtedly he would be made an example of under the "ley fuga," and desperate to the extreme, he succeeded in killing some of his guard that night, took one of their horses and a gun and escaped to the mountains, beginning his career as a fugitive from law and justice and, in the eyes of the world, a bandit.

A reward was offered for his capture, and this was increased as time went by until $10,000 was offered for him, dead or alive. However, [because of] the fact that he was befriended by people who knew his history and therefore sympathized with him, and that he developed an almost uncanny sagacity in eluding his pursuers, he succeeded in preserving his life for the following sixteen years. He naively states that during this period he lived on the country, though for a considerable time he was patio boss at Mina Vieja, near Chihuahua. Most of these years, however, he rustled cattle and supplies, sometimes alone, sometimes in company with kindred spirits, never killing except to save his own life. At the conclusion of his narrative of his life, which he told me some three years ago, he said he did not wish his worst enemy to be compelled to live the life he had, a hunted coyote during all these years.

At the outbreak of the Madero revolution he gathered a band of trusty followers, led them with more or less revolutionary success until he met Madero at the first taking of Juarez, who then pardoned him for his former crimes and made him a colonel.

Since then he has never wavered in his allegiance to the principle Madero advocated, and regards Madero as his martyred saviour.

When Madero was elected president the only reward Villa asked for was the concession of the bull-ring and meat market in Chihuahua City, which was granted him and with which he was occupied up to a short time before the Orozco uprising started. When this was brewing, Governor Gonzales of Chihuahua, who trusted Villa absolutely, asked him to bring his men into the city to act as its guard, but at this time Orozco showed his hand, revolted with his troops and began his famous revolution. He then and there became the sworn enemy of Villa. Villa fled to the mountains with his men, shortly afterward took Parral, was driven out by Salazar, but was at a ranch ten miles away when the alleged looting of Parral, which was really done by Salazar, took place. He then went to Mapimi, joined forces with Tellez, the federal commander at that place, came back to Parral with Rabago, joined Huerta at Jiminez when he was on his way north against Orozco, and where the trumped-up charge of insubordination was brought against him by Huerta. . . . Huerta had him court-martialed and ordered shot, and I imagine since then many's the time he has wished he had carried it out. However, at the intercession of Emilio Madero, Villa was sent to Mexico City a prisoner of war; finally escaped from the penitentiary, where he spent months of imprisonment in study, made his way with one companion across Mexico to the border and into Texas.

He remained quiet in El Paso until Madero was murdered, when he crossed with seven men and began his spectacular career.

NEVER IN COLD BLOOD

In his bandit days his notoriety was so widespread that nearly every crime committed and unaccounted for in northern Mexico was charged to him, and, while there is no doubt but that he participated in many, it was physically impossible for him to have accomplished everything in that line his enemies accused him of, and he, of course, says that he never committed murder in cold blood, only killing those who were seeking him for that same purpose.

In personal appearance he is about five feet ten inches in height, weighs about one hundred seventy-five pounds, is well developed and muscular, has a very heavy protruding lower jaw and badly stained teeth; a rather dandified, moderately heavy mustache of the heavy villain variety; crispy, kinky black hair of the negroid type, which is generally tousled. He has the most remarkable pair of prominent brown eyes I have ever seen. They seem to look through you; he talks with them and all of his expressions are heralded and dominated by them first, and when in anger, or trying to impress some particular point, they seem to burn and spit out sparks and flashes of fire between the hard-drawn, narrowed and nearly closed lids.

He is a remarkable horseman; sits his horse with cowboy ease and grace, rides straight and stiff-legged, Mexican style, and will only use a Mexican saddle. He loves his horse; is very considerate of his comfort, probably due to the fact that they have aided him in escaping from tight places so many times. . . .

He dresses very commonly, has none of the Latin desire for pomp or show of any kind, and is never so happy as when he is performing some rough-riding stunt or attending a cock fight, one of his pet diversions.

He is very democratic, realizes he is from the peon class, mourns his lack of educational advantages, and whatever may have been his incentive when he joined the Madero revolution, he is certainly now imbued with the belief of the principles the Constitutionalists are fighting for,—for the betterment of the masses and the foundation of self-government.

He married legally a new wife in Torreon some few months ago; the wife he had in El Paso and who is now living in Chihuahua was bound to him by church marriage some years ago, and this is not considered legal in Mexico, so he has a valid excuse for his recent trial. His morals, however, are not worse, if as much so, as most of his class.

He never willingly breaks his word and he never drinks a drop of liquor of any kind, two very rare and commendable virtues seldom found in a Mexican.

His rather picturesque, commanding figure on horseback, coupled with his romantic and adventurous past, tend to make him the idol and almost a demigod among the common people, and his hold on them is simply marvelous. Where "Don Pancho" goes they will follow, and his very name means more in inspiring confidence of his friends and instilling terror to his enemies than armies of lesser known and admired men.

Many of the other generals of his class are naturally jealous of his fame or notoriety, and by the better class he is tolerated as a necessary evil. Due to these two facts, there is bound to be a break very soon, because of the well known incompatibility which always comes to the surface among Mexicans. Of all the

men now in the limelight in Mexico's troubled affairs he stands
head and shoulders above them all, and with supervision by the
United States, which I believe he would accept, he is the only
one worth counting on. He has developed very fast in the last
few years, and especially so in the last few months. He is a
remarkable man in many ways. Surrounding him with proper
influence, developing him with proper coaching, and with the
assurance of fair play on the part of others, I feel that he is the
biggest man the present disturbance in Mexico has developed.

His comprehensive grasp of details, his untiring energy, his
steadfast purpose, his wonderful personality as a leader of men
and his demonstrated military ability, mark him to be a factor
that must be considered in Mexico's future.

WRITTEN MARCH 5, 1914
                         HAVE NO REASON TO CHANGE IT *YET*

5

Pecos Bill, The Original Typical Texan

He is as big as all outdoors and lives somewhere in the West. With his strapping wife Sue Foot Slue, his wild riding horse Widow Maker, his mean pet coyote Baby, and an old hen Henrietta and her three little chicks Tom, Dick, and Harriet, he is at odd times a jack-of-all-trades, a cowboy and a rancher, an oil field worker, a digger of tunnels, a doer of a thousand deeds of derring do, and always, day in and day out, the nonpareil Texan of Texans. He lives only in the existence given him by tellers of tales, by dreamers of fantastic dreams; but he has already been here so long that he may stay forever. He will be remembered well after nearly everybody now alive is dead and gone. Who is he and where did he come from and how did he get that way are questions whose answers lie in the legend of Pecos Bill, the most fabulous character of the sprawling plains of Texas.

For Pecos Bill is a culture hero. He is a fictional character, the product of folk imagining. Unlike the great human figures of actual history, he never lived in the speaking flesh, never had a true beginning, and will never have a predictable end; in fact, he has never existed except in the mystery which is the living myth. As a culture hero, however, he is a tremendous source of inspiration, an ever-flowing spring brimming with the wonderous stuff of legends. In this manner the folk hero transcends history, because he is one person who represents many, because he, in the expression of his personality, embraces the spirit and the characteristics of a whole people. So was the legendary hero of old, the Hercules of the Greeks and Romans, the Beowulf of the Anglo-Saxons. So is he today, the Paul Bunyan of the North, the colored John Henry of the South. In the Southwestern region the culture hero of a booming empire of farms and industry, of cattle and oil, is Pecos Bill, the big brawny boy from Texas.

Pecos Bill was born but for one purpose. As the embodiment of the sterling qualities of the Texans themselves, he was born to perform the stupendous feat of conquering a vast land and harnessing its resources. In his composition there is some of the roughness of the frontiersman, of the Davy Crockett of yore, as well as some of the daring of the modern speculator, of the Glen McCarthy of today. To Texans, he is at once a recollection of their great past and a reminder of their future glories. His story is a tale of marvels, of prodigies as large as Texas herself.

The saga of the folk hero of Texas begins this way. He was born on the eastern side of the state near the Sabine river, and nobody now remembers the exact name of his "paw" or "maw." They were strong healthy people of frontier stock, and Bill, as he was first called, was at birth no sickly, puling weakling but a fine, active child. As an infant, he with his own hands choked a snake to death and stole his eight rattles; as a mere boy, he with his knife killed a terrible bear and skinned him. Bill grew tall and tough, lean and lanky, loud and proud—a typical Texan. And then he started adventuring, striking out as a youth for the land of purple sunsets. When people in West Texas first saw him around Pecos, they thought he was a coyote, not a man, although he had no fur and no long tail. But they knew for certain that he was a man when he boomed:

> I'm wild and woolley and full of fleas
> And never been curried below the knees
> And this is my night to howl—Yippee!

With a song on his lips big Bill then swam into the wide middle of the Pecos, swallowing so much water in his crossing that thereafter the river remained hardly more than a trickle. To commemorate the watery event, the brawny boy was there and then christened Pecos Bill, the name he wears to this good day.

Big Bill was not a mite tired after swimming the Pecos, but he was a little water-logged. With a mighty heave he spewed from his mouth the last of the river water, which landed near Galveston to form the Gulf of Mexico. Then, to show how easy it was, he jumped back across the Pecos, whose bed was pretty dry now anyhow after all the water he had drunk from it. Elated at drying up the river, whose overflows had made a swamp of the early Trans Pecos area, he turned a few handsprings between Odessa and Midland, and everywhere his fingers pressed into the soil an oil well immediately started gushing. With two strides forward and two back, he grabbed up steel pipes in Dallas, nuts and screws in Fort Worth, and rigged up a field of fine derricks as pretty as you please. All the things Pecos Bill did in West Texas he did in a big way and did them in a hurry.

After that, he started ranching. He spread out his huge arms as far as they could reach and then whirled once. All the land now lying in this circle he took for his own. He then quickly set about revolutionizing the cattle business. He first created from a part of this property the famous Perpetual Motion Ranch, so-called because it ran itself after he stocked it. The other half of his property he called the Circle Mountain Ranch. It was built around a steep mountain, one so steep that he had to import from El Paso a special brand of cattle whose legs were short enough on one side to allow them to graze circularly around the mountain to its top without falling off. Bill was the most remarkable rancher of early Texas history, for he never lost even so much as one steer. The reason for his success was the new type of fencing he brought to the plains: he built his fences deer high, hog deep, and bull strong.

Pecos Bill was also responsible for other important improvements that helped the ranchers. Like the typical Texan, he was original, enterprising, inventive. In fact, besides inventing the first lariat, which he made by tying together the tails of ten rattlesnakes tightly, he was the man who fed his stock the new feed enriched by vitamins grown successfully on April 1, in the year of the Texas Centennial, on a former cotton patch near Lubbock (and later also at Leveland). For the first time in recorded history, his heifers bore two and three calves. His triumph, however, was an old cow named Patience, for in the winter of 1950 she had five calves at once. Patience was also the first cow to give pure homogenized milk, a product now justly celebrated around the world. Before he quit punching cattle, Pecos Bill constructed twenty large water tanks, largely for irrigation purposes, which water he had flown from the Rio Grande in nineteen airplanes hired from Peyote Field. He was able to save money on the twentieth by riding on the last plane himself with his mouth full of water. The final feat he performed for ranching was to wipe out with his bare hands nearly all of the last cattle rustlers, the hideous Hell Gulch Gang, whose few survivors fled away to Austin and there entered politics.

In recent years Pecos Bill has been delving in the oil business and hotel trade. He dug a tunnel from Houston to New York, placing first a big pipe line in it to pump oil. The oddity of the pipe is that it contains a greased chute which connects with the Empire State Building. Money placed in the chute in New York reaches Houston just as soon as Bill presses a green button in his headquarters in the Saint Julian Hotel. Bill's Hotel Saint Julian is a circular arrangement, like his notorious Circle Mountain Ranch. The elevators inside, which run up its hundred winding flights, are, however, all gracefully curved to match the symmetry of the exterior.

Such, then, is the saga of the folk hero of the Lone Star State. He came into being through the oral stories of the old timers of Texas. In most respects he is a young culture hero, for he is a later creation than either Paul Bunyan or the colored John Henry. The first time I heard of him was about 1920, when my uncle, in Colorado, Texas, told me about Bill's going to sleep with his double-barrelled shotgun propped upright beside him. When Bill woke, he found it had rained a regular West Texas rain, because one barrel was powder dry and the other plumb full of water. Pecos Bill first appeared in print in 1923, in the old *Century Magazine,* in a tale by Ed "Tex" O'Reilly. But since then he has appeared there often. Besides poems, plays, and paintings about him, he is the subject of more than eight books and forty-five articles. He is one man of folk origin who is certainly making literary history.

Pecos Bill is here to stay. From time to time reports come in of his death, but these must be thoroughly discounted. For Bill, whose longevity is not untypical of the Texans of yore, is a most hardy soul. So the yarns keep pouring in, each taller than the last. Right now, from San Antonio to Alpine, the folks say that Pecos Bill, sensitive to the traffic problems in Brewster County, is putting in a subway system in the Big Bend Country.

6

Trailing Ambrose Bierce

Shortly after the strange disappearance, in 1913, of Ambrose Bierce, American author and journalist, one report, among many, stated that at the outbreak of the World War he was training with English soldiers in Lincolnshire; another, that he had died early in battle on the French front (*Bookman,* August, 1925, p. 642). But the most persistent rumors appear to place his death in Mexico.

One of the earliest accounts depicts Bierce dying before a firing squad in Icamole, east of Chihuahua, in August 1915 (Starrett, V. *Buried Caesars.* Chicago, 1923). A later version of this states that the Mexican officer who ordered the execution possessed a snapshot of Bierce (*American Mercury,* September, 1925). Unfortunately no one has been able to produce either the Mexican official or the snapshot. But it was reported several years later, on the other hand, that Bierce had been seen in San Luis Potosi in December, 1918. Here again, however, confirmation is sadly lacking; for the Mexican who supplied this tale was murdered in a love scrap in Los Angeles before his remarks could be checked and corroborated.

Nevertheless the rumor that Bierce died in Mexico has continued to flourish, and I have encountered it many times during the past ten or twelve years of intermittent investigations. On October 2, 1928, John Cullen, of the New York *American* (with which Bierce had been associated) wrote me that Ambrose's death "in all probability was caused by a bullet fired by a follower of Villa." But no reason is given for this belief. Possibly Mr. Cullen was influenced by a statement made in the *American Parade* (October, 1926, p. 43) by Adolphe de Castro, Bierce's collaborator on *The Monk and the Hangman's Daughter,* that "Bierce was shot to death by Villa's orders."

In 1929 I met Mr. de Castro in New York. He gave me at that time substantially the same account as appears in his *Portrait of Ambrose Bierce.* He was not at all certain that Bierce had actually been murdered at Villa's command; indeed he implied, as he does in his *Portrait,* that Ambrose's death might have been hastened by excessive drinking. De Castro was in some respects less sure of what had happened than he had been in 1926.

The latest story, and by all odds the most exciting, is told by Tom Mahoney (*Esquire,* February, 1936), who represents Bierce as a supporter, not an enemy, of Pancho Villa. According to Mr. Mahoney, Bierce went along as a regular member of the army when Pancho raided a northern Chihuahua *estado* and fell in battle at Ojinaga. The bodies of the soldiers were piled together and then burned; and there were, therefore, no remains. The great advantage of this report over all others is that it successfully removes any possibility of a *corpus delicti.*

From what base in actual fact do these many accounts derive? Precious little, it seems to me. Bierce's letters are proof that he was in Chihuahua, but none of these makes any real contribution to the essential riddle.

When in 1935 I moved to Alpine, center of the Texas Big Bend, I determined, therefore, to visit Chihuahua and Ojinaga in the hope of uncovering any relevant information. I went first to the home of Señora Luz Corral de Villa, Pancho's widow, but received no inkling of a clue. Quite obviously Villa might have known Bierce without informing the Señora, but this would appear unlikely if, as has been argued, Pancho and Bierce were at all intimate.

Shortly afterwards I called on the American Consul, who had no personal information whatever regarding Bierce, but who kindly permitted me to copy from the files the records in his possession bearing on the case. These records, appeals first by newspaper and then by radio, reveal that the United States Government in 1930 made a serious effort to get at the facts.

I had no better luck in Juarez or Ojinaga. At Ojinaga I talked with old-timers, border patrolmen, prospectors, and desert rats, but I discovered nothing about any *gringo* dying for Villa on the battlefield.

Now the Mexican is notorious for preserving traditions and for telling tales, and inasmuch as no informant among them in Ojinaga could furnish a single datum, it is my conclusion that the spreading belief that Bierce died in Mexico rests at present on no substantial proof whatsoever and should thus be strongly opposed.

On the other hand, I have no evidence of what *did* happen to him. Perhaps he went on to South America as he had planned. The late Walter Neale, whom I knew well, insisted that his friend died in the Rockies. And it is true that in 1911 Bierce had written: "At my age a fellow should go into his room and begin dressing for death. My room is Yosemite Valley."

After moving to El Paso, Texas, in 1946, I made anew repeated efforts to trail "Don Ambrosio," as the Mexicans style him. A trip to Yosemite Valley in 1960 yielded nothing—nothing, that is, except the impression that when Bierce vanished Yosemite would have been an ideal place for anybody to disappear. From 1960 to the present, I have from time to time broached the mystery of Bierce to the numerous Mexican personages I know and have interviewed in that romantic republic. But none of these many probings ever produced the results I wanted.

The late Elias Torres, who wrote more on Villa than any other writer, always held that the American was slain at Villa's command. But when "Don Ambrosio" sought to run away from it all in Mexico, he was a man not only up in years but a heavy drinker (*catarrene muy borracho*). He certainly sojourned for a period in Chihuahua City, addressing letters from that state capital to his daughter in Los Angeles. Newsmen of the Chihuahuan *El Heraldo* advertised his description in their pages and sought out informants to identify him. Their efforts failed, as no testifier proved able to pick out Bierce's photograph from some dozen of different individuals submitted to their scrutiny. The American Consul in Chihuahua City in those hectic days— a gentleman named Marion Letcher—may have had knowledge of what transpired, but Mr. Letcher long ago retired to live in

Italy. I wrote to the ex-Consul in Italy but never heard from him. Somewhere today, in Mexico or elsewhere, there must live a survivor of the Revolution who knows what happened. Hopefully, I continue to this hour to ask questions of all such people I hear of or encounter.

In the total absence of any major datum that an impartial investigator would consider conclusive, I have almost forsaken hopes of unearthing a worthwhile lead. In the Revolution of that day, disappearances occurred often and usually without notice. Moreover, Bierce seemed bent on self-destruction and openly said so. My present thought is that Villa did not murder this *Americano,* whose disappearance must rank among the greatest of mysteries. I rather think that age and alcohol together with likely privation and possible exposure to the elements account for his end.

Jesse James's Chivalry

According to a report by my former student, Mr. Ray Gregory of Columbia, Missouri, his grandfather, Mr. Cliff Gregory, once encountered the notorious hold-up artist, Jesse James, on a train going from Columbia to Kansas City. Having heard that the outlaw was chivalrous to women, Mr. Gregory slipped his wallet to his wife for safekeeping when he saw Jesse board the train. Thus he saved his greenbacks, and all the robber got from grandfather Gregory were the few loose coins he had in his pockets. Jesse made no demands for money on grandmother Gregory; instead, he gave her a kiss. The outlaw repeated this performance of robbing the men and kissing the women with all of the train passengers. The grandfather therefore had only kind memories of the James boys, for he was proud of having outwitted Jesse and having retained possession of his money. The grandmother enjoyed remembering her experience, too. In the opinion of the Gregory family, Jesse James measured up to the best traditions of the gentlemanly badman. His talent for train robberies has long been established. His treatment of women, as manifested in this story, exhibits an element of chivalry in his character that deserves to be better known.

Myths of Pershing's Mexican Campaign

Beloved Mexico, in our country
When Carranza governed from the dais
Twelve thousand Americans passed
Wanting to punish Villa for an error.[1]

The Punitive Expedition of 1916, in which General Pershing chased Pancho Villa deep into Mexico for his raid on Columbus, New Mexico, resulted in the creation of many songs and myths among the Mexicans.[2] This folklore, extolling the prowess of both Villa and his Mexican competitor, Carranza, has distorted history in picturing General John J. Pershing's strategy as wholly awkward and useless. It also has recorded the intense, if unwarranted, hatred the natives came in many instances to nurse for the cavalrymen who entered the state of Chihuahua in search of the bandits.

Interest of the Yankees in the Mexican campaign has been reflected in a recent novel and in several songs. The American novel about the Expedition was *They Came to Cordura,* by Glendon Swarthout. This book, later made into a film with the same title, appeared in 1960. Founded on Pershing's pursuit of Villa, it concerned a few minor fictitious events before and after the last cavalry charge in Mexico at Ojos Azules, Chihuahua. The plot presented Major Thorn, Awards Officer of the campaign, ordered by General Pershing to escort five cavalrymen slated for the Medal of Honor across the barren state of Chihuahua to Cordura and safety. During this trek, they encountered many hardships and personal problems, which enriched the story. Almost entirely imaginary, the tale tended to glorify life in the desert and to underemphasize the nearness of an enemy —Pancho Villa.

Oral tradition also appeared in songs cavalrymen sang. At the outset they felt rather jubilant about the chase. They thought it would be a lark. Much to their disappointment, it lasted on and on. But during the Expedition, the troopers sang a number of happy, tuneful verses "on the spot" as they traveled along. One of those they sang, "El Paso, I Love You," was composed by Dr. Corinne McCarthy. Its verses described the attractions of the border, the salubrious clime and imposing mountains, the sapphire blue of the sky, and the golden mesas stretching to the sunset. Then it concluded with a reference to the Great River.

> El Paso, El Paso, I love you,
> To you I'll ever be true,
> You're set like a Gem,
> In a Queen's diadem,
> On the banks of the Rio Grande.

A second song, "Camping on the Border," also by McCarthy, explained how many of the Yankees grew homesick for Pennsylvania, Michigan, or elsewhere in their "tents pitched on the desert, in the sun's white glare." Its verses echoed with farewells to Massachusetts, Rhode Island, "Old New Jersey, and New York 'cross the way." A tristful note crept into the refrain of these Americans who had come so far away from their homes.

> 'Mid the cactus and the sand,
> Along the Rio Grande,
> We're camping,
> Camping on the border land.[3]

Another one, "The Militia Border Patrol," complained that the land was hot, the wind strong, and the chances of getting shot rather strong. It also reported how heavy a sixty-pound pack became to a foot-soldier. The verses concluded with bitter reflections on eating "hard tack" and tramping endlessly through the sand.[4]

Stanzas like these epitomized the hopes and high spirits of the Americans as they prepared to chase Pancho Villa back into Mexico. But after the pursuit started, they began to tire easily, both of the land and the food. Bone weary from marching over rocky earth, they trudged along and composed a dirge of their own about their hardships.

> We left the border for Parral
> In search of Villa and Lopez, his old pal.
> Our horses they were hungry
> And we ate parched corn.
> It was damn hard living
> In the state of Chihuahua
> Where Pancho Villa was born.[5]

As the hounding of Villa quickened, tale bearers sprang up everywhere. They told how Villa transformed himself into a little black dog that barked at the heels of General Pershing's soldiers and threw them into helpless confusion. They told how he changed himself at will into a desert plant and so escaped detection as the weary cavalrymen dragged by. They told how the ghost of his deceased mother came to him in the night to warn him of the enemy's approach. They bragged how he misled the Yankees by reversing the shoes on his horses so that he appeared to be returning from the direction toward which he was fleeing.

One of the wildest stories to issue from Fort Bliss concerned a letter written by a woman in California to Pershing. In it she wrote that Villa often visited her at night and that, for a consideration, she could arrange to permit the Americans to capture him. Now unobtainable, the letter supposedly lodges in a "secret" file of the General's papers at Fort Bliss. Of the same character, another story represented Pershing in 1917, after the Expedition, offering the adventurer Emil Holmdahl in El Paso a sum of $10,000 if he would assassinate Villa. Holmdahl decided not to try it. He told "Black Jack" Pershing, allegedly so-called because of his attachment to Negro troops, that Pancho would be difficult to isolate from his omnipresent bodyguards and that, besides, he liked the bandit. The tallest yarn of all depicted Pershing and

Funston hiring Villa at Fort Bliss in 1916 to raid Columbus for $80,000, so that they could train their troops in Mexico and fool Germany into believing the Americans would be unable to come to Europe to aid the Allies.

Another story developed after Villa received a wound at Guerrero, when he battled the Carrancistas, not the Americans. With a hole in his leg, Villa had to hide until his wound had healed well enough to travel. His bodyguards, known as the Golden Ones, took him to a cave in the Sierra Madre foothills. While hiding there, Mexicans claim that he sat and watched the American soldiers who camped below him. As usual, the Yankees sang to keep their spirits up. One of these tunes greatly mystified the Mexican chief because he could not understand it. The Americans kept repeating, "It's a Long, Long Way to Tipperary."[6] Villa, not being able to understand English, fancied their words said in Spanish, *"Se jalo el buey con tapadera,"* which much amused him because he interpreted the song to say, "The Ox Got Drunk with Blinders On." Could it be, he thought, that the Americans were describing their own stupidity in not being able to find him?

Both the Americans and Mexicans had mixed feelings about the Punitive Expedition. Folklore, not fact, presents Villa as used to living in the wildwood and enjoying Pershing's pursuit because he liked playing "cat and mouse," particularly when he could play the "cat."[7] This he did by disporting himself in the towns, to all of which he had access, while the tiring troopers plodded on in the dull country to which their movements had been restricted. Villa was in his own land and knew it well, which gave him a distinct advantage. Villa was so sure of himself, people claimed, that he masqueraded as an American, in an American uniform, under the American flag.[8]

The Yankees found the Mexican climate enervating. Not being used to the wind and sand, they often became discouraged. Meanwhile, Villa irritated them. In one tale, the troopers sat down to eat breakfast. About that moment Villa came riding up. Quickly dispersing the *gringoes,* Villa sat down in their places and ate their breakfasts, later on taking to the hills. The Mexican folk say that during the Expedition Villa put on weight eating American ham and eggs. Another story says the Americans were anxious to get Villa because he had cached $100,000 in his money belt, and that they tried to entice him to eat breakfast with them. None of the Yankees minded losing a few vittles if they could only get their hands on that money belt.[9]

"The Corrido of Pancho Villa" brags of the brave natives and labels the *gringoes* cowards. Its opening stanza declares that Carranza "let the Americans pass 10,000 soldiers, 600 airplanes, looking for Villa, wanting to kill him." Subsequent stanzas mention the false report of his death, Villa's airplane, his prisoners, men who lost their ears, the big feet of the Yankees, and the chagrin of the Americans when forced to return to their land.[10]

So ran the verses of the *corridos* of northern Mexico. In them the natives appeared ever courageous, ever victorious; in them the Yankees always looked red and shamefaced as they retreated homeward. But did the Americans have no hero to be extolled by the makers of myths?

As a match for Villa, the Yanks had a man who beat him, by name Colonel S.R.H. "Tommy" Tompkins, a fighting officer about whom folktales still circulate. He was the elder brother of Major Frank Tompkins, who had met the Mexicans in Parral. After the withdrawal of Pershing, Villa attacked Juarez on June 14-15, 1919. Tompkins then commanded the 7th United States Cavalry. He and his men crossed from El Paso into Mexico, vigorously assaulted the Villistas, and put them to full flight. The bandits quailed at the sight of the cold steel shining from the bayonets drawn by the advancing Americans.

Tompkins was not a strict disciplinarian. In many instances, he favored the enlisted men in preference to his officers. In one folktale, a junior officer reported that he overheard the enlisted men calling him a "Pink-Whiskered S.O.B." Tompkins replied that as long as his troops respected him for what he was, he did not care what they thought of his whiskers.

When involved in a serious problem, "Tommy" Tompkins reportedly often treated the difficulty as a joke. This may have been to release some of the tension in his men. One hilarious incident involving Tompkins and his younger officers occurred as the Expedition crossed the border into Mexico. Not knowing the country well, they became confused. Noticing this condition, a lieutenant pulled out a map. Unknown to him, the map was one ordinarily used for practice maneuvers on the Gettysburg battlefield in Pennsylvania. Two or three times the Expedition had been perilously close to becoming lost. The map thus seemed all important. After studying it intently, Tompkins finally snapped, "Now we're getting somewhere!"

In order to prevent his troops from pillaging the Mexican communities which they passed through, Tompkins kept his troops out of all towns. When a few of his enlisted men stole a pig, his punishment was to bury the pig in front of his own tent in plain view of everyone. In this folktale the feet stuck out of the ground just enough to entice everyone who saw them. After burying the pig, Tompkins departed on a reconnaissance mission. When he returned, the pig's feet stood up precisely where he had buried them—except that one leg stuck out in the wrong direction. The men obviously had stolen the pig and eaten it. Upon seeing this, Tompkins dismissed the matter from his mind, regarding it as a good morale factor for his troops.[11]

Tompkins was a rough but just officer. Although his language waxed profane, the men liked him. He drew complete loyalty from all of his subordinate officers as well as the enlinted men.

The yarn about Pershing himself most likely to have impressed Villa told how the American General in the Phillippines put to the torch all the men, women, and children of Mindanao.[12] Exaggerated tales of "Black Jack" Pershing's cruelty and the toughness of officers like Tompkins may explain why Villa ran instead of meeting his opponents in open battle.

The Mexicans, however, do not speak of Villa's "running." To them, he was a fine guerrilla leader. To them, his bravery in battle compensated for his flaws of character. Many songs told of his valor, delineating him as a strong man with a warm heart. At the commencement of the Revolution, he first came to public notice because he tried to help the *peons* of northern Mexico. They armed themselves and flocked to him, willing to go anywhere to battle with him if he would only free them. Because he did try to help them, they looked up to and revered him. The *corrido*, "Pancho Villa," surpassed all others extolling his bravery. Its rhyming stanzas reported that he began his rise with a group of peasants. It continued with his escape from the Yankees, a deed that made him a legend, and then told of how he performed like a *toreador* in out-maneuvering his pursuers.[13]

In view of these paeans to Villa, it is no wonder that the masses held him in high esteem. Moreover, he always remained steadfast in friendship. When he picked a friend, that friendship endured. Robert E. Lee Fogle, an engineer on the local trains around El Paso in 1916, stated, "He would take his shirt off his back and give it to you if he liked you, or if he didn't he'd snatch the same shirt off and revile you."[14] Men also admired him because of his demonstrated military acumen. If he had received a formal education, he would have developed, they say, into one of the really great generals of the world. As it was, he held a magnetic spell over his soldiers. Their extraordinary courage and willingness to fight until death contributed much to the prestige of their leader.

Pancho Villa, very *mujeriego,* had a strange power over women.[15] He had at least eight wives. These women, from first to last, were Luz Corral, Juana Torres, Pilar Escalona, Asuncion B., Austroberta Renteria, Maria Amalia Baca, Manuela Casas, and Soledad Seañez. Señor Salvador Caballero B., celebrated historian of Chihuahua, asserted that Villa had a total of thirty-two wives. Ramon Piñon Acosta, of El Paso, stated that when Villa died "he left more widows than there are crosses in the cemetery."

During Pershing's chase, Villa did not live with his legal wife, Luz Corral. In 1915 he had sent her out of Mexico by an American friend, and she sojourned briefly in San Antonio, Texas, before moving for a much longer stay in Cuba. Señora Luz Corral thus knows less about the Punitive Expedition than Soledad Seañez, whom he married in 1919, when the resurgent Villa boasted of his eluding Pershing and grew so brazen as to attack Juarez and incite the Yanks against him once more. A full account of the loves of Villa would comprise a book in itself. His conquests were legion. In Mexico today, the poor *peons* remember his generosity, the rich, his daring antics, his troops, his military genius, but the women will never forget his virility and sultry desires. But Villa observed certain reservations about women. Even though a polygamist, he would not allow them to grace his camp as they did that of the Carrancistas. This fact separated him from the rest of the lawless bands that roamed the wilderness of the northern states of Mexico during the Revolution. Because Villa had certain morals (he liked the Mormons), one *corrido* vaunted with justice that

> Even though you may not like it, I repeat
> In a plain unvarnished way
> That chicks like Pancho Villa
> Are not born every day.[16]

After the Americans left Mexico, Villa stormed around a while and showed off his power to lead men victoriously again at the battle of Juarez in 1919. Something, however, had gone out of him during Pershing's chase. He remained in the public eye, it is true, but with this major difference; people originally had thought of him as a hero; now they regarded him as a fugitive. When he received an opportunity to retire, he seized it. He commenced leading a normal life at Rancho Canutillo, Durango. The blood-thirsty thief, who had thousands of deaths to his account, became a model of sobriety, industry, and domestic virtues. Then havoc hit him, struck him heavily. After living such a riotous life, his death could come in only one way—with violence.

The bird image fitted Villa and stuck to him to the end. Esequiel Martinez, author of the ballad *"La Muerte de Francisco Villa,"* used it when describing him as a *"Pollito fine."*

> He was a fine baby chick,
> And there was no other in the nation;
> And because they were afraid of him
> They killed him by treason.[17]

The figure of a bird reappeared at the last as Villa's image of doom. The folktale goes that a gambling debt over fighting cocks precipitated his demise. Villa, much addicted to the Mexican national sport of cockfighting, had run seriously into debt. Instead of paying his obligation to the cock fancier Meliton Lozoya, he publicly threatened to kill the man. Full of fear and trembling, Lozoya set about trying to save himself. He soon found other parties who had deep enough grudges against Villa to want him killed.

Meanwhile, Villa settled down in Parral to a normal life with his wife Soledad Seañez, and there he became in some ways a respected citizen of his community. The men of Parral deferred to him and the women there looked up to him. But his work of slaughtering had wound against him the clocks of damnation; the inevitable had to come.

On July 20, 1923, while riding into Parral from his home in Canutillo in his Dodge automobile, seven men ambushed and killed him and his personal guards, Miguel Trillo, Daniel Tamayo, Rosalio Rosales, Tomas Medrano, Claro Hurtado, and Ramon Contreras. The seven murderers were Meliton Lozoya, Juan José Saiz, and his cousin José Saiz Pardo Pardo, two of the Guerra brothers, Ruperto Vara, and Salas Barraza.[18] Only one Mexican survived the ambush, but he never talked much. This man, Villa's cousin Ramon Contreras, escaped from the death car with an injury in his arm. He later lost the arm and died in 1955. Different tales exist as to who actually committed the crime. Many volunteered their names to try to get publicity. Did a Mexican try to get revenge for his family that Villa had wiped out? Villa, still considered a threat to politicians, like Gabriel Chavez, General Plutarco Calles, and President Obregon, might have been killed for political causes. Did a group of old, unforgiving Carrancistas annihilate Villa and his right-hand men? Did an American kill him just for the recognition? The best answer is that Obregon and Calles hired the job done because they feared Villa might return to power and also were tired of paying him a large pension.

Historians, with respect for facts, would probably say that to murder such a tyrant was justified. But after the deed, ballad writers painted in words a sympathetic picture of the dead *hombre*. *"La Muerte de Francisco Villa"* made a long story out of the killing.

> Gentlemen, bear in mind
> And be very attentive
> That on the twentieth day of July
> Villa was assassinated.
>
> In the year nineteen hundred,
> In its twenty-third year,
> They killed Pancho Villa
> At Hidalgo del Parral.

Twelve succeeding stanzas reverted to his exploits in the Revolution before turning to the fatal hour of his assassination. As may be seen below, the *corrido* next specified the day as July 20, retold known facts about the death car, mentioned the men who accompanied him, and named the section of Parral where the tragedy transpired. According to this source, he was shot when leaving Parral for his ranch at Canutillo.

> The morning of the twentieth day
> He left for his ranch
> From the city of Parral
> Where he lost his life.
>
> Villa passed in his car
> That he drove himself
> Without knowing that traitors
> Were already waiting for him.
>
> In a section near the entrance
> Called Guanajuato,
> Passing by a lonely house
> The terrible assassination was committed.
>
> When passing by that house
> Various fusillades were heard.
> Villa with Trillo and his guards
> Perished all together.

Nearer the end, *"La Muerte"* evidently alluded to Meliton Lozoya and Salas Barraza in enumerating only two murderers:

> Two infamous assassins
> Instantly bore down upon
> Villa and his soldiers
> And shot their already dead bodies.

The ballad, sympathetic to Villa, asserted that government troops pursued the culprits toward the town of Santa Barbara. At the close, verses declared that Mexico always will miss and need Francisco Villa. More related to the Expedition, the third stanza before the end referred unrepentantly to the seventeen Americans killed at Columbus.

> In the town of Columbus
> He left his traces;
> Only seventeen gringoes
> Were what he left there.[19]

In 1926, three years after Villa's burial, a strange and evil event befell his remains. The deed occurred ten years after the Punitive Expedition, but it related to the major aim of that often forgotten chase, namely the apprehension of Pancho.

On the dark, cold night of Friday, February 5, 1926, five defilers, said to be his own henchmen, entered the small cemetery in Parral, opened the grave of Villa, and decapitated his corpse. The head was then borne through the city streets on a long pole. Next day a report reached El Paso that the head had been seen in Bosque Bonito, Chihuahua, en route for Columbus, New Mexico. This hearsay harmonized with a note that had been left in the violated grave to the effect that the defilers were carrying the skull to Columbus for a $5,000 reward. The horrendous deed shocked most of the Mexican people. Nobody except a *gringo,* they said, could have performed such a fiendish trick. The man everybody in Parral suspected was Emil Holmdahl. They ignored the real culprit, General Durazo, who performed the excavation. Holmdahl, a soldier of fortune with no military status whatever, had gone with Pershing into Mexico. In El Paso earlier, he belonged to the Adventurers' Club, a fast-moving band of soldiers of fortune. Holmdahl sported a black diamond ring on his finger, wore flamboyant clothes, and attracted attention wherever he went. After the Expedition, Mr. Joe Goodell, the owner, gave Emil a free room in El Paso at the Sheldon Hotel, simply in repayment for his drawing power and influence over prospective patrons. Suspicion, then, fell on this man.

Fables replaced facts in the ballad "The Beheading of Villa," which ignored the actions of the Mexican General's grave diggers and focused the blame completely on the Americans.

> The gringoes no longer respect
> Even the peace of the grave:
> They have desecrated the tomb
> Of Pancho Villa in Parral.

In this *corrido* Holmdahl, of Teutonic descent, received the epithet "Saxon huckster." Other verses asserted that he removed the cadaver, cut off the head, and defiled the body.

> He broke the concrete
> With an iron crowbar

> And removing the loose earth
> He withdrew the corpse from its crypt.
>
> He then cut off the head,
> Poor human remains,
> And leaving the grave open,
> The American fled.
>
> The mutilated body
> Thrown into the pit
> Was discovered the next day,
> Oh! What an excess of evil![20]

What was Emil Holmdahl's motive? Well, why not revenge? The *corrido* declared that "If you desire to claim the head, Offers may be made at Columbus." But there may have been another motive. Mr. Goodell "roomed" Emil free at the Sheldon Hotel (now the Hilton), but he had to have money for food and drink. Legend also has it that a Science Institute in Chicago made an offer of $5,000 for the head because the Yankees wanted to study his brains. Old Villistas in Juarez claim that American scientists shrunk his head to the size of an orange in order to study it better with a powerful microscope.

However that may be, Mr. L. M. Shadbolt, also a member of the Adventurers' Club, recalled in 1957 a meeting he had in 1927 or 1928 with Emil Holmdahl in the Sheldon Hotel. "Emil was light on funds at the moment" and thirsty. They shuttled to Juarez day and night. This continued for five days, until Shadbolt and his associate Clyde H. Creighton did not feel very well. Then "in strode Holmdahl, a bundle wrapped in newspaper under one arm and a bottle of Don Jose Cuervo under the other." Suddenly Emil said: " 'Say, I got something to show you guys.' With that, holding one edge of the newspaper wrapping his bundle, he gave a casual flip—and out rolled General Villa's head."[21]

Perhaps the Punitive Expedition of 1916-1917, the vengeful pursuit of the Villistas, came thus to its final end in El Paso in 1927-1928. One by one their leaders had been killed. Pablo Lopez had been executed long ago. An American private had shot the great Candelario Cervantes, who led the raid. Holmdahl himself had killed Julio Cardenas. Only Villa had escaped them, to fall a victim of a Mexican fusillade. Cheated of the privilege of killing him themselves, did the Americans consider the Columbus score settled at last when in this legend Emil Holmdahl displayed the skull of Villa to his startled El Paso friends in the old Sheldon Hotel?

Although Mexican resentment of the Expedition can be at least partially understood, one cannot condone the disservice that native folklore has done in seriously misrepresenting what actually happened. When celebrated historians have incorporated these myths into their pages as facts,[22] serious damage to American prestige has resulted. Until Mexicans revise their histories, these false impressions will be repeated from textbook to textbook, instructing the impressionable youth of a proud Southern neighbor to picture the emaciated figure of tall Uncle Sam as a sneaky, murderous ambusher and a ghoulish violator of the grave.

Let it be remembered that Mexicans, not Americans, ambushed Pancho Villa and riddled him with bullets. The ballad *"La Decapi-tacion"* erred therefore in making the Yankees guilty of his death.

> The Yankees were not able
> To defeat him in a fair fight,
> So they cut off his head.[23]

The man who stole Villa's skull, according to the historian Ing. Oscar A. Martinez, was, not Holmdahl, but Brigadier General Francisco R. Durazo, then chief of the Garrison at Parral.

At other times folk literature more closely regarded the truth. When Carranza failed to run down Villa after Pershing's withdrawal, Don Adolfo de la Huerta met with the fugitive and persuaded him to retire from war and politics in return for the gift of the Hacienda de Canutillo, Durango. The verses of *"La Muerte"* reported these transactions verbatim.

> In nineteen hundred twenty
> When the war ended,
> Don Adolfo De La Huerta
> Conferred with Villa
>
> And he asked for guarantees,
> This brave leader;
> And the government gave him
> The ranch at Canutillo.[24]

A poem on his surrender, *"La Rendicion,"* reiterated the datum on his retirement to Canutillo, near the town of Las Nieves.[25] Nobody will question his presence at Columbus, to which he came after saying farewell to most of his soldiers. *"Los Combates"* reported that he came to see the Americans.

> *Decia don Francisco Villa:*
> *Adios, adios, Mexicanos;*
> *Ya me voy para Columbus*
> *A ver los Americanos.*[26]

The Punitive Expedition proposed to return the guerrilla's Columbus call. One trouble the Americans had concerned false reports of his death, but the major difficulty centered on determining his whereabouts. Mexicans have unanimously denied that he lolled at ease in the home of Pedro Alvarado when Frank Tompkins entered Parral. But all the circumstances at Parral, even the spirited defense by the green-eyed Alsatian beauty, reflected authentically his amorous proclivities. *"La Persecucion"* described Villa's pursuit and offered advice on where the Americans could locate him. The city specified, interestingly, was Parral.

> And if they want to make a social call,
> He is in Parral; they can see him there.[27]

Perhaps the *Americanos* had a valid reason, after all, in entering that city.

Humble literature holds a prominent place in the saga of Pancho Villa's escape from the Punitive Expedition. Imaginative as Mexicans are, folklore in the years to come will likely hold an even larger place. But it has already presented a false picture, representing him as "a countryside hero."

The actual reason why Villa ran so fast was that he had become obsessed with fear for his personal safety. In Mexico City, Francisco I. Murgia tried to assassinate him on October 27, 1914.[28] After that, he became afraid of everybody. He would change sleeping places several times during the night through fear that some of his followers would assassinate him in his sleep. He made his cooks taste first the food they had prepared for him before he would eat it. A year later, October 9, 1915, he told the pro-Villa editor of the El Paso *Times* that "I am here in Juarez." He still feared for his life and jumped at his shadow. He said: "Here maybe I shall die, and probably soon . . . they may murder me on the highway; they may assassinate me while asleep in my bed."[29] During that same year Frank M. Lynch and Lee H. Crews, of the El Paso Bank and Trust Company, where Villa had his money, went to Juarez to deliver the General's payroll to him. They found him in his tent groveling under his cot, his pop eyes rolling in fear.[30] The strain of waiting for somebody to shoot him had almost driven him mad. Only when backed by overpowering numbers did he splutter and strut. The naked truth is that Pershing harried Villa closely, killed his chief officers as well as most of his men, and kept him on the run. Only in folklore did Pancho Villa personify the Lion of the North.

NOTES

The present work reached completion through three grants (1961-63) from Organized Research, Texas Western College, El Paso. These funds enabled the author to go to Mexico, visit the scenes described, and interview many of the people mentioned herein. Special thanks for courtesies in Parral, Mexico, belong to Don Felipe Brown and Ing. Horacio Fernandez.

[1] C. Herrara Frimont (ed.), *Los Corridos de la Revolución* (Mexico, D.F., 1946), p. 64; Donald F. Fogelquist, "The Figure of Pancho Villa in the Corridos of the Mexican Revolution," *University of Miami Hispanic-American Studies* (Coral Gables, Florida, 1942), pp. 11-22.

[2] Haldeen Braddy and John H. McNeely, "Francisco Villa in Folk-Songs," *Arizona Quarterly*, X, 5-16 (1954).

[3] The songs by Dr. McCarthy are quoted through the courtesy of Mr. Chris Fox, El Paso, Texas.

[4] I have been unable to identify the author of this song or to obtain permission to print its verses.

[5] This song is quoted through the courtesy of Mr. John W. Breen, Columbus, New Mexico.

[6] Américo Paredes, "The Ox Got Drunk with Blinders On," *Western Folklore*, XX, 42 (Jan., 1961).

[7] Dr. Arthur L. Campa, University of Denver, Denver, Colorado.

[8] Villistas supposedly mixed and mingled in the towns with the Yanks, who of course could not tell one Mexican from another. Haldeen Braddy, *Cock of the Walk* (Port Washington, N.Y., 1970), p. 149.

[9] See 7.

[10] Vincente T. Mendoza, *El Corrido Mexicano* (Mexico, D.F., 1954), p. 93.

[11] Lt. Col. Bertram C. Wright, El Paso, Texas.

[12] Maj. Herbert W. Conklin, El Paso, Texas.

[13] E. Guerrero (ed.), *Corridos Populares* (Mexico, D.F., 1915), p. 18. Most educated Mexicans contend that the masses never favored Villa; the songs of the folk thus must be interpreted as exaggerations.

[14] Mr. Robert E. Lee Fogle, El Paso, Texas.

[15] Haldeen Braddy, "The Loves of Pancho Villa," *Western Folklore*, XXI, 175-182 (July, 1962).

16 Mendoza, *op. cit.,* p. 68.

17 Frimont, *op. cit.,* p. 82.

18 William V. Morrison and C. L. Sonnichsen, "They Killed Pancho Villa!," *Frontier Times,* XXXIV, 6-10, 48-50 (Winter, 1959-60). Barraza, it may be noted, had made several prior attempts to kill Villa as early as 1921; Teodoro Torres, Jr., *Pancho Villa, Una Vida de Romance y de Tragedia* (San Antonio, Texas, 1924), p. 220. Lozoya allegedly had tried to kill Villa beforehand, too. In the first prepared ambush Villa arrived on the scene just as school let out and filled the streets with children so that the murderers did not fire at him. A few weeks later Lozoya had better luck. Villa entered Parral "from Canutillo" through Plaza Juarez onto Calle Riva Palacio (now Maclovio Herrera), and here he was shot. The bullets riddled the right hand side of the car opposite the driver, which shows that the vehicle was turning a corner to enter Parral. For these last data, I am indebted to Mrs. H. F. Keeler, of El Paso, who grew up in Mexico. There yet remain many witnesses in Parral who testify that he was leaving that city for Canutillo when he was killed. The truth is pretty hard to come by in Mexico.

19 Frimont, *op. cit.,* p. 79, eighteen Americans died at Columbus.

20 Haldeen Braddy, "The Head of Pancho Villa," *Western Folklore,* XIX, 25-33 (Jan., 1960).

21 *Ibid.,* p. 32.

22 Joaquín Márquez Montiel, *Hombres Célebres de Chihuahua* (Mexico, D.F., 1953), p. 235.

23 See 20.

24 Frimont, *op. cit.,* p. 80.

25 E. Guerrero, *"La Rendicion de Villa,"* from a print.

26 Frimont, *op. cit.,* p. 63.

27 *Ibid.,* p. 65.

28 Jesse Ed Rascoe, *The Treasure Album of Pancho Villa* (El Paso, Texas, 1962), p. 16.

29 John Middagh, *Frontier Newspaper* (El Paso, Texas, 1958), p. 177.

30 Mrs. Herbert W. Conklin, El Paso, Texas.

9

The Underworld of El Pablote
and La Nacha

The most notorious character in the modern era of the Southwest bears the name of La Nacha. She is now an aging grandmother, the widow of El Pablote Gonzalez. According to both the
El Paso Police and Federal Bureau of Investigation, she has done
more damage in the Southwest than Lucky Luciano, the exiled
narcotics king of the twenties. According to criminals in El Paso,
she long has acted as a queen of the dope traffic and a fence for
stolen merchandise. Her rule over the Southwest has lasted for a
period of thirty-seven years, a reign occasionally interrupted by
jail sentences and pitched gun battles.

La Nacha's real name is Ignacia Jasso, viuda de Gonzalez, who
was himself the first borderland king of narcotics. She is known
around the globe by the diminutive of her Christian name, La
Nacha. In her own devious ways, La Nacha has become as infamous on the border today as the bandit Pancho Villa was in an
earlier epoch. When a young woman, she married a gangster
gunman, El Pablote Gonzalez. El Pablote then led an underworld
narcotics ring in Juarez, Mexico, where no one challenged his
power. He originated the Mexican version of the one-way ride,
from which there is no return. These one-way trips led to the
piedras (rocky terrain) south of Juarez, and anyone who went
there never returned alive. One hundred and three deaths resulted

from El Pablote's famous "trips." The ex-owner of La Nacional Restaurant, Mr. Danino, recently described the narcotics king. He said that "Pablote was a *gigante,* over six feet tall and always surrounded by his *pistoleros.* When he used to enter my restaurant on South El Paso Street, all my customers would leave their food for fear that they might offend him in some way. They took off through the door without saying anything."

On the night of October 30, 1931, El Pablote met his death at the hands of Special Officer Robles, of the Mexican Police. His demise came as the result of a gun fight in the La Popular Cafe in Juarez. The officer fled across the border in fear of his life. During this time, La Nacha was placed in prison on a narcotics charge. There she publicly swore vengeance to kill her husband's assassin.

La Nacha's long and versatile career began in 1924, when she was first jailed on a narcotics violation. From that time on, it became one jail after another until the death of her husband, when she took over his trade. In the eyes of the law, La Nacha is just as ruthless as and much more intelligent than El Pablote. Nevertheless, after her ascendancy, she was immediately released each time that officers arrested her.

Early in the recent thirties she allied her forces with Enrique Fernandez, the so-called Al Capone of Mexico. After his long reign of terror, the government sent several special investigators to break up the gang. There was a gunfight in Juarez, and Fernandez was shot in the foot. All of the officers went scurrying back to Mexico City, except one, who was thrown out of a car in front of the El Paso Police Department and riddled with bullets. Enrique Fernandez and La Nacha finally had a disagreement. The near end of Fernandez came with his ambushment near the Downtown Juarez Bullring. He barely escaped with his life and fled into the heart of Mexico. His survival proved short-lived, for he soon met death from gunfire on a crowded street in the Mexican capital.

After years of shootings and street brawling, the Juarez Mayor Bermudez told his police force to "Bring La Nacha in or turn in your badges."

Meanwhile, the United States Federal Officers had a plan to lure her into the United States. They sent two representatives, posing as Oklahoma narcotic peddlers, to buy a large supply of

dope. The undercover agents accompanied La Nacha to a morphine factory in Guadalajara and then to Jalisco, where they
found hundreds of opium poppy fields hidden in the mountains.
Here they encountered two of La Nacha's right hand men, "El
Abogado" (The Lawyer) and "El Chemico" (The Chemist). The
agents failed to lure La Nacha to the United States, but they did
receive delivery of $8,000.00 worth of morphine and so soon
arrested "The Lawyer" and "The Chemist" at San Antonio, Texas.

The American Government agents, however, determined to
continue their investigations. They tried again but without avail.
The Federal District in El Paso, Texas, under the advice of
Assistant United States Attorney, Holvey Williams, cooperated
by indicting both La Nacha and her runners. This attorney observed that under article 377, title 18, "Anyone found guilty of a
conspiracy contrary to the laws of the United States is subject to
indictment and extradition even though they have never entered
the United States." He further had this to say about her smuggling
of contraband drugs: "She clearly sent the delivery to the United
States and violated the War Time Laws of conspiracy and should
have been extradited by the Mexican Government."

In 1942, La Nacha finally fell into the waiting hands of the
Mexican Government. After many long hours of vigilance, the
Mexican police apprehended her in the act of giving a shot of
morphine to an addict. Under wartime law, she was compelled
to enter the Mexican prison at Tres Marias Island, where she
remained for the duration of World War One, or for two years
and three months. Of her, the prisoners said: "She made the
best tortillas of anyone we have ever had to cook for us." On
February 4, 1943, she was allowed to leave the prison to attend
her son's wedding. All of Juarez attended. Everyone was griev-
ing because the "poor mother" could not be present, when in
she walked, accompanied by four armed guards. After her release
from Tres Marias Island, she remained in hiding without anyone
being able to discover her whereabouts. Prison officials and
prisoners alike say that in 1944 she changed her way of life,
becoming very religious. It seemed as though La Nacha had
reformed. Some of the prisoners used to pray that she would
be released, because, they claimed, such a good person should
not be left in prison.

In 1950 La Nacha returned to Juarez, supposedly converted

to a better life. She did nothing but read the Bible. Yet criminal operators still found her the biggest fence in all the Southwest. In 1954 she was again arrested, during the big crackdown on narcotics, but soon won her release with an *amparo* (a special immunity).

In 1955, Ruben Salazar, an El Paso reporter, went with a man whom he described as a "hypo" and watched her give him a shot of heroin. He later appeared before a Senate Investigation Committee on Narcotics and told all he knew. Mr. Salazar is now working in Los Angeles, California, and does not dare to return to Mexico. In late 1955 La Nacha turned in the Juarez Chief of Detectives for trying to make a deal with her. She stated that she was no longer in business and resented his accusations. In the same year police accused her of taking stolen diamonds from thieves who had robbed Shain's Jewelry store in El Paso. Nothing came of these accusations, and the charges were all ultimately dropped.

Recently in Albuquerque, New Mexico, policemen became interested in La Nacha's activities when two young junkies were found dead from overdoses of heroin. The boys were eighteen years old each. They had told their friends that they went to Juarez and there purchased a large amount of heroin from La Nacha.

On January 16, 1961, a preacher from Albuquerque came to Juarez to try to convert her. He said, "My mission is to take this woman from hell and convert her to the ways of God and keep her from ruining the lives of young people." He claimed that he earlier had converted "La Concha," a bootlegger from Cheyenne, Wyoming. La Nacha told him, however, that "I am too far gone; God can do nothing for me now." This Reverend, Alberto Sandoval, said that God told him to see her. He also testified that he talked to the priest at the El Rosario Catholic Church in Juarez and that the priest reported she was a loyal church member.

Today La Nacha deals only in American money and sells a *papel* of heroin for $5.00. In her home she has modern furniture with all the latest conveniences. Her house is cluttered with Saints and filled with her children and grandchildren. In a recent interview she gave every appearance of being a sentimental grandmother—and a handsome widow of good repute.

The foregoing data, garnered from underworld sources as well as the El Paso lawyers, Joe Rey and son, may serve as a background for the following stanzaic folksong on El Pablote and La Nacha. Material of this kind is hard to come by, and the investigation failed to unearth any further *corridos,* though others may exist or now be in the process of composition. The present folksong, copied down in a Juarez cantina for a consideration, tells a more or less accurate story of the historical facts just reviewed. It forms a not unimportant addition to the small corpus of underworld narcotic folklays already known.

EL CORRIDO DE EL
PABLOTE GONZALEZ

Gentlemen, I am going to sing a song with a fine expression
About the secret deeds of El Pablote, king of morphine.
He was always drinking and throwing money away,
And with gun in hand threatened the whole world.
There was no one who could stop him, not even the police.
He relished the fact that he could do whatever he wanted.
On October 4 in the night El Pablote, or Pablo Gonzalez,
Cowardly killed the special officer Teodoro Alvarez.
They took him prisoner and he was truly a prisoner,
But since there was money he obtained his liberty.
His liberty caused him to run to Chihuahua and ended
When he was accused of the death of Villareal.
On October 30 in the night, I am going to remind you,
El Pablote was found drinking at the Popular Cafe;
And there he pulled out his gun in his fist, saying:
"I am used to having an owl (policeman) for breakfast very
    early."
The special officer there was a man of action,
And seeing that the man was drunk paid almost no attention—
But Pablo shot Robles. When he saw himself attacked,
He also began to shoot, and Pablote fell wounded.
He shot a second time and parted his heart,
And there ended the secret deeds of dying El Pablote.
His wife, called La Nacha, was struck with bad luck,
Because they put her in prison when El Pablote died.
When she came out of prison at his tomb she took an oath,
And there on her knees she told him of her revenge.
I don't want to lie because it is not convenient;
It is not the same story which all people say.

In this world, gentlemen, life is just an illusion.
We know that to every saint must come his death.
It was not because they were poisoners that they died;
It was because they made so many people die.
Now with this song I ask my leave, plucking a rose.
Here is the end of La Nacha and Gonzalez.

10

Artist Illustrators of the Southwest:
H. D. Bugbee, José Cisneros, and Tom Lea

H. D. Bugbee illustration from THE HERALDRY OF THE RANGE by J. Evetts Haley. Canyon, Texas, Panhandle Plains Historical Society, 1949. Courtesy of Carl Hertzog.

The richly variegated culture of the Southwest is today most graphically illustrated in other regions of the United States through its pictorial arts. In southern New Mexico, the Statue of Cristo Rey, the masterpiece of Urbici Soler, stands atop its peak near El Paso as a beacon to visitors who come to the crossroads of the Southwest. The same influences which brought and kept Soler here have similarly attracted artists in other media.

Tom Lea

Chapter heading from *THE WONDERFUL COUNTRY BY Tom Lea. Copyright 1952. Courtesy of Little, Brown & Co. (Boston).*

Double spread drawing from *FORTY YEARS AT EL PASO by W. W. Mills. Copyright 1962. Courtesy of Carl Hertzog, Publisher (El Paso).*

Full page drawing from **THE LONGHORNS** *by J. Frank Dobie. Copyright 1941. Courtesy of Little, Brown & Co. (Boston).*

José Cisneros

FRAY MARCOS DE NIZA

Full page illustration from THE JOURNEY OF FRAY MARCOS de NIZA by Cleve Hallen-
beck. Dallas University Press, 1949. Courtesy of Carl Hertzog.

Three particular examples of this newer generation have distinguished themselves as artist illustrators. H. D. Bugbee, José Cisneros, and Tom Lea have come to typify the best aspects of Southwestern art. Their illustrations, given enduring life by the individualized settings of the typographer Carl Hertzog, go far beyond the regional and momentary. They evoke the spirit of the land, the pageant of its history, and the strength of its early settlers.

H. D. BUGBEE, lately deceased, made his home in Canyon, Texas, where in his illustrations he became an oustanding archivist of the cattle country. In J. Evetts Haley's *The Heraldry of the Range* (1949), Bugbee's work depicts the range lands and such workaday scenes as the remuda and the roundup. A hard-driving realism suffuses Bugbee's chuck-wagon scene. Although of New England origin. Mr. Bugbee came to the Southwest in his youth. He adapted completely to the Western milieu, in time becoming an illustrator for *The Cattleman, Country Gentleman, Field and Stream,* and other national magazines. He long served as Curator of Art at the Panhandle Plains Historical Museum.

JOSÉ CISNEROS, who came from Durango, Mexico, to El Paso, Texas, has explored the pageant of history in drawings made for such typical regional publishers as the Historical Society of New Mexico, Southern Methodist University, and the Texas Folklore Society. His flair for re-creating the costumes and heraldry of the past has brought him into collaboration as artist with Fray Angelico Chavez of Santa Fe. A genius at map-making, Mr. Cisneros has taught himself his craft. Having little chance for book learning, he has acquired his education by reading all the books on history available to him. His genius for penetrating history to resurrect scenes of special flavor and compelling conviction is displayed in the full-length drawing of the Fray in Cleve Hallenbeck's *The Journey of Fray Marcos de Niza* (1949). Recently Cisneros has illustrated books for New York publishers, including one for Random House on Captain Cortés (1960) in the World Landmark Series. The career of José Cisneros began with the encouragement and recognition of Hertzog and Tom Lea.

TOM LEA, a native El Pasoan, has chronicled the Southwest in galleries of portraits of early worthies and scenes of pioneer life. Characteristic examples appear in his monumental work on *The King Ranch* (2 volumes, 1957). Here his collaboration with Hertzog resulted in unusual chapter titles and a new color process. Known internationally as a writer rather than as an artist, Mr. Lea first studied at the Art Institute of Chicago. In time the young artist was to make the name Tom Lea famous in a field far removed from the law, in which his father had earlier made the name famous. Before World War Two, the artist Lea had achieved substantial success in the four media of portraits, scenes, murals, and illustrations. During the War years, he served as special correspondent for *Life*. Subsequently, he turned to writing, producing works like *The Brave Bulls* (1949), *The Wonderful Country* (1953), and *Hands of Cantú* (1964). It is as a book-illustrator that the artist Lea is featured here, and he can be grouped with Bugbee and Cisneros for thoroughgoing realism. Lea's penchant for authentic detail and fidelity to basic truth are displayed in the three reproductions of his book illustrations which precede. Mr. Lea selected the three drawings included here as examples of his work as a book illustrator over a period of more than twenty years.

II

PALAVER

1

Cowboy Lingo of Texas's Last Frontier

In a remote corner of Texas, on the border of Mexico, there is a land where the cowboy is probably still as much in evidence as ever before; for here the flourishing business of raising cattle has always been and continues to be the principal means of livelihood. The Longhorn has been replaced by the pedigreed Hereford, and of course the *six-shooter* has gone completely. But in other and important ways life on the range remains the same. The cowboy still appears with his boots, saddle, and spurs; he still rides fence when fences need mending; he continues to ride the chuck line when visiting one ranch after another during off-season or when without a job; he still eats at the chuck wagon and spins tall tales about the campfire at night. "Cow country," the ranchers call it, and cow country it is and probably always will be. Nature made it for that alone.

This cattle country is a part of Southwest Texas lying west of the Pecos River, and is commonly known as the Trans-Pecos; or, among the folk, simply as the land "West of the Pecos." This is the stomping ground of Pecos Bill, legendary cowboy hero. Within this larger area there is a well-defined section called the Big Bend, a region embracing the Davis mountains in the north, the Chisos in the east, and the Chinatis in the south. Since the state of Texas is so large, the Big Bend is pictured on most maps at the bottom of the page,—a roughly triangular section, set off to itself as a sort of appendix to the vast commonwealth, of which, as a result of the winding course of the Rio Grande, it is really an integral part. Yet there is a certain appropriateness in regarding the Big Bend as an appendage to the state, because topographically, culturally, and economically it is markedly different from other, more populous regions of Texas. In fact, this very isolation of the Big Bend has made its culture strongly individualized and highly indigenous.

The most interesting aspect of this frontier country, at least to the student of language, is the lingo of the cowboy. His diction is rich with his own coinages, colored with native slang, and variegated now and then by the influence of the Mexican tongue. The language of the cowboy in the Big Bend may hardly be called a separate speech, but his lingo is at first likely to bewilder the greenhorn or hayseed, as the tenderfoot is impartially called.

Since the horse figures so prominently in the life of the cowboy, the greater share of the cowpuncher's inventiveness has been expended in developing a "horseology," or vocabulary about the horse. For example, an *owl head* is an animal that can not be trained either to work or to ride. A *stick horse* has to be forced to do everything he does. A *cold-blooded horse* is not a thoroughbred animal. The *night horse* is one staked near the cowpuncher's bed for immediate use in some such emergency as a stampede. A *cold-jawed horse* is one difficult to rein in or stop, because he ruins the rider's leverage by getting the bits between his teeth and holding on to them tenaciously. A *mocky* is a young mare, and perhaps the word develops from the fact that she mocks the *bronco-buster* in being frisky and mettlesome. A *top horse* is the best of the group. A *cutting horse* is one especially trained to separate or "cut" a single animal from a whole herd. (I have seen one cutting horse who could "cut" a hen from a big flock of chickens.)

Some of the other terms about horses are probably more familiar than these. An *outlaw* is a killer, a *salty horse* is a vicious beast, a *cantankerous horse* is unruly, and a *hame-headed horse* is stupid. A *mount* is one horse put aside for special riding jobs, while a number of horses so corralled compose what is generally termed a *remuda*. The word *cavvy* seems to be a variant of *remuda*, and *cavvy* is probably to be explained by the fact that good riding horses are kept close for roping and herding young calves. A *roller, snorter,* or *roarer,* as he is variously described, is an animal whose excitability appears to be due to the growth of small polyps in his nostrils which cause him to snort or to roar.

Many of the more colorful Western terms are associated with the cowboy's taming of wild horses, sometimes as a part of routine business and at other times as a relaxation from work at the rodeo. Used in its strictest sense, the *peeler* refers to the cowpuncher who rides into the herd and "cuts" out the horse desired. The next problem is to saddle the pony, or, as the cowboy says, "to put on *the ellum* (*elm*) and screw it down." Other words for saddle besides *ellum* include *hull* and *cack*. The horse objects to a saddle just as he does to thorny cactus on his back; hence the use of the colorful *cack* for saddle. On cold mornings practically all young broncos pitch a little or *frog walk* when first mounted. When a rider *frogs* a horse, he mounts him, and then proceeds to calm him or to correct his *frog walking*. Once the cowboy has firmly settled in the saddle and is riding the bronco, he is said to have *found his seat;* but if the rider is thrown off, the spectators use a form of understatement in saying he was slow *hitting* (*catching, finding*) *his saddle.* If the bronco-buster retains his seat but loses his foothold on the stirrup, he simply *blows his stirrup.* When the bronco commences to buck, he *wrinkles his spine, unwinds, folds up,* or *boils over.* When the bronco gets his head between his knees, the cowboys say that he *swallows his head,* and when the horse starts pitching from this position, he *breaks in two.* He is a skillful cowboy who rides the horse and *fans* him by whipping the pony with his hat. As long as the rider does not deign to scratch the bronco with his spurs, he is *coasting on the spurs.*

The born bronco knows several styles of pitching and bucking; the horse knows these stunts instinctively, for once he is trained or taught, he is tamed or *broken,* as cowpunchers say. If the pony bucks in circles and figure eights, he is a *pioneer bucker,* probably so-called because he appears to be looking for new territory to pitch in. But if the horse eschews *pioneer bucking* and does all his pitching in one spot, he is described as *bucking on a dime.* A good bronco can shift from one gait to the other quickly, and a sudden shift in bucking style is known as the *double shuffle.* The horse is *fence rowing* when he bows or humps his back and permits his front legs to come down together, first on one side and then on the other. He is a *pile driver* when he jolts his rider by coming down with all four feet closely grouped and legs as still as ramrods. He is *sun fishing* when he bucks high in the air; he is *swapping ends* when he turns completely around in one upward pitch; and he has a *watermelon under his saddle* when he bows his back so much that the front part of the saddle lifts somewhat from his body. When the bronco pitches a rider high enough in the air that light can be seen between the cowboy and the saddle, the rider is in a dangerous position, the horse is beginning to get the better of him, and he is said to be *seeing daylight*. The cowboy violates the rules of the game if he catches hold of the pommel or any part of the saddle in order to stay on the pitching horse; and if he does so the spectators say he is *squeezing the biscuit, shaking hands with grandma, grabbing the nubbin,* or *reaching for the apple.* Less vivid terms to describe the same act include *pulling leather* and *clawing leather.* Sometimes the *bronc-* or *bronco-buster* decides to *thumb his mount;* that is, after the wild horse stops pitching, the rider sticks his thumbs into the animal's shoulders in order to goad it on to its final pitches; and thus he tames or *breaks* the horse more readily.

There is, however, a difference between bronc-riding and contest riding. In contest riding the cowpuncher may use his spurs to excite the horse, but once the horse is pitching, the rider must hold on only with his knees and legs. It is against the rules to hold on with the spurs; these must be free and in plain sight. In bronc-riding, on the other hand, the rider may use his spurs at any or at all times.

Story and song have helped to make many words in the cowboy's language popular, so that today *maverick* and *dogie* are everywhere pretty well known. The *de-horned* cow and the *muley* cow are likewise familiar phrases, and all but the new stream-lined trains are equipped with handy *cow-catchers.* But it is somewhat more difficult to understand the lingo a rancher might use in giving his cow-hand the following instructions: "The boys say there are some cows on the lift down on the Rio Grande. I reckon you'll have to ride bog today and tail 'em up." If you understand this lingo, you know "cattling" (i.e., the cattle business). What the *straw boss* (assistant foreman) means is this: The cows are sick or stuck in the mud and can not stand on their feet; therefore they are *on the lift.* To gain a standing posture, cattle get up on their hind feet first and then lift up their fore feet. This is a distinct peculiarity of the cow. About the best way to help cattle gain their feet is, then, to lift them up by the tail, so that their hind part rises first, and thus enables them to get up the rest of the way by themselves. *To ride bog* is to ride the banks of the river, usually after a flood, to see if the cows are stuck in the mud.

Even for the cowboy there are different names. He is indifferently called *cow-hand, ranch-hand, cowpuncher, rawhide, waddie,* or *cow-waddie.* The Texas cowboy is less frequently called *waddie* or *vaquero,* probably because of the connotation of the words, *waddie* apparently referring to a *gun-toter* and *vaquero* being a Mexican word for cowboy. In the Texas Big Bend *buckaroo* seems not to be used, although the word is common elsewhere in the West, especially in Montana.

Vivid words and phrases are also in common use in the daily life of the cowboy. Food is *chuck,* biscuits are *sinkers,* chicken dumplings are *slickers;* deer meat killed out of season is, euphemistically, *goat meat.* A hash or goulash composed of tripe, kidneys, haslets, etc. is happily called *son of a gun* (Slumgullion). One of the most pungent phrases used by the cowboy is *wild mare's milk* for hard liquor. The cowpuncher does not "roll a cigarette"; instead he *builds a smoke.* Similarly, instead of preparing a rope for a toss, he says he *builds a loop.* The cowboy's *bedfellows* are rattlesnakes, tarantulas, and centipedes. Finally, when a cowboy dies or gets killed, it is said that *his spur has rung its knell.*

As the Big Bend is bounded just across the Rio Grande by the states of Chihuahua and Coahuila, there are naturally quite a few Mexicans in this part of Texas. But these Mexicans as a rule know very little English, and Texas cowboys are frequently equally ignorant of Spanish. The result is that a compromise is arrived at between the Texas cowpuncher and the Mexican *vaquero.* Most of the ranch terms are of course English, but a few are Mexican, and a number are a cross between the two. A few outstanding examples may here be referred to.

The Mexican word *segundo* (Spanish for "second") is often used instead of foreman, who is second in command to the rancher. The cook is frequently called the *cocenero,* and *Sancho* is a favorite name for a pet lamb or kid. One phrase commonly used is especially interesting; namely *dally man.* Cowpunchers are ordinarily either *tie-hard* or *dally men*. The "dally man" does not tie his rope to the pommel of the saddle, but very adeptly loops the rope or gives it a turn about the saddle horn. Instead of saying "give it a turn," the Mexicans say *da le vuelta;* and the Texans have compromised by calling this type of *roper* or *rope-thrower* a *dally man*. It may be added that along the border *riata* is as common for "lariat," as is *lazo* for "lasso."

The vocabulary given here is selective, not exhaustive; but it nevertheless seems worthwhile to have discussed even briefly the language of the cowboy as it has been spoken and as it is now being spoken, especially when nowadays there are so many romantic stories and popular songs which largely misinterpret the cowboy and his lingo. The Texas cowboy remains in most ways a true son of the border country; his cheery greeting to a horseman to *light and look at his saddle* is about the most hospitable invitation to dinner to be encountered; and probably nowhere today is there a better region for the study of the Western spirit and the language of the cowboy than the Texas Big Bend. Wherever writers of Western thrillers found the corrupt *lassoo* for "lasso," it certainly was not West of the Pecos.

2

Smugglers' Argot in the Southwest

The lowest pass to the north, El Paso, Texas, has been a favorite rendezvous for smugglers since the time of the Spanish conquistadors. At this 'sensitive point' on the Texas-Mexico border there have been three peak periods of activity in the twentieth century: first, the turbulent days of the Mexican Revolution (1910-14); second, the hectic years of Prohibition (1919-33); and third, the sensational present era of illegal traffic in narcotics (especially since 1950). Each of these periods has contributed special words describing its own characteristic activities.

During the Revolution the rebel Pancho Villa rampaged up and down the Rio Grande, frightening the Mexicans into smuggling their cattle and anything else they had, including prostitutes,[1] across the border into Texas. They sold everything cheap, for they knew Pancho would confiscate whatever he ran into. During Prohibition El Pasoans went over to Juarez, not only to drink, but to bring home large supplies of contraband liquor. For a while it was sold in Juarez on the streets to motorists in the traffic lanes bound for the Texas side. When Mexican authorities tightened down in 1930,[2] *rumrunners* came into the picture and engaged the police in pitched gun battles while smuggling their merchandise over the river. Since the outbreak of the Korean conflict, smugglers have carried munitions unlawfully into Mexico and dumped numberless aliens and all types of narcotics into Texas. "La Nacha," queen of the Juarez dope ring, has stayed on her side of the border, but the impact of smuggled drugs has been felt throughout Texas and, indeed, in other parts of the nation.

Smuggling at the Pass of the North today has both dangerous and relatively inoffensive aspects, because smugglers may be either professional criminals or petty offenders. Anybody who sneaks by the busy customs men at rush hours without paying duty on a taxable product becomes guilty of a crime thereby. Such petty *border running* is termed *jam.* The minor offenders are said to be men of the type who cheat on their income taxes or women of the sort who cannot resist a bargain or a sale. Women are rumored to be talented at selecting *annexations,* quantities of merchandise to be taken over the border, and at concealing *candy,* small pieces of jewelry. When a female acts as a criminal lookout, speakers of the argot refer to her as *bright eyes,* whereas a male spotter might be called almost anything from an *aguador* (Spanish for *water bag*) to a *soldier* (one who stands guard). The chief offenders are professional smugglers, who constitute a criminal class and speak an underworld argot. Well equipped and ably organized, they do a sizable volume of illegal trafficking each year all along the Mexican border in taxable or prohibited goods.

Recent smuggling, as reported by the Treasury Department, has mainly involved five significant commodities. These five are, in ascending order of importance, aliens, watches or their springs, war materials, jewelry, and narcotics.[3] Attempts to bring either aliens or enemy spies into Texas now have sharply declined. Occasionally, visitors from out of town still try to smuggle *perdidas* (Spanish for *prostitutes*) across the river. There continue to be a few housemaids unlawfully entering Texas from Cordova Island, a Mexican area north of the Rio Grande. These rather harmless crossings, effected by *amusers,* or accomplices (so called because they are small-timers and hence amusing rather than worrisome), have always occurred throughout the Texas-Mexico country and have certainly been going on long enough to account for a number of terms used by smugglers.

Yet other words have derived from the smuggling of watches, jewelry, and war materials. As for watches, the premium is on those of Swiss manufacture, and the probability is that these rarely come into the Southwest in *bundles*, or large quantities. There exists some traffic, however, in *buttons,* or small amounts. The same statement holds true for jewelry, particularly diamonds, which usually reach New York City, the diamond center, not overland from Mexico, but by sea or air routes from Belgium or Brazil.[4] Instruments of war, on the other hand, pose another question and return the focus, importantly, to the Southwest. Importations into Mexico from the United States, happening as they do with some regularity, were particularly serious during the recent emergency of the Korean conflict. Today, munitions persist in passing illegally across the international line, throughout the Southwest as well as at Tijuana, Baja California,[5] so that *gunrunning* appears a steady phenomenon of the borderland.

To *run* merchandise successfully, the *sneaker* needs an *Adam,* or partner, one who is an *ace* or a *major;* that is, a man who can be depended on. He further needs a *lagger,* or contact man, and, to avoid detection, may hire the services of a *jigger moll,* a female lookout. Sometimes he utilizes a *jacker,* an expert at camouflage. Men who wade the river with contraband goods strapped to their backs are identified as *burros* or *mulas,* both being Spanish words for donkeys. If they sleep in the open overnight, they use *Mexican zarapes* (actually, newspapers spread out like a blanket). A *stop* is a place to *fence* goods, and a *swagman,* the fellow who receives illicit materials. The *pullers* (*fences*) may be handling *milk ropes,* pearl necklaces; *muggles,* an impure or poor quality of sap that comes from a marijuana bush; or *the queer,* counterfeit money. The place where prohibited goods are assembled before being taken *under the bridge* is designated the *dump.* Mail and contraband are received at a *drop.*

If the smuggler has any doubts about his operations, he will look for *eels,* or spies, in his *ring.* He also will seek out the opinion of his *hawks,* lookouts. He then may station at a dangerous spot a *walking tree,* a watchman. If he still remains worried, he may make a *dry run,* a test to discover the whereabouts of his *family men,* the sellers of smuggled articles. The really careful operator will send forward a *doaker,* a man to draw attention away from the actual smuggling, or, better yet, carry with him a *pregón* (Spanish for *proclamation*), a pretty girl who draws the eyes of everybody to her own person. What he fears most is a *finger louse,* a person who informs for government agents only; or a *red shirt,* a man who refuses to obey orders. The phrase to describe a Negro stool pigeon is *faded bogey.* If the operator becomes frightened, he will return to his side of the border in a *bootlegger turn,* or in a hurry; for he has respect both for *chotos* (Spanish for *suckling lambs*), the police and for *los panchores* (Spanish coinage for *fat border patrolmen*).

The major difficulty in the Southwest today stems from the narcotic trade. The largest port of entry between Brownsville, Texas, and San Diego, California, El Paso bids fair, at the moment, to become the undeclared dope capital of America. Of all seizures in 1954, the most important was said to be that at El Paso on August 28 of ten ounces of high-purity heroin from Dr. J. Blas Sotelo, a Mexican physician, who operated an "anti-alcohol" clinic in Juarez. He was arrested by a customs agent working undercover and later sentenced to serve five years. Worse yet, in January, 1955, a former United States customs inspector was caught delivering 300 grains of heroin at the International Airport.[6] More recently, R. S. O'Brien, chief narcotics agent in El Paso, raided an apartment near the International Bridge, where he found a female peddler's letter to her male accomplice. It reported that she had left at ten in the evening, that no customers had come, that she had taken a small paper full of heroin, and that she had left a dose for him in the syringe:

Dear Chuy,
    I cut out at 10.
    No birds.
    I took a little *chiquita,* so I can sleep.
    The shit is in the gun.

For almost a quarter century now, bands of juveniles have figured sensationally in the dissemination of narcotics, bringing to modern border running a luridness hard to match even in the epoch of the rambunctious Villa. Since about 1931, when their nefarious activities first won publicity, *pachuco* gangs have continuously smuggled narcotics into El Paso from Juarez. Interesting enough, their charter of organization is reported to require that each member must understand the lingo of dope

addiction to be initiated.[7] Young apprentices at the trade bear
the name of *choir boys.* Although composed largely of Latin
Americans, *pachuco* membership includes persons of all races.
From El Paso to Los Angeles, both Negroes and Anglo-Americans may be seen wearing their identifying tattoo signs on hands
or forearms, these marks constituting a special brand of secret
communication in themselves. *Pachucos* also employ a highly
individual, bilingual argot, or *caló.* Since many of them 'run'
for dope rings, their speech has left its unmistakable traces among
smugglers.

Corruption among erring policemen of both El Paso and
Juarez has abetted smuggling, which helps to explain how its
argot has gained widespread use locally. Late in 1954 two gun-
packing Mexican officers crossed to El Paso from Juarez in a
stolen automobile and created a disturbance at the junction of
Copia and Pershing streets. When apprehended, the *hopped-up*
Mexican policemen, or *arms,* were found to have hidden their
contraband marijuana cigarettes in their car where it had stalled.[8]
In April of 1955 a top newspaper reporter exposed the narcotic
orgies then regularly occurring at the city jail in El Paso itself.[9]
Soon afterward, on June 19, three thieves broke into Shain's
Jewelry Store, or *ice palace,* in downtown El Paso and stole
$1,700 worth of valuables, or *collat* (probably from *collateral*).
Upon his capture, one of them confessed that he smuggled the
loot to Juarez and there traded it for heroin to the Mexican
dope ring led by the notorious woman known as "La Nacha."[10]

Southwestern operators are accordingly of all shades, kinds,
and descriptions. They will do practically anything to cheat the
United States of its import duty—from *planting* a package on the
automobile of an innocent party[11] to lining the casket of a dead
man with drugs.[12] If they are dope addicts as well as smugglers,
as often they are, they may utilize their own persons from top
to bottom by hiding *cachuchos* (Spanish for *caps;* capsules)
either under wigs or in a *rectum stash.*

Still they get caught—if not by border patrolmen or customs
inspectors, then by officers of the Bureau of Narcotics. Agents
frequently secure information from clues furnished by *bat carriers* or *belchers* (informers). Agents also sometimes hire a
decoy, whose name is always *Conny.* The Federal government
maintains at near-by La Tuna, Texas, a well-conducted prison

to correct *boneheads,* or lawbreakers, once they are tried and convicted. This *hutch* with its inmates, or *geezos,* is familiarly known on the border as *La Tuna Tech.*

The lure of easy cash brings *rumrunners* from everywhere to the fabulous Rio Grande. At an early date they used only horses, and some of them still do. In the rough terrain of the southern Trans-Pecos, a wide territory, livestock *stray* from Chihuahua and Coahuila. The *chili chasers,* border patrolmen, ride horses when chasing *wet* cattle across arroyos or *biyookies* (a distortion of *bayous*) and also when *rimming up a gunyon,* riding up a canyon. The pursuers attempt to *double team* (surround) the pursued. They are bound to catch him if his mount *turns a wildcat,* stumbles and falls. But if the horse is not a *dead head,* he may save his rider. To escape the vigilant border rangers, a smuggler's horse must travel fast and *lay his belly in the sand.*[13]

The elite smuggler from the East is more likely to own fast automobiles, known loosely as *mule trains,* or even an airplane.[14] This bold robber of the government means business. He speaks a dramatic argot in keeping with his profession, because he risks being chased, fired upon, and killed, not for a hundred dollars or so, but for the *heavy* stuff.

The words which came into the argot during the Mexican Revolution, it may be said in conclusion, include such particular expressions as *Chink runners* and *yellow goodsmen.* Pancho Villa so mistreated the Chinese in Chihuahua that they hired smugglers to convey them to the United States. Prohibition contributed even more words, especially the phrase *rumrunning,* which covers any and all types of smuggled articles. In those days a *rummer* was a specialist at importing illegal liquor; a *rum beak,* a judge who could be bribed; a *squawk woman,* a female informer; and a *third rail,* a reliable clue. Today the emphasis on traffic in narcotics has produced a special argot for drugs;[15] however, some of these words still definitely belong to the vocabulary of the smuggler. These include *dead money* for poor counterfeit bills; *deck* for two small sheets of paper with narcotics between them; *gum* for crude opium; *hospital* for a pick-up point for drugs; *mezy*[16] for the sap from a marijuana weed; *still* for a Federal decoy station; and *married,* applied to opium to which foreign substances have been added. What lies ahead in an age of air transportation is uncertain. The *naranja* or *regio montaña,* Spanish for the brains of an outfit (i.e., 'better half' and 'ruler from the mountain,'[17] respectively), will probably then be peddling *dolly verden* (Spanish *de la verde*), or marijuana sap, more briskly than ever.[18]

NOTES

[1] Owen P. White, *Them Was the Days* (New York, 1925), p. 73.

[2] El Paso *Post,* August 12, 1930.

[3] Chester A. Emerick, *Statement of the Deputy Commissioner of Customs* (Washington, D.C., February 7, 1955), pp. 2-7.

[4] *Ibid.,* pp. 6-7.

[5] United Press, June 22, 1955.

[6] Emerick, *op. cit.,* p. 5; El Paso *Times,* April 5, 1955.

[7] George McGrath, "Secrets of the Pachuco Terrorists Exposed," *Police Gazette,* CLIX (1954), 8-9, 30.

[8] El Paso *Herald Post,* October 30, 1954.

[9] *Ibid.,* May 9, 1955.

[10] *Ibid.,* June 20, 1955.

[11] Such an experience happened to a personal friend of mine, who prefers to remain anonymous.

[12] My informant is R. S. O'Brien, Bureau of Narcotics, El Paso.

[13] See my article, "Big Talk of the Big Bend," *Texas Parade* (July, 1955), pp. 40-41.

[14] On March 31, 1954, two smugglers of tungsten were arrested in a twin-engine Cessna at an airfield near the Arizona-Mexico border, and the violators admitted numerous previous unlawful flights (Emerick, *op. cit.,* p. 8).

[15] See my paper, "Narcotic Argot Along the Mexican Border," *American Speech,* XXX (1955), 84-90.

[16] *Mezy* is perhaps a distortion of *marijuana* incorporating the Dog-Latin element *-ez-,* which I commented in an earlier article. According to Lieut. Art Islas, of the El Paso Police Department, it is a clipping of *Mesican,* variously spelled, which is a variant of *Mexican.*

[17] On this individual, sometimes called "The Man from Montana," in older lore, see Wolfgang Fleischhauer, "The Ackermann aus Böhmen" and "The Old Man of the Mountain," *Monatshfete,* XLV (1953), 189-201; and "The Old Man of the Mountain: the Growth of a Legend," *Symposium,* IX (1955), 79-90.

[18] For many of the words used in this study, I am indebted to local officers of the Border Patrol, the Bureau of Customs, the Bureau of Narcotics, the Federal prison at La Tuna, and especially to Alvin Clark, a former student, and to R. S. O'Brien, Supervising Narcotics Agent, El Paso.

3

Tall Talk of the Texas Trans-Pecos

As claimed by Ripley and advertised by the local chamber of commerce, Alpine, Brewster County, Texas, is the largest city in the largest county in the largest state in these United States. With an area of approximately six thousand square miles and a population of some six thousand Texans and Latin-Americans, this region of the so-called Trans-Pecos abounds in picturesque scenery, frontier conditions, old legends, and tall talk. Since there is about one square mile per person, it seems altogether natural that the lingo of the natives should match in at least some part the superlative vastness of the country. Distances in this area seem so great because of the sparse habitation that even the hardened traveller may complain that the mileage is wrongly reckoned. To account for this, the native always explains that the miles were measured 'by cowhides with the tails thrown in.'

To this good day 'cattle-raising' remains practically the only occupation in the Trans-Pecos, so that cowboys and horses, boots and saddles, are everyday sights. The vocabulary of these people is thus greatly influenced by the colorful conditions surrounding ranch life. For example, cowboys living a rough and hardy existence occasionally develop into 'tough hombres.' The special phrase employed to describe this 'customer' is that he is 'tough as a boot and twice as high.' If this particular cowboy has committed all the vices either inside or outside the law, it

is said that he has, like a 'salty' (wild) horse, 'gone the gaits.'
If this cowpuncher has 'played checkers with his nose' (been
in jail) or is otherwise not to be trusted, the rancher may adopt
'horseology' by stating that 'he won't do to tie to.' On the other
hand, if this 'wrangler' is playful but not vicious, the 'pusher'
(foreman) may claim that 'he'll do to ride the river with.' The
river is the Rio Grande, not Jordan, and this expression means
that the 'cow-waddie' could be relied on even for 'rustling'
contraband from Mexico to Texas. If there is any question as to
the veracity of the speaker, that is, if you are 'jubious' (dubious),
the narrator gives strongest assurance by repeating: 'I'll take a
paralyzed oath.' If a Westerner is vexed with someone who is
'showing out' (bragging), he is capable of saying quite a few
things; but he usually says: 'You'd better high-tail it outa here,'
by which he means 'git going.'

In the free, open, and democratic West, picturesque diction is
by no means restricted to the 'men folks,' for ranch women have
their special phrases too. For example, when the 'tenderfoot' wife
displays her inability to cope with ranch life, her neighbors assert
that 'she don't know beef from bull's foot.' If this new lady has
been previously married, her neighbors say that 'she's been on
the carpet before.' If the lady wears city rather than ranch
clothes, the people tell her: 'Out here you've got no more use
for them than a hog has for a side saddle.' If it appears that the
newcomer may prove satisfactory, the women admit that 'she
can count ties' (repair a barbed-wire fence). But 'between you
and me and the gate post,' if this visitant appears 'stand-offish'
or 'dresses fit to kill,' there are a few 'plain speakers' who will
'vow and declare' that she is nothing short of 'a son of a so-and-
which.'

More so than anywhere else, life can be dull and monotonous
on the ranch, and even under the best circumstances, there is not
a great deal to do unless you travel some of those long West
Texas miles to a regional city. Therefore sometimes the 'boys
unlimber for a little stud and draw.' If you ever play poker way
out West, it will be wise 'to come full handed' (with plenty of
money), not 'half shod' (with little money), as some optimists
do. And if you think you are not getting a 'square deal,' why
then 'don't be clabber-mouthed (silent) about it.' However, if
you talk too much, that is, if you 'have a busy lip,' then some-

body may 'cut your water off,' 'take your meter out,' or 'comb your head with a six-shooter.' In any case, 'take it standing up' (bravely) and 'don't die with your heels up' (be shot in the back). Tell your partners 'just how the wind's a-blowing and the dust's a-flying' or 'exactly how the cow ate the cabbage over the back fence on a windy day.' In general, however, it is wiser not to 'get a shuck in your snoot' (become angry).

Although the ranch spouse may be 'dead set' and 'tooth and toenail against it,' there are occasions when her husband may imbibe so much that he 'gets quite a hearing' and reaches home, vows his help-meet, 'a-seeing elephants and a-hearing owls.' Accordingly she queries: 'What the hum do you mean, you hunk-abo' (bohunk)? Being thus 'corralled' the inebriate may try to 'latch on' (be agreeable), but since he is pretty obviously 'snooze-marooed' (drunk), he may be instructed either to 'angle in' (enter) or to 'drag up' (leave).

When a cowboy prepares for the weekly dance on Saturday night, he 'gets dressed up like a sore toe.' Then he selects his favorite 'taw' (dancing partner), who may be a 'satchel' ('honky-tonk' employee), a 'smooth hide' (city dame), or the 'old stand-by' (usual escort). Above all he avoids the 'slab-sided' (fat) girl, to whom he even prefers the 'scantling' (thin girl). At dancing he may be 'tender' (inexperienced), in which event he explains his inactivity as 'hossing around.' But the gay *vaquero* is usually faithful to one sweetheart, it not being 'in the cards' to 'roach,' 'short pot,' or 'cabbage' on her.

In a wide border territory like the southern Trans-Pecos, it is perhaps to be expected that some smuggling should occur. At all events, if cattle 'stray' from Chihuahua or Coahuila into Texas, these cattle are pronounced 'wet.' Similarly a smuggled article may be termed 'wet.' Or one may hear it whispered that a certain *señor* is a 'wet' Mexican. In the rougher terrain the 'chili chasers' (border patrolmen) use horses to give chase across 'biyookies' (i.e., arroyos, from bayous, used ironically) or to 'rim' (ride) up a 'gunyon' (canyon). The pursuers attempt to 'double team' (encircle) the pursued. They are certain to apprehend him if his horse 'turns a wildcat' (falls) or 'tumble-sets' (somersaults). But if the horse is not a 'dead head' (inferior), he may save his rider.' In order to escape the border rangers, however, the horse will have to 'lay his belly in the sand' (travel rapidly).

Some few of these words and phrases may be found in other sections of the country, but since the vocabulary used in the Trans-Pecos is largely conditioned by the physical environment of the folk, it is most frequently quite original. Now the Westerner is famed for his reticence, and reticent he is. The only thing to remember, and this reflects credit on both him and his speech, is that when he does have something to say he says it in a lively, virile way.

4

Narcotic Argot Along the Mexican Border[1]

Illegal traffic in dope occurs sporadically today all along the extensive border between Mexico and the United States, from Brownsville, Texas, to San Diego, California. According to reports of the United States Department of Justice, the smuggling of drugs across this border was gradually increasing even prior to Pearl Harbor. These reports further state that since December 7, 1941, Mexico has replaced Manchukuo as a chief source for the unlawful traffic in opium and other similarly dangerous narcotics.[2] Near the middle of the wide area comprising the Mexican border lies El Paso, the largest port of entry into the United States and the base of the largest of the American customs agencies, this station controlling the southwestern region of Arizona, New Mexico, and Texas. Since the legal trade with Red China now has ceased and the illegal greatly abated, the Mexican border has become a main focus of interest for the dope smugglers and the Federal agents trained to apprehend them. What is the nature of the language of the drug addicts with whom both border smugglers and narcotic agents are concerned?

The vocabulary of Mexican border dope argot contains many old terms previously used by addicts negotiating with peddlers whose products came from the Orient as well as a large group of newer terms, some of them Spanish, that are used by addicts now buying drugs that derive from Mexico. To understand the present diversity of the narcotic argot heard along the Mexican border,[3] it is necessary to review the definitive vocabulary lists which have been already printed, for these glossaries contain terms common to narcotic speech wherever it is spoken.

In attempting a chronological survey of the character, extent, and quality of dope argot, attention must be called first to an article by David W. Maurer, "The Argot of the Underworld Narcotic Addict," which was published in *American Speech* in April, 1936.[4] This earliest linguistic treatment of the subject included a total of 235 terms in common use at that time by known drug addicts. A second article by Maurer, entitled "The Argot of the Underworld Narcotic Addict: Part II," appeared in *American Speech* in October, 1938.[5] This second and fuller exposition of the subject contained 273 new terms in addition to those already cited. Finally, in 1954 Maurer and Victor H. Vogel published a rather comprehensive glossary in their book entitled *Narcotics and Narcotic Addiction.*[6] This list contained 539 entries, 31 more than the total of 508 represented in the two earlier articles. But these figures do not accurately exhibit the number of terms exactly involved. For one thing, the glossary in the book omits 14 terms included in the article published in 1936 which may be specified below in the interests of completeness:

CHILL, *v.* To submit to arrest without struggling or resisting.

HIPPED, *adj.* [Said of] an opium addict who has smoked so long while reclining on one side that one hip is slightly atrophied.

MARK A CONNECTION, *v. phr.* To locate or make contact with a peddler. An addict who has *marked a connection* knows where he can get dope when he needs it.

MEZONNY,[7] *adj.* [Said of] one who 'has his money working' and is about to get his goods from the peddler.

MIZAKE THE MIZAN, *v. phr.* To get the 'dope' from the peddler. The phrase is a distortion of *make the man.*

MT. SHASTA, TO BE FROM, *v. phr.* To be addicted to narcotics and presumably to be highly exhilarated.

RATION, *n.* A shot of dope.

RIZOLIN, *part.* A phrase meaning 'the stuff is rolling,' or 'your order is filled.'

SACH (variant of *satch*), *n.* The method or place of conceal-
ment of the drug when the addict is about to be arrested.
SIZENDIZUP, *v. phr.* The coast is clear and the sale may
proceed. The phrase is a distortion of *send up.*
SNIFTER, *n.* An addict who inhales cocaine.
SUGAR, *n.* Like *sweet stuff,* a euphemism for drugs.
TAKEN, *part. adj.* Knocked out with drugs.
WITCH HAZEL, *n.* Heroin.

Moreover, the glossary by Maurer and Vogel also omits five
terms listed in the article published in 1938, which also may be
quoted to complete this review:

AD. (*Add.*), *n.* A narcotic addict, especially a needle addict.
BINGO, *n.* A ration of narcotics injected hypodermically.
BLOODSUCKER, *n.* A physician charging high fees.
GOZNIK, *n.* Narcotics.
PIPIE, *n.* An opium smoker.

In the three glossaries thus far reviewed—the two articles of
1936 and 1938 and the book of 1954—there is actually a total
of 558 terms. These 558 entries do not comprise all the known
terms now being used by narcotic addicts. So much is clear from
the fact that in 1953 Harry J. Anslinger and William F. Tompkins
included a fairly impressive glossary in their book *The Traffic in
Narcotics.*[8] This glossary runs to a total of 378 terms. Of these,
Maurer and Vogel's book of 1954 contains all but 193. Since
these 193 entries are not included in either the two articles by
Maurer or the book by Maurer and Vogel, they may be regarded
as additional words in the argot, bringing to 751 the number of
terms in the dope argot that are now in print.[9]
    There remain some 83 terms used on the Mexican border which
do not appear in the printed sources just mentioned and which
are therefore entitled to be separately listed and glossed in this
review. These 83 new terms, being partly English and partly
Spanish, constitute a kind of international dope language. When
they are added to the 751 from printed sources, the number of
terms known in the argot reaches the total of 834. These hitherto
unprinted terms now may be explained as follows:

BABY DOLL, *n.* Heart stimulant; possibly an alteration of
barbital.

BAD GO, *n. phr.* A poor amount for the money paid.

BEAT THE DOUGH, *v. phr.* To run away with the money.

BE ON THE NOD, *v. phr.* To be half-asleep from drugs.

BLUE GRASS, *v.* To return to the narcotic hospital in Kentucky for further treatment.

BOREDOM BEATER, *n.* A person smoking marijuana for pleasure.

BOY, *n.* Heroin, as opposed to *girl,* cocaine,[10] and *Doña Juanita,* marijuana.

BRIDGE, *n.* A holder for marijuana cigarettes.

CACHUCHA (Sp.), *n.* A capsule of drugs; probably from the Chilean use of the word, which means a small comet.

CAN YOU DO ME GOOD? Will you sell me drugs?

CARANJAL (Sp.), *n.* A person who is looking for a drug; possibly from Cuban *carañuela,* a tramp in a play; or, as one Hispanist informant suggested, from *carango,* a kind of flat fish in the West Indies.

CARRIE NATION, *n.* Cocaine.

CARTUCHO (Sp.), *n.* A small package of marijuana cigarettes; from the Spanish word for cartridge or roll of coins.

CHALKED UP, *part. adj. phr.* 'High' on cocaine.

CHOCOLATE, *n.* Opium (from its brown color).

COOL, *adj.* Quiet.

CRIPPLE, *n.* A marijuana cigarette.

CRUZ (Sp.), *n.* Opium; possibly from *cruz de mayo,* red Mexican herb of the heath family.

DAGGA (Sp.), *n.* A marijuana cigarette; probably from Spanish *daga,* a stove or furnace of a brick kiln.

DICK SMITH, *n.* An addict who is a lone wolf.

DOÑA JUANITA. *See* BOY.

DOPE DADDY, *n.* A peddler.

ELI LILLY, *n.* Morphine; from the name of a legitimate commercial company.

FIEND, *n.* A morphine devotee.

FINE STUFF, *n. phr.* Good marijuana.

FISH, *n.* An addict who pimps.

FLEA POWDER, *n.* A reduced, cut-down, or weakened ration of a drug.

FOREIGN MUD, *n. phr.* Cooked opium (from its color and odor), raw opium smells like a freshly broken green twig and not like mud.

FRANTIC CHARACTER, *n. phr.* An addict nervous for dope.

FRISKY POWDER, *n. phr.* Cocaine.

FROGSKINS, *n.* Paper money.

GEORGE, *adj.* Trustworthy.

GIRL. *See* BOY.

GOLDEN SPIKE, *n. phr.* The hypodermic needle.

GONG BEATER, *n.* An opium addict.

GOOD GO, *n. phr.* A fair amount for the money paid.

GREEFO (Sp. *grifo,* literally 'faucet'), *n.* An addict. There is also a Spanish word *griffa* meaning 'weed'; hence marijuana; among Creole Negroes, the same word means 'snuff-colored.'

HACHE (Sp. pronunciation of the letter *H*), *n.* Heroin.

HAND TO HAND, *adj. phr.* Delivered immediately.

HARD NAIL, *n. phr.* Needle.

HARD STUFF, *n. phr.* Opium.

HAY HEAD, *n.* A marijuana smoker.

HEAT'S ON. The law enforcement agents are closing in.

HI GATE. Hello there.

HYGELO (origin obscure; possibly from a Sp. coinage suggested by the English spelling of *high-low*), *n.* A morphine addict.

INFLUYENTE (Sp.; a variant of Castilian *influente*), *n.* A 'big shot' in opium or other drug rings.

JENNY BARN, *n.* The women's ward in a narcotic hospital.

JIVE STICK, *n.* A marijuana cigarette.

KNIFE IN ONE'S ARM, *n. phr.* Injection with a crude or makeshift needle.

LEÑO (Sp. for 'piece of firewood'), *n.* A marijuana cigarette.

LUSHER, *n.* A decayed drunkard who mixes marijuana with liquor.

MARY JANE, *n.* Marijuana.

MILK SUGAR, *n.* Medicine.

MISS THE CHANNEL, *v. phr.* To stab the arm but miss the vein.

MOJO (probably from Sp. *mojar,* 'to celebrate by drinking'), *n.* A euphemism for morphine.

MULE, *n.* Marijuana mixed in whisky; hashish fudge is mentioned in *The Alice B. Toklas Cook Book* (New York, 1954).

NARCO, *n.* The narcotic hospital in Lexington, Kentucky.

NARCOTIC ZIPH, *n. phr.* The language of 'dope' addiction.

PACHUCO (Sp. coinage), *n.* A young Mexican gangster or smuggler.

PAPEL (Sp. for 'paper'), *n.* Any drug rolled in paper wrapping.

PISTOLA (Sp. for 'pistol'), *n.* A syringe.

POLLETA (Sp. coinage, for the Sp. usually means 'little chicken, little boy or girl'), *n.* A small bottle of dope in liquid form.

PUT TO THE MOUTH, *v. phr.* To swallow (the evidence).

RIDING THE WHITE HORSE, *ger. phr.* Drugged dreaming; many boxes of drugs have the figure of a white horse on the outside.

SEDOL (possibly from Sp. *sed,*[11] 'thirst'), *n.* Morphine.

SHOOT BELOW THE BELT, *v. phr.* To inject in the hips or legs.

SHORT BUY, *n. phr.* A small purchase.

SISTER-IN-LAW, *n.* A prostitute.

SNEAKY PETE, *n. phr.* Marijuana mixed in wine.

STACK, *n.* A package of marijuana cigarettes; one cigarette or one dose of one ounce is a 'piece' or a 'stick,' from German *stück.*

SWING INTO HIGH GEAR, *v. phr.* To get 'high' on drugs.

TEA HEAD, *n.* An addict of drugs in liquid form.

TORCH UP, *v. phr.* To light up a marijuana cigarette.

TURN ON, *v. phr.* To smoke a package of marijuana cigarettes.

TWO-ARM HABIT, *n. phr.* The confirmed addiction of one who injects drugs in both arms.

UZZFAY, *n.* Dog Latin for *fuzz,* a name applied to one of bewhiskered Uncle Sam's narcotic agents.[12]

WAY DOWN, *adj. phr.* Said of an addict, depressed between dosages.

WEEDLY, *n.* A woman who smokes marijuana; that is, a 'hay-headed girl,' as was pointed out to me by Jack Salem, of the El Paso radio station KTSM.

WIGGED, *adj.* Said of an addict, with a muddled head.

YESCA (Sp. for 'inflammable tinder'), *n.* Marijuana.

ZOL, *n.* A marijuana cigarette.

ZOO, *n.* The jail.

ZOOK (underworld term), *n.* A worn-out prostitute addicted to drugs.

No doubt the list could be extended, by further inquiry, to as many as a thousand or more words,[13] but the present objective is not to compile a dictionary of dope argot. For the purpose of this paper, enough examples have been reviewed to afford four or five generalizations that adequately describe the basic nature of the argot of drug addiction:

1. Narcotic ziph is an oral language so closely related to jive talk and other underworld lingos that such expressions as *zook* for prostitute, *Dick Smith* for a 'lone wolf,' and *Hi gate* for 'Hello there' are frequently used by nonaddicts as well as by addicts.

2. Narcotic ziph contained a number of words that are now obsolete, such as *bending and bowing* to describe an addict being stimulated by drugs and *a Brody* for a spasm feigned by an addict in order to get narcotics from a physician. A few others are in the process of becoming obsolescent, such as the phrase *foreign mud* for opium, which now has been pretty universally shortened to *mud*.

3. Narcotic ziph is a growing or increasing language, because its speakers are adept at coining new words to replace the obsolete ones. They create these new words partly from the intellectual pleasure derived in doing so and partly from fear of detection by persons who might overhear them and inform against them. In early times the Persians used for *hashish* such euphemisms as 'the green parrot,' 'the mysteries,' and 'Master Sayyid' because of the evil repute of the drug and its association with the dreaded Assassin sect.[14] Today addicts use such simple linguistic devices as Dog Latin, puns, and the system of inserting *ez* or *iz* after initial consonants or consonantal clusters.

4. Narcotic ziph is replete with expressions that exhibit a poetic order of creative imagination. It employs such figures of speech as *blue heaven* (sodium amytal), *golden spike* (needle), and *yellow jacket* (a barbital), the euphemism *Chinese needle-work* for dealing in opium, the metaphor *riding the white horse* for a drugged dream, the metonym *weekender* for an occasional user of drugs, the personification *Benny* for benzedrine, *boy* and *girl* for heroin and cocaine respectively, and synecdoche in *frogskins* for paper money, *finger stall* for a hiding place for drugs, and finally *hard nail* for the needle used for an injection.[15]

5. Narcotic ziph tends to be, not a regional tongue, but an international language. Its words come from the speech of many nations and include such expressions as the American *Bay State* for syringe, the Chinese *yen-shee* for the residue of opium in the bowl of a pipe, the English *foreign mud* for opium, the German *stück* for a ration of an ounce, the Hebrew *skamas* for drugs, the

Italian *capo* for a leader of a drug ring, and the Spanish *yesca* for marijuana.

Any word in the extensive vocabulary of the drug addict, it may be noted in conclusion, would probably be readily understood along the border today. For, despite the vigilance of understaffed law enforcement agencies, the menace of dope is much nearer than before, at least geographically. Its home base is no longer Burma, China, or some other country far beyond the seas; now the international smugglers entering the United States cross over the bridge or walk across a boundary strip of land. This is shown by the fact that the Federal Bureau of Narcotics recently apprehended, in New York City, fourteen men of a dope ring that handled millions of dollars in drugs from its headquarters in Montreal, Canada, and Mexico, D.F.[16] Yet more recently, when United States Customs agents testified in El Paso, on September 17, 1954, before Senate investigators, the important witness, R. S. O'Brien, of the Bureau of Narcotics, told of the phenomenal increase on the border in the illegal drug traffic that year. In describing where border addicts received their dope shots, Mr. O'Brien said that they went to 'injection specialists' in El Paso and especially to 'shooting galleries' in Juarez, Mexico.

NOTES

[1] This paper was read at the Present Day English group meeting of the Modern Language Association in New York, December 27, 1954.

[2] Walter R. Creighton, *Narcotic Investigation and Narcotic Law Enforcement* (Division of Narcotic Enforcement, State of California, 1950), pp. 3-6.

[3] For the foregoing information, I am indebted to Lawrence Fleishman, supervising customs agent at El Paso, and especially to R. S. O'Brien, supervising agent of the Bureau of Narcotics, El Paso.

[4] XI, 116-27.

[5] XIII, 179-92.

[6] David W. Maurer and Victor H. Vogel, M.D., "A Glossary of Terms Commonly Used by Underworld Addicts," *Narcotics and Narcotic Addiction* (Springfield, Ill.: Charles C. Thomas, 1954), pp. 262-92.

[7] The insertion of [əz] or [ɪz] after an initial consonant or consonant cluster is a device for disguising a word or phrase.

[8] Harry J. Anslinger, U.S. Commissioner of Narcotics, and William F. Tompkins, U.S. Attorney for the District of New Jersey, "Glossary," *The Traffic in Narcotics* (New York, 1953), pp. 305-16.

[9] Probably additional terms could be gleaned from other books now in print, although I do not propose to give a bibliography of the subject here. Certainly a widespread scholarly interest in narcotics and the speech of narcotic addicts is indicated by the number of new books being published in this field today (see *An Index to the Publishers Trade List Annual*).

[10] *Girl* for *cocaine* appears in the printed lists.

[11] The word *sedol* may be a shortened form of *sedatol,* a medicine.

[12] *Amdray* for a dram of narcotics illustrates Dog Latin also; see Alfred R. Lindesmith," "The Argot of the Underworld Drug Addict," *Journal of Criminal Law and Criminology,* XXIX (1938), 261-78.

[13] In compiling my list, I relied partly upon a brief article in the El Paso *Herald Post* (November 29, 1951), but chiefly upon aid from Messrs. W. R. Bain, of the El Paso police department; Lawrence Fleishman, supervising customs agent; Allen Moore, a student of Texas Western College; and especially R. S. O'Brien, supervising agent of the Bureau of Narcotics.

[14] Charles A. Nowell, "The Old Man of the Mountain," *Speculum,* XXII (1947), 500, n.12.

[15] This fourth conclusion was added at the suggestion of Professor T. M. Pearce, of the University of New Mexico.

[16]. United Press, August 13, 1954.

The Anonymous Verses of a Narcotics Addict

The literature[1] on drug addiction contains a corpus of poems of both folk and literary origins. Among the more popular narcotic poems and songs of recent time are such familiar titles as "Chinatown, My Chinatown,"[2] "Cocaine,"[3] "Cocaine Lil,"[4] "Honey, Take a Whiff on Me,"[5] "Irene,"[6] "Minnie the Moocher,"[7] "The Old Dope Peddler,"[8] "Why Don't You Be Like Me?"[4] and "Willie the Weeper."[5] Interesting as these materials are, they clearly reflect their literary quality in being written, with the exception of a few words, in conventional English as well as in being either composed or edited by writers who are not addicts. Of more importance to the student of drug argot is such a rarer verse specimen as the short excerpts from an untitled ballad cited in *American Speech* by the noted Professor Maurer in 1938.[9] Saving this excerpt, avowedly the composition of an addicted user of drugs, no representative group of narcotic verse, so far as is known, has ever appeared in a learned journal for the linguistic record. Since evidence of the currency of this underworld argot has rested hitherto mainly upon oral sources, it obviously would be valuable to have written proof in the form of the original verses of a known addict to enlarge the present knowledge of the argot as well as to afford a fuller file on its folk usage.

In this connection, it is possible to submit, through permission from Mr. R. S. O'Brien,[10] Special Agent of the Bureau of Narcotics, the texts of six poems about narcotics by an anonymous Creole woman who is a confirmed user of drugs. However short on literary merit, her verses lack nothing in realistic downrightness or revealing autobiographical disclosure. For the student of current English, they possess primary significance, for they represent the writing of an established addict and show narcotic terms, here explained in the footnotes, to be an integral and natural expression of her working vocabulary. The full texts of these original poems appear under her following six alliterative titles.

I. MARIHUANA MIXUP

It happened a long, long time ago;
I thought I knew a lot.
I had a feeling I must go
And blast[11] some crazy[12] pot.[13]
I smoked and smoked and then
I was floating in the sky.
I smoked some more and got a buzz[14]
And knew that I was high.[14]
I floated down the avenue,
Just laughing all the time;
And then it was I really knew
That blasting[11] weed[15] was fine.
My feet were two feet off the ground,
And I was in the air.
Later, I began coming down;
I didn't feel so hot;
I made it slowly back to town;
I capped[16] me some more pot;[13]
I stashed[17] the stuff in someone's hall
And went on home to bed.
My old man[18] knew about it all,
But nothing much was said.
The next day I got busted[19]
As I walked out of the door.
Someone I had trusted
Gave my name into the law.
I knew I could beat the case
If the cops could be bought,
And next day with a smiling face

I made it from the court.
I found myself some cash;
Then I went on to the meet;[20]
From there picked up my stash.[17]
The same old story repeats, you know.
I think I know a lot.
I got a feeling I must go
And blast[11] some crazy[12] pot.[13]

II. NARCOTIC NOEL

'Twas the night before Christmas,
And all through the pad[21]
Reefers[22] and cocaine
Was all that we had,
When down the chimney came sniffing Sam
With his little black book
In the palm of his hand.
He said, "Man, two caps[23] of 'H'[24]
Is all that I got,
And you know how that goes;
I'm gonna shoot[25]
Them myself."

III. BOP BUBBLE

The drums are beating faster
Than the beating of my heart.
The rhythm gets more frantic,[26]
And it tears my soul apart,
And in the background I can hear
The wailing of a horn,
As the night is drifting on
Into another dawn.
So I sit here, and I'm nodding;[27]
And I hear Lester[28] blow.
I dig[29] the blasting of his sax;
The sound's both sweet and low.
The music's really getting hot.
It's setting off a spark;
It's ready to explode right now
In this inviting dark.
Yes, this is my world always,

With the best kicks[14] I have known;
And when I get the feel of it,
I'm by myself alone.
Then I'm cut off[30] from all of you,
Though I know deep down within
That it gets me as it gets you
Way underneath your skin.

IV. MEDITATION

As I sit here alone in my little jail cell,
I'm looking real beat and feeling like hell.
The feds[31] got me busted[19] for one little sale;
So here I am with my ass in a jail.
I'm sick as a dog, got the shakes and the twitches.
I can't get a fix,[32] the sons of a bitches.
They don't know what it's like for a junkie[33] to kick;[34]
I just wish they knew what it's like to be sick.[35]
But they ask you those questions
And tear you apart.
Who's your connection?[36] And how did you start?
Man, all these questions are getting me down.
I wonder what's happening with the junkies[33] in town.
I bet they're capping[16] right now from their man[36]
And shooting[25] up as much shit[24] as they can.
I wish someone would bring some horse[24] in this place;
I'd be pacing these floors with a smile on my face.
And even though the hi[14] wouldn't last,
It'd still goof me out.
I'd live over the past;
I'd think of the streets and the things I could do,
Remember old times, both happy and blue.
So you have your freedom
And do all your dirt;
Then wonder why you had to be hurt.
Well, I've done all the doing
I'll do for awhile, so I'll just take it slow[37]
Till I come up for trial.

V. JUNKIE'S JOY

Last night I had a date
With this guy,

And he inquired if I got hi.[14]
I told him "No"
But said, "Let's go;
I'll be a junkie."[33]
I went along with him to cop.[16]
It took so long I blew my top.[38]
But he came through
With a big one, two.[39]
Man, what a junkie.[33]

VI. CRADLE CAPERS

I knew it not then,
But when I was one,
My life as a junkie[33]
Had just begun.
Since ma was a viper
And daddy would snort,[40]
I'd watch from the sidelines
And really get brought.[41]
Time went by,
And at the age of two
I'd seen so much
I knew just what to do.
Since ma was a viper
And daddy would snort,[40]
There wasn't much more
I had to be taught.
On the day I was but three
I started blasting[11] some crazy[12] tea;[15]
But I wasn't satisfied,
Strange as it seems,
For I'd see spikes[42] and droppers[43]
Whenever I dreamed.
On my next birthday,
When I was four,
I hopped on my tricycle
And went off to score.[44]
It was then I discovered
From my connection[36]
That I was young
And needed protection;
But I got a new man,[36]
And by the time I was five

I'd shot[25] so much shit[24]
I was more dead than alive.
Since ma was a viper
And daddy would snort,[40]
And I was a junkie,[33]
We were bound to be caught.
So I played it cool,[45] and when I was six,
I decided to go back to blasting[11] those sticks,[46]
Or my health would be ruined then.
What could I do
With veins that collapsed[47]
And had abscesses[48] too?
So I played cool[45] until I was seven;
That's when I found myself
Floating in heaven.
That morning I capped[16] some morphine at last,
And from that day on
Things were moving too fast.
A whole year went by, and then I was eight,
I went uptown to see
Where I could get straight.[49]
I got there; and some cat,[50]
He just winked at me
And offered to cap[16] some fabulous "C."[51]
So you know what happened;
And when I was nine,
I bumped into an old friend of mine.
I told him I split from my pad[21]
Awhile back,
So he felt sorry for me
And gave me some smack.[52]
Things were real frantic,[26]
And when I was ten,
I spotted this stud in an opium den.
His face was all sallow
And yellow and drawn,
But he told me he felt like
He knew I was cool,[45]
And he said I was ripe
To start blasting[11] opium
From a water pipe.
I took a few pokes,[11]
And, man, I got stoned.[53]
I goofed[36] and just wanted

To be left alone.
Then somebody said, "Chick,
You 'bout ready to fly."
So I flew off the table
And blackened one eye.
But I didn't care
He'd just been reborn.
If I did have that fall.
I was so stoned[53] I was blind.
Man, what a ball!
Twenty-four hours later I finally came down
And made a decision to go back downtown.
I wanted some more
Of that fabulous "O";[54]
And ever since then
It's been go, go, go.
Time has gone on,
And now I'm eighteen,
But I make it my business
To stay on the scene.[55]
And if I don't get hi[14]
When I go to score,[44]
That's all right.
I just use a little bit more.
Yesterday I shot[25] some real wild shit,[24]
But I had a hard time getting a hit.[56]
Since my veins are all hardened,
I'll have to skin pop[57]
And cut down a little[58]
Each day till I stop.
Although I say that right now to myself,
I know junk[24] is one thing I never can shelf.[59]
I'll never be able to give up that hi,[14]
So I'll just be a junkie[33]
Till the day that I die.

The general impression one receives from all the poems is that the anonymous author uses standard, rather than regional, speech. A possible indication of the writer's Southern origin (*i. e.*, Louisiana) appears in "Bop Bubble" (No. III, lines 6, 8), where *horn* (hawn) rhymes with *dawn;* but the sound (cp. VI, 68, 70), which could be only an imperfect rhyme, does not give the verse either a regional or a dialect flavor. The narcotic argot itself would be understood by an addict anywhere in the United States or even by foreigners intimate with the illegal traffic in drugs. These several texts are thus further evidence of the fact that "Narcotic ziph tends to be, not a regional tongue, but an international language."[60]

The six narcotic poems afford an excellent contemporary illustration of folk literature by an anonymous poetess of unmistakable folk status.

NOTES

[1] David W. Maurer and Victor H. Vogel, *Narcotics and Narcotic Addiction* (Springfield, Ill., 1954), pp. 254-255, 293-294.

[2] William Jerome and Jean Schwartz, New York, Remick Music Corporation, 1906.

[3] M. E. Henry, *Folk-Songs from the Southern Highlands* (New York, 1938), p. 140.

[4] John and Alan Lomax, *Best Loved American Folk Songs* (New York, 1947), p. 291.

[5] John and Alan Lomax, *American Ballads and Folk Songs* (New York, 1938), pp. 186, 184.

[6] John and Alan Lomax, *Negro Folk Songs as Sung by Lead Belly* (New York, 1936), p. 237.

[7] Cab Calloway, New York, Mills Music Publishers, 1931.

[8] Tom Lehrer, *The Tom Lehrer Song Book* (New York, 1952), pp. 51-53.

[9] David W. Maurer, "Argot of the Underworld Narcotic Addict: Part II," *American Speech* (1938), XIII, 181, note 6.

[10] Mr. O'Brien, who collected the verses in Arkansas in 1956, said that the Creole woman, an octoroon, came from Louisiana.

[11] smoke, by cupping the hands and drawing deeply.

[12] good, fine, excellent.

[13] marihuana in a cigarette or in a pipe bowl.

[14] feeling of elation ranging from euphoria to intoxication.

[15] marihuana, a plant or weed.

[16] To "cap" may mean to open a capsule of a drug or to buy a drug. The verb "capped" appears to signify "got possession of" or "brought," whereas "to cop" or "copped" may mean "to steal" or "stole." To "cap" also may refer to filling a capsule.

[17] A "stash" is a "hidden package"; to "stash" is to "hide"; "stashed" means "cached."

[18] According to Mr. O'Brien, a "hustling girl" calls her procurer her "old man."

[19] arrested by the police or federal agents.

[20] the meeting place with the seller.

[21] sleeping quarters, bed, cot, or apartment. When she says "I split from my pad" she means that she left her home or her "old man" (O'Brien).

[22] marihuana cigarettes.

[23] ampoules, capsules.

[24] heroin; usually "junk" and "shit" also mean heroin.

[25] inject with the hypodermic needle. "Sam" may be the name for any dealer in drugs who is an addict himself. He may have had a "reader," or a prescrip-

tion, when he bought the heroin. If so, he might logically call the box he carried it in his "little black book."

26 faster; a "frantic" character is an addict: to be "frantic" is to want a drug or, in a special sense, to desire coition.

27 succumbing to a drug.

28 Probably from Lester Young, a famous saxophone player.

29 to listen or to understand. Mr. O'Brien cited "I snap you" as synonymous with "I dig you."

30 removed; insensible from narcotic intoxication.

31 federal narcotic agents.

32 a shot with a needle.

33 an addict (pl. -s).

34 to quit the habit.

35 to suffer the "shakes and twitches" of the withdrawal syndrome; synonymous with "having a monkey on your back" (O'Brien).

36 peddler, who may be referred to as "the man," "the man from Montana" (a variant of "the old man of the mountain").

36 pass me out. "Goofed" means knocked out from overdosages, generally from barbiturates (O'Brien).

37 suffer the withdrawal without complaining (O'Brien).

38 became angry, lost my head. [The first stanza of "Junkie's Joy" has been omitted because of its objectionable vulgarity (Braddy).]

39 two injections, two spasmodic physical reactions; evidently he had the so-called "two-arm" habit.

40 sniff cocaine or heroin. "Viper" would seem here to mean one who sniffs a powdered drug.

41 instructed, taught.

42 needles, the hypodermic needle being often called "golden spike."

43 Eye-droppers, substituting for needles, are sometimes inserted in a rent in the flesh.

44 make a successful purchase or injection of a drug.

45 quietly; to act carefully and not arouse suspicion (O'Brien).

46 marihuana cigarettes or bundles of them.

47 darkened, flattened veins from numerous punctures and hot solutions injected into them (O'Brien).

48 from shooting impure "medicine": opium poisoning obtained from smoking it or "cooking" paregoric by evaporation in a spoon to get the opium from it (O'Brien).

49 The phrase means, not "to go straight" (conform to the law), but "to get the stuff" (purchase narcotics) [O'Brien].

50 musician.

51 cocaine.

52 She probably means that he gave her "money" for buying drugs or that he selected customers for her services as a prostitute.

53 completely intoxicated.

54 opium.

55 the place where drugs are available.

56 inserting the needle in her hardened veins.

57 inject into the epidermis.

58 a futile reduction treatment (O'Brien).

59 give up, quit.

60 "Narcotic Argot Along the Mexican Border," *American Speech* (1955), XXX, 89.

6

Wild Mare's Milk

In 1937 I cited *wild mare's milk* as a euphemism for *whisky* in 'Some Southwestern Cowboy Lingo,' *American Speech* (XXII, 153). The phrase then was submitted as a contemporary Southwestern coinage, but further inquiry shows that the expression has had a rather long literary history though not with the precise meaning of *whisky*.

It is doubtful that the cowboys of the Southwest drew the expression from some schoolboy knowledge of the famous nineteenth-century romance *Sohrab and Rustum*. But the reference should be mentioned. There Matthew Arnold spoke of the Tartars of Oxus 'who from Bokhara came and Khiva, and fermented the milk of mares' (II. 120-21).[1] Here Arnold alluded to a practice among certain Oriental people of fermenting mare's milk and honey. These Orientals won celebrity as 'mare milkers,' their intoxicant being named *kumiss*.

There remain further important references to *mare's' milk* as a euphemism for an intoxicating beverage. The Elizabethans Beaumont and Fletcher used the phrase in *The Knight of the Burning Pestle*. There a character called the Wife recommended both this drink and a cordial for their medicinal value: 'Faith, the child hath a sweet breath, George; but I think it be troubled with the worms; *corduus benedictus* and mare's milk were the only thing in the world for't' (III, iv, 29-33).[2]

A yet earlier mention of the drink occurs in the thirteenth-century *Travels* of Marco Polo. There the medieval Polo talked about the Tartars and reported that 'their drink is mare's milk. prepared in such a way that you would take it for white wine; and a right good drink it is, called by them kumiz.'[3] Eastern tribes made much ado about the concoction. On the twenty-eighth day of the moon in August their astrologers scattered mare's milk in the wind as an honor to all the spirits and idols whom they adored.

Probably the first citation in English occurs in the ninth-century Anglo-Saxon narrative 'The Voyages of Ohthere and Wulfstan.' There King Alfred described the Balts, whose land abounded with honey. He said that 'the king and the richest men drink mare's milk, and the poor and the servants drink mead.'[4] Mead, as is well known, is honey fermented with water, whereas mare's milk is honey fermented, not with water, but with the milk of camels or mares. These two drinks, mead and kumiss, were favorites with the Balts, for King Alfred stated that since there was 'mead enough' these people brewed no ale whatever. Presumably, these Asiatic customs became known in England through such accounts of explorers as Alfred's report on Wulfstan.

The ultimate origin of the Westernism *wild mare's milk* seems thus to be the ancient East. Significant references appear in the Persian saga of the Old Man of the Mountain, the Oriental legends of Paradise, the religious works of early Greece, and especially the Bible with its promised land of milk and honey.[5]

NOTES

[1] Sir Arthur T. Quiller-Couch, ed., *The Poems of Matthew Arnold* (Oxford, 1926), p. 201.

[2] Felix E. Schelling and Matthew W. Black, eds., *Typical Elizabethan Plays* (New York, 1949), p. 579.

[3] George B. Parks, tr., *The Book of Ser Marco Polo the Venetian* (New York, 1927), p. 82.

[4] As translated from James W. Bright, ed., *An Anglo-Saxon Reader* (New York, 1948), p. 42; see also F. P. Magoun, Jr., and J. A. Walker, eds., *An Anthology of Old-English Prose and Verse* (Cambridge, Mass., 1948), p. 58.

[5] Parks, *op. cit.*, p. 50; Vergilius Ferm, *Ancient Religions* (New York, 1950), pp. 148, 156, 176; and King James Bible, Numbers 13:27, 14:18, 16:13; Exodus 3:8. In England, Mandeville in the fourteenth century wrote about the Old Man's paradise of milk and honey (Josephine W. Bennett, *The Rediscovery of Sir John Mandeville* [New York, 1954], p. 45).

7

Riding the White Horse

Hop heads know their opium brands:
Cocks or mules bedeck the cans.

Narcotics, an indissoluble link with prostitution and smuggling, have long influenced social mores on the Mexico-Texas border. Among drugs, none is more ravaging than heroin. Labels most often found on its boxes display such figures as the Dragon, the Eagle, the Elephant, the Fox, Hadji Ala Baba, the Kicking Mule, the Lion, and especially the White Horse. The contour of the box is square; the content, diacetylmorphine. This fine white crystalline powder is obtained by treating the morphine base with acetic anhydride. The powder comes out so fine that it will practically disappear when rubbed into the skin. It acts quickly if rubbed into a mucous membrane, the eye or mouth, or if sniffed; and even more quickly when injected into the veins with a needle. In 1956 an infant borne by an addicted El Paso mother showed symptoms of heroin poisoning at birth. For its worst effect, heroin makes people violent and murderous. For its best effect, it surpasses morphine by producing euphoria, a feeling of well-being.

Grandpa had a horse, papa a car, and son an airplane. The West had changed. The lines of the poet Cummings are true to life in a vital way now, because "Buffalo Bill's   defunct." For today Westerners easily may find themselves enmeshed in a drug ring "riding the White Horse," mired deep in a dope den listening to the popular strains of the juke-box song "Hajji Baba," which name (Hadji Ala Baba), as already mentioned, forms a trademark on boxes of crystal white heroin.

"Horse" comes expensive; and in order to support his habit, an addict needs a sure source of money. Thievery and pickpocketing help, but the danger of apprehension remains great and the monetary amount of the return variable and uncertain. The best device for the addict is to introduce a man with a steady salary to the same habit and live off of him. Another favorite practice is to "hook" a woman with the habit and have her work for him as a prostitute. The woman destined for this end may start as the mistress of the addict or even as his wife.

Cunning as a fox, the "Ad" man ordinarily devotes a little time to the selection of the prospective prostitute. He selects a girl highly temperamental or perhaps emotionally unstable—a personality who during her menstruation period stands in particular need of a "boost." In one instance an addict married a country girl from Montana and brought her to live with him in Silver City, New Mexico. Her first experience with "H" came when she menstruated. Feeling that "Hache" lifted her over the worst tide of her period, she came gradually to rely on regular shots of the stuff. Not too long after her initiation, the full dosage of heroin began to have physiological effects on her body. She stayed constipated most of the time. Her ovaries began to dry up so much that her menstrual glands finally ceased to secrete. One of the mental results beginning to make itself felt simultaneously was a heightened desire to be abused and mistreated. The inner masochism of her subconscious rose to the surface. She sank with ease, yieldingly, into a periodless prostitute who serviced her gentleman customers all days and nights of the month. Meanwhile, her addicted husband took her earnings from her to maintain his increasingly expensive habit.

The worst manifestations of drug addiction occur among erring juveniles. Although the majority of them escape the ultimate deterioration of the heroin habit, juveniles go to Juarez to frequent dirty bars and cheap jive halls. Owners of such establishments contend that they can not hire policemen to be on the look-out for the droves of dope-pushers who throng to such places to barter their wares in dark corners or smelly latrines.

Nor do such places look especially dangerous to the uninitiated eye of the casual beholder. All he sees is a group of hep-cats drinking soft drinks like Coco-cola or 7-Up. He does not see the goofballs dropped into their drinks nor the short brown cigarettes they alternately puff with their Camels or Chesterfields. Even an undercover agent can be misled unless he knows the folk-ways of the bops.

The observer begins to "pick up" when a "cube" (3-D square) is told to "clik," and he sees him take his "toy" to the dance floor. If he "digs" the "hard speil," he can learn a lot by keeping his "gims" open and his "flaps" cleaned out.

For instance, the "grape cat" who refuses to "goo" represents a "wino" who will not eat his food. He is a "capon" with a "copper nose" and a "tush-pusher" who will take you to a "fine dinner"—an effeminate man with a drunkard's red nose and a procurer who will conduct you to a pretty girl. If you refuse to go, you are a "square" who does not "flip the chick." Maybe a "crazy gate" like you wants the "pride" (best). You ought to "rock." There is no use saving "gold" for the "cold meat party" and "dust bowl" (funeral and grave). The best thing for you to do is to "slip him some skin with the long five" (shake hands) and stop acting like a "creaker" (oldster). In other words, be "cool, daddio," and "float" (pay your way) before the "Davy Crocketts" (draft boards) get you. "Hey, gate," stop that "dribble" about "deep six" (the grave) and "fall out for in there" (be surprised by a thrill). "Come to school before you're melted out."

For another instance, the "dicty" (aristocrat) who drove up in the "cattle train" (Cadillac) just had an "expense" (new-born baby). His "head chick" has stayed at home with her "hoop" (ring). He needs a "main queen" with plenty of "headlights" (bosom), a "doll" who is really "Mary" (capable). Before he "drills out by cow express" (walks out), he ought to "mush" (kiss) that "banter" (pretty girl). What she needs, they call "bread" and "deep sugar" (money and sweet talk). She is "foxy on Four-and-one" (clever on Friday) and always after that "cholly" (dollar). With those "stilts" of hers she will get a new pair of "gam cases" easily. If he has the "corn," she has the "cave" (room); and by Saturday night she will have him at the "ice palace" (jewelry store). Hear that "riff"? Put a "demon" in the "piccolo" (juke box).

Brown needle men know the art
To heat the spoon and feed the heart.
Faster draws the rapid breath
Till the white hour of their death.

That's it—or how it usually starts.

2

Marijuana is the Mexican name of *Cannabis sativa,* or Indian hemp. Top leaves and stalks as well as blossoms from the plant grow rich in resinous glands that produce the drug. It may be brewed into a tea and drunk; mixed with spices or chocolate and eaten; or rolled into a cigarette, as usually in the United States, and smoked. Taken alone, it does not produce hallucinations but only intensifies thoughts, fancies, and desires which the addict already has. Taken with liquor, it becomes dangerous and leads to crime. Thought not to be as habit forming as other narcotics, it is much more widely used today than any other drug. For a description of its results on one experimenter, see U. S. D. Quincey, "Confessions of an American Marihuana Smoker," *Discovery* (1952).

On the border the ranch hand has always sung his "Cow, Cow Boogie" for a special reason, because "He was raised on loco weed." Or sometimes he may drink "mule," marihuana mixed with whiskey. In other lands people often eat it as candy. In 1954 Gertrude Stein included the recipe for "hashish fudge" in *The Alice B. Toklas Cook Book* (British edition only). "Mule" and "sneaky Pete" (wine with marihuana) better characterize the El Paso menu.

As for other words in border narcotic ziph, many of them naturally have a Spanish or Mexican origin. Those heard frequently around El Paso include *"cachucha"* for a capsule of drugs, *"caranjal"* for a person looking for narcotics, *"cartucho"* for a small package of marihuana cigarettes, *"cruz"* for opium, *"daga"* for a doped cigarette, *"Doña Juanita"* for marihuana, *"grifo"* for an addict, *"mojo"* for morphine, *"pistola"* for a syringe, and *"yesca"* for marihuana.

That other linguistic origins also figure in the speech may be easily shown. "Boy" and "girl," heroin and cocaine respectively, derive from Anglo-Saxon. The word *"yen,"* meaning yearning, came into English long ago from the Chinese language. Yet other words came from German, Hebrew, and Italian, such as "stack" for a ration of an ounce, *"skamas"* for drugs, and *"capo"* for the leader of a drug ring. Negroes have contributed, among others, the word "ofay," Dog or Pig Latin for foe, or white man.

American expressions of course compose the majority. Many of these appear self-explanatory, being but a figurative means of saying a plain thing. A "bad go" is a poor purchase; "to beat the dough," to run away with the money; "to be on the nod," to be half asleep from drugs. Similarly, "to blue grass" means to return to the hospital in Kentucky as patients needing free drugs; a "boredom beater'" signifies one who smokes marihuana only rarely; and "Can you do me good?" means Will you sell me drugs? As for the paraphernalia and products, a "bridge" stands for a cigarette holder, "Carrie Nation" for cocaine, "chocolate" for dark-colored opium, a "cripple" for a cigarette, "Eli Lilly" for morphine, "frisky powder" for cocaine, "frog skins" for money, "golden spike" for the hypodermic needle, "hard nail" for a puncturing instrument, and "Mary Jane" for marihuana.

The people associated with the drug business include "Dick Smith," an addict who is a lone wolf; the "frantic character," one who becomes nervous for dope; and "George," the man who always remains trustworthy. "Tea heads" like their drugs in liquid form, but they later take to using shots and even develop the "two-arm habit." Both men and women stay "wigged" (muddle-headed) with "zols" (marihuana cigarettes), which they either "turn on" or "torch up." Prostitutes get "way down" when they encounter a narcotic agent. They associate him with bewhiskered Uncle Sam and call him "Uzzfay" (Dog Latin for fuzz). They know the agent will take them to "Jenny Barn," the woman's ward of a drug hospital.

Marihuana has long been associated with the Mexican Border, where hardly anything would be easier to obtain. In Juarez the pleasure seeker can get it on the streets or even in jail, if he chances to land there. On December 5, 1960, Police Chief Herrera Orozco, of Juarez, made a new seizure of the weed in a cell of the *carcel.* He remarked to the El Paso *Herald-Post,* "It's easier to get marihuana inside the jail than out." Mr. Reuben Salazar, a courageous reporter for the same *Herald-Post,* found in the fifties that conditions were equally bad in the El Paso jail. In other words, peripatetic marihuana pushers appeared everywhere on both sides of the Rio Grande.

3

> That *muchacho* near the shelf
> Will steal the caps and kill himself,
> But his sister lithe and strong
> Will puff the weed and kick the gong.

Morphine, the principal alkaloid of "mother" opium, forms a definite chemical substance. Manufactured in many places, it derives from raw opium by various processes, the main one consisting of digesting the opium in limed water and recovering the morphine from the solution. The morphine base finds itself freed by the addition of alkalis. To obtain morphine salts, the alkaloid, or base, receives treatment with hydrocholoric, sulphuric, or tartaric acid. Morphine will turn red when treated with nitric acid, which is the usual preliminary field test.

Those who take "M" find the first reaction to be one of extraordinary well-being and vigor, accentuated in persons of unbalanced mental and physical functions. But addiction to the drug injures the user. Although later doses may produce satisfaction and feeling of normal health, addiction requires even larger quantities to gain an effect. When the cells can no longer assimilate the drug, death results.

Among dope fiends, the death symbol becomes omnipresent. Masochism is sometimes practiced as a foretaste of death, a negative pain. In the mind of an addict, his drug transcends all. He hates it and, to accentuate the positive upsurge resulting from an injection, loves it, ambivalently. But chiefly he loves it. Hence his name for the drug is a transcendent, sublime expression, the word "soul."

Though its usage is declining today, morphine in the earlier epoch of Reconstruction, after the Civil War, became the main support of wounded, mutilated soldiers who received inadequate treatment from ill-equipped surgeons. The incidence of accidental addiction of soldiers serving in the Orient is not so rare. Veterans of World War II as well as the Korean Conflict, former bed

patients of William Beaumont General Hospital, El Paso, have
been known to seek the drug on the border. In 1955 a former
paratrooper died in Juarez from overdosings of heroin. Deaths
occur in other manners, too. Dope peddlers want to keep their
customers at all costs. The drug fiends are said to "belong" to the
pushers; and if a fiend causes trouble, he may be given a lethal
portion, or "hot shot," which will cause his death.

> The man astride the topmost hill
> Supports himself by shot and pill.
> When you fumble a trifle later,
> Snap him then, sad alligator.

Addicts testify that drugs enable them to relive the past. They
depend on them to recapture some lost experience; to know some
thrill never experienced before; to go back, way back, to a child-
hood past. Their minds whirl with mad ideas that twist and turn
about in their heads.

4

> When Del Toro pumps the forge,
> Then Dick Smith is really George.

Opium may be recognized in its raw state by its outer appearance of compound vegetable matter, such as leaves and twigs; by
its soft brown exterior color; and by its characteristic odor, a
heavy, sweet smell. Opium is usually trafficked in one-pound
bricks, covered with red and white wrappers.

Although many Chinese addicts live to a ripe old age, other
races do not. Opium is a soporific, inducing pleasant but fantastic
dreams. Later, symptoms of poisoning develop, with death often
the result. Relatively unknown to Chaucer and Shakespeare,
opium has been often discussed by more recent writers.
Baudelaire, DeQuincey, and Edgar Allan Poe lived to report
their experiences with it because they took it in diluted form, or
infrequently. What Poe used was laudanum, which may have
occasioned the dreams he narrated in his story, "Ligeia." The
Englishman Thomas DeQuincey ate opium in cake form, recount-
ing the whole experience in *Confessions of an English Opium-
Eater.*

The Frenchman Baudelaire smoked the stuff, sucking on citrus fruit between puffs to keep his mouth wet. He wrote on the subject lengthily in his famous work called *Paradis Artificiels*. Other recent authors who have revealed their sensations after taking drugs include Hart Crane, Walter Duranty, and Aldous Huxley. The most descriptive statement on the results of smoking opium came, however, from an old addicted border prostitute. She said: "You never forget it—once you've 'slept with the Chinaman.' "

Nearly all countries cultivate poppy fields for the medical use of opium and its derivatives. Such projects are known to exist, or to have existed recently, in both Mexico and the United States. The legal employment of drugs as pain-relievers occurs everyday, in particularly large quantities during periods of war or other disasters. But the illegal employment of opium is also a worldwide phenomenon. The presence on the Mexican border of contraband opium is therefore no more a matter of surprise than would be its appearance in distant Burma.

Traditionally, Chinamen have been the principal addicts of opium. "Chinatown, My Chinatown," a song said to be written about the Chinese colony in New York City, pictured a Wall Street derelict dreaming that he was "a millionaire." The Chinese had a flourishing colony in the Mexican state of Chihuahua until Pancho Villa came to power there. Villa ran most of them northward to the Rio Grande, where they waded across to safety in Texas. That happened nearly half a century ago. Today many of these refugees as well as their descendants live in El Paso and Juarez. None of these people have engaged in criminal activities connected with opium, but far different conditions once prevailed. The El Paso *Lone Star* reported on January 20, 1883, that opium joints were doing heavy business at the Pass. According to the *Evening Tribune,* October 18, 1893, El Paso then had more Chinese residents in terms of percentage of population than any two other cosmopolitan corporations in Texas—and also more opium dens. Between then and now, no doubt more than one erring Chinaman has "bootlegged foreign mud." One such story may be heard around Deming, New Mexico.

> By thieves and pushers quickly rooked,
> The blue-eyed girls are firmly hooked;
> And few of them recall their names
> Or pulseless flesh that lit their flames.

This tale concerns a Chinaman who made a lot of money selling opium in both El Paso and Juarez. He married a beautiful young Anglo wife after he had given her the habit of "lacing" her whiskey with opium in liquid form. She became so frantically addicted, after graduating to opium suppositories, that he had to move her to Deming, away from her source of supply. One report says that she finally ran away from her husband and went into the Mexican state of Sonora, where by toiling as a prostitute she was able to resume and support her habit.

For a consideration, one may visit a border opium den today. The spectacle affords something to remember, as the scene is one of dignity, quiet, and reserve. Here no be-bops gyrate on the floor; drunks do not pound on the tables; *mariposas* do not embrace the startled tourists. The pipe smokers arrange themselves on the carpeted floor in a sleeping posture, supine. The head of one rests on the stomach of another, four to a square; and the pipe is passed backward and sideways to each succeeding smoker. No music reaches their hideaway, for they hear the strains celestial; no nude girls, teeth painted red and skin anointed, clutch their arms or legs, for they dream of far-fairer maidens. The saffron figures look immobile and withdrawn, yellow enamel mannikins of an artificial otherworld. Now and again, but seldom and not hurriedly, black attendants remove a sleeping smoker from the square to place him on a couch, where his dreams last on and on. His place on the floor is then quickly taken by a new inhaler. After a short while, the air becomes murky in the already gray room with its softly-tinted walls.

The lasting sensation of the non-addicted observer is the insufferably sweet odor of the opium, the lemonish taste in the mouth, the lifelessness of the entire scene of corpselike figures. The heavy scent of something like incense endures and almost chokes him as he stumbles out the door into the bright, drilling sunshine of Borderland.

5

What goes on in coky's mind?
What goes round in coky's head?

This pains his brains:

"Something was wrong with her last night. The main thing I saw was that her mouth was on the top of her head, and she kept moving straight upward from where she stood on the floor as if she had defied the law of gravity and was going to eat the grapes and apples and pears that were painted on the wall paper on the ceiling. I kept dragging her down by her bare knees, her knobs, trying to get her to keep them on the floor and stop screaming and start to praying like she ought to, like we both ought to. And she kept going straight up, throwing her arms up over her head, and whether going up to the ceiling or simply getting taller by the minute until she just filled up the middle of the room like a pillar of stone that you built there to hold the house up. And me? All I could do was to grab her yellow knobs and pull her down till they were on the floor. But after that, she was really all right, serene, really 'in there.' We could hear the dawn breaking as though you were tearing a cardboard box apart, little by little, and then with a big, long-sounding rip. A hot flash blinded my eyes as the sun illuminated the glass window on the upper half of the door; and a parching fever coursed up and down my dry flesh; but as soon as I drank a glass of tap water, I heard the bird on the roof sing, not loud and fierce at first, and then so piercingly loud that the blood beat like thunder in my ears. I know I suddenly felt a trickle of blood run down the back of my head to the nape of my neck, and then under my collar and down my back, spreading fan-like till it dried out; but all I wiped away was a trickle of water from my chin, which spilled when I drank the full glass of cold water from the water faucet. And the bird's voice became so loud he sounded as big as an eagle; and I thought, strangely and without any reason, that he was up there on the roof to hold the sky up, to keep it from breaking through the ceiling and flooding through the door where the sun was now pouring as though you had loosed every flood gate there ever was, into that door that was an irrigation ditch cascading all the distance from Ysleta a spouting river of chartreuse sunshine all over the room.

Both Mabel and Mary, all are prone
Before La Nacha on her throne.

"When whoever he was came back from wherever he had been,

he grabbed her off the ceiling, for I was on the green bed on the blue floor; and he took her, with the multi-colored ceiling wallpaper sticking out from all around her, and left. Or sat down in the azure chair in the yellow corner across the brown room with his gray coat pulled up so close around him and her wallpaper wrapping sticking out everywhere that I could hardly see him— or them, that is. From the angle I looked from on the bed, I could not tell anything for certain until I turned on my side and saw only a chair there. She had gone all right, gone with whoever he was that always came and took her and then brought her back, wild-eyed and tired, scarred up a little about the face where he kicked her, and retorn on her insides where she broke her rib, really cracked it, jumping up at the ceiling as she did last week or last month or last night, or whenever it was. And her nose was on the top of her head, her red, red nose.

> Look upon her seated there,
> Sharpened eyes, drilling stare.

"And all of them, whoever he was and the bangsters who came along, opened up the quarter-ounce bottle and inhaled it through the nostrils; and dropped some, for she leaned down and sniffed it through the mucous membranes of her nasal passages, her two-horn honker, until she, haptically, got contentment and stopped flying up to the ceiling but laid herself down and flipped open her flesh-pocket before all of them, whoever he was and everyone of those black bangsters, while Peter Prospero, the big boy, talked on nosology; until it looked like they couldn't leave, one after the other, as they crowded down around her on the floor. What a bender with big bloke, those bangsters had! Later, Mrs. White aced in with a bingle, all chalked up with Cecil. When her flesh-pocket started flopping and swooshing, it looked like the singing bird couldn't hold up the roof anymore, for the sky came crashing through it, so that she now stuck to the ceiling at last, pancaked and flattened as a bloody piece of plaster, and the bright lights, red, green, and gold, brown, and black, went flashing everywhere. She didn't come to until I held the bottle right up close to the rent in the middle of her head."

8

The Pachucos and Their Argot

An article relating to the argot of the dope addict appeared in the *Southern Folklore Quarterly*[1] recently, in which a liberal number of English coinages used by the drug addict were featured. The interest manifested in this specialized speech has prompted the extension of this investigation into the cognate diction found among the *Pachucos* in El Paso. The Committee on Organized Research, Texas Western College, has made available financial assistance with which to continue the study into the mores and language of this anti-social group.

A full history of juvenile delinquency in the United States would have to include a chapter on the *Pachucos,* Latin-American youths from the Texas-Mexico Borderland. One story, somewhat lacking in evidence, says that they led a social protest movement dating from about the outbreak of the Revolution in 1910. According to a recent interview with Professor Rafael Cravioto Muñoz, of Pachuca, Hidalgo,[2] they began to organize into gangs in the United States in the 1930's. At first they appeared as harmless, overdressed juveniles, wearing long watch chains and sporting the ducktail hair-do. Later their use of marihuana, or *cannabis sativa,* involved them with the police. When the narcotics laws were stiffened in 1956 to encompass *cannabis,*[3] the *Pachucos* suddenly found themselves mired in crime, though they never unified into a syndicate, as depicted in Wenzell Brown's novel

Teen-Age Mafia (1959). Their impact has been felt in Arizona, California, New Mexico,[4] and Texas, particularly in El Paso.

Mr. Ramón Villalobos, a noted police reporter for the El Paso *Times,* once lived for a time on the West Coast. According to him, in the 1940's many *Pachucos* moved from El Paso to Los Angeles, which they called *Losca, Califa.* In California large-scale warfare broke out between the *Pachucos* and the *Califas,* two zoot-suit gangs of teenage hoodlums. When the *Califas* suffered defeat, all zoot-suiters on the West Coast adopted the name *Pachuco* for their own designation. In those days many youngsters who lived in Los Angeles and who planned a trip to El Paso used to say: *"Voy al Pachuco,"* "I am going to El Paso." Further testimony to the same end comes from Thurston Scott, in his novel *Cure It with Honey* (1951). He said: "The toughest *Pachucos* come from El Paso but don't get smart until they pass through Losca." A gangster from New Mexico may be called a *Manito,* one from El Paso a *Pasiente,* and a youthful one from either El Paso or Los Angeles a *Pachuco.*

The underworld folkways of these juveniles feature street brawls, strong-arm robberies, rapes, and especially dope peddling. In 1957 the actress Marie McDonald, known as "the Body," described her alleged attackers as zoot-suited *Pachucos.* Individual members of the gangs often become addicted to marihuana or heroin, but both addicts and non-users "push junk" wherever possible. They bend all their efforts on getting at the money. To maintain their own ever-growing drug habits, the addicts have to do a steady trade in narcotics, with the result that they often initiate younger juveniles into the same practices. As they gain strength and prestige, the gangs enlarge the area of their nefarious doings, making their dark, disruptive influence felt even in the United States Air Force, whose pilots fly to many regions distant from California and Texas.

In 1954 *Pachucos* operated as airmen at the Air Force base in Chanute Field, Illinois. Photographers took pictures of cadets whose hands, forearms, and shoulders displayed characteristic markings. The markings most commonly used turned out to be "L O V E," and "I L O V E." Others signs included the figure of a diamond, a small cross on the nasal bridge, blue dots below the eyes or in the center of the forehead, and a long arrow pointing up the forearm to a heart. Some cadet airmen sported on their knuckles "E P T," which Illinois officials correctly interpreted as designating the airmen's point of origin, that is, El Paso, Texas. A subsequent Texas investigation, held at Sheppard Field, Wichita Falls, disclosed in 1954 that a stockade prisoner bore tell-tale *Pachuco* tattoos on his hands and arms. About the same time 25,000 men underwent screening at Lackland Air Force Base in San Antonio. A number of these also had tattoo markings, several of which could be linked to the symbols used by *Pachucos* in their secret society, the most popular one being a cross with bars placed between the thumb and index fingers, with each cross (or "ray") representing six months or more in jail.

An excellent place to study the *Pachucos* from El Paso is nearby Ysleta. In October, 1955, at the Ysleta bridge just out of Zaragoza, Mexico, Mr. Louis Giallanza, of the Texas Liquor Control Board, stopped a few boys who were returning to Texas. Mr. Giallanza noticed a number of markings on the young men. One of them, named Alfred, had five marks on the fingers of his hand which, together, formed the letter "E."

"What does the 'E' stand for?" Mr. Giallanza asked.
"My name," the boy replied.
"What is your name?" Mr. Giallanza said.
"Alfred," the boy said.

That was all the boy would say about it, though he clearly belonged to a delinquent class. Mr. Giallanza found, next, that another fellow in the same group had an "E" on his right hand as well as a question mark, "?," on his left. The name of the second boy was Pete, so that the letter "E" did not serve as his initial either. Perhaps it referred to the locality of the city of El Paso. After that, two or three lads remained for questioning. One of these had a heart tattooed on the back of his hand with a large cross inlaid over it. This one had long sideburns and used cosmetic paint and lipstick on his face and mouth. Yet another lad had an arrow pictured on his arm; it pointed upward to the word "MOTHER." The last lad had a key delineated on his arm, the meaning of which he refused to divulge. For weapons, the painted young men carried daggers, rubber hoses, and broken oar handles. Their whole demeanor suggested both sexual perversion and aggressive belligerence, two qualities not usually linked by arm-chair psychiatrists.

In more recent years policemen in El Paso have discovered the gangs to be very secretive, closely organized, and tight-lipped. The members remain faithful to the criminal code from fear of reprisals by their leader. Their main reason for being loyal stems from the aura of holiness suffusing their bizarre initiation. They swear by the cross or take an oath in the cemetery above the graves of their mothers. Their weapons have holy names, as *santo niño* (holy child) for a black-jack. In point of fact, a discernible Christian atmosphere surrounds their society, because members must believe in God, wear a miniature crucifix about their necks (or a similar pendant from the left ear) and know the four points of the cross. Their misconstruction of the noble spirit of Christianity turns them into religious fanatics. For these reasons, they have won and merited the disapproval of both Americans and Mexicans alike.

The *Pachuco* operates mainly at night, and his favorite weapon has become the knife. Less conspicuous than a gun and easier to hide on the person, knives form a required part of the operating equipment. The sound of a gun would arouse the law, but knives can be manipulated silently, without fear of apprehension by policemen or night-walkers. From incessant practice, he becomes artistic in the handling of a shiv. Short of stature, he compensates for his lack of heft by making the shiv his "equalizer."

Frequenters of bars, pool rooms, dance halls, and brothels, these Border boys fancy *mambo* music more than rock and roll. They dislike competition from rival gangs, fighting all who invade their territory or who try to steal their customers. Energetically they ply their trade, which is to push dope, procure girls, and smuggle contraband goods over the Rio Grande. They earn better money from narcotics than the Teddy Boys of London and the Stilyahi of Moscow gain from petty thievery. Like the Teddy Boys, these Latin Texas "teens" pay great attention to dress. On October 1, 1959, the Wholesale Clothing Manufacturers Association declared the Teddies "the best-dressed males" in London. The Border delinquents also have their own music, a "*Pachuco* Hop." To its strains they can dance all night, and frequently do. Dressed in expensive ebony-colored clothes, atop "cloud 8" from marihuana, these brunet adolescents comport themselves as the aristocrats of the Borderland underworld. Their clothes follow an individual fashion. The boys wear dark peg pants, long black coats, a sombre long-sleeve sport shirt buttoned at the neck, and black shoes with steel taps on heels and toes. This uniform constitutes their dark armor of the street.

Men appear inclined to accept effeminacy among the *Pachucos* for what it is. Women react more strongly, feeling disgust in the presence of the abnormality. A well-known El Paso public school teacher, Mary Thurston, upon seeing a typically well-dressed *Pachuco,* had this to say about him.

> The black coat collar was turned up in back and seemed to emphasize the long wavy lines of a hair style that smacked definitely more of a coiffure than a hair cut. The coiffure appeared incongruous with male clothing. The black, heavily-oiled hair, set in intersecting waves combed into a duck tail at the nape of the neck, glinted with sapphire and amethyst lights. As it turned slowly to the side, the head showed no inconsistency in the care that had been given to grooming or the toilette. Time, infiinite pains, vanity and love of the sensuous had gone into this masterpiece.
>
> As he walked forward to meet a friend, thin metal taps on heel and toe resounded with a sharp staccato accent. I could see a pair of black pumps polished to the highest glaze. A long double-breasted coat reached below his hip line. Dark shirt and black tie completed his sombre color scheme, colors which seemed alien to the bright cheerfulness of the Border country.
>
> When he looked upward to speak to his friend, I for the first time saw his face fully. Immediately I felt revulsion for this strange and somehow fascinating creature. His face looked too delicately modeled, his eyebrows too neatly trained, his appearance too consciously perfected for him ever to hold the slightest physical attraction for a woman in any walk of life. As he and his male companion walked out of sight, the androgynous impression remained, that and a faint wafting of a perfume, not lavender but lilac perhaps.

There appears the anomaly represented by the *Pachuco,* a boy both fierce and fragrant.

Homoeroticism is a practice that the boys may learn from the jails which they infest, although most of them remain heterosexual. They like staying in the calaboose, because there they can serve long terms and so accumulate "rays" to tattoo on their hands as souvenirs of their imprisonment. Sometimes the Mexican jails also have beautiful *lángaras,* Anglo-American girls, like seventeen-year-old Patricia Arthur. In 1955 the Juarez newspaper *El Fronterizo* described one of her nocturnal sprees. In Mexican jails the law and the lawless then mingled freely and intimately, Patricia Arthur managing to bear a child during her prison term. For the other part, the homoerotic *Pachucos* disport themselves with "Boise boys" or teenage nancies.

Disgusting as some of their habits were, Border boys at the pass of the North in the 1950's found much to do outside the jails. They "ran" for smugglers, "fed the fences" stolen goods, and filled their pockets with the "heavy stuff." In 1959 the Border Patrol discovered a pound of contraband heroin worth $75,000. Living in heroin heaven, the *Pachucos* loved their "holy" organization. By one means or another, they planned to stay in the drug business forever.

Today the *Pachucos* in El Paso have virtually disappeared as an organized group, but they have bequeathed to society several gangs of imitators. These imitators wear tattoos, dress "cool," and speak the "junkie" argot. No longer is racial extraction an accurate means of identifying an original, because today the gangs include Anglo-Americans, Gypsies, Hawaiians, Indians, Japanese, and Negroes. This is particularly true of Los Angeles. Nowadays an investigator will run across the sobriquets of *Pocho* and *Tírili* more often than he does the name *Pachuco.* The word *Pocho* has been variously explained. Perhaps it developed from *"Pochi"* (or *"Pochio"*), a word associated with the Yaqui Indians in Sonora, Mexico, and meaning "short" or "incomplete," which could apply to the boy's stature. The word may be related to *"Pochocho,"* which refers to an animal with a short tail or, vulgarly, to a stupid person, as a Latin who speaks Spanish haltingly. Mexicans from the state of Sonora brought the word with them to California, for soon *Pocho* became synonymous with anyone who was in any way incomplete, as someone *"que no es ni es."* Yet another meaning of *Pocho* is "decay," as *"Aquello que está en periodo de putrefacción."* Still another is "poacher," the term applied to an unwanted alien in the United States. But the most likely explication appears to be "pokey," since these Mexican delinquents are slow, or "pokey," about conforming to the mores of American society. *Pocho* thus could be construed as a pun on the word "pokey." Or perhaps the reference applies to the jail, for all of these youngsters are habitues of jails, or "pokeys." Anyway, today the term refers to Mexicans who have been unable to do a good job of imitating the Yankee. On the other hand, *Tirili* developed in the El Paso area. It is a short form of *"Tirillento,"* a term widely used in Mexico as well as South America and one which means over-dressed. On the West Coast it has been used to describe a gigolo of Asiatic or Filipino origin. *Tirili* aptly describes the flamboyant dress of the Border type. The influence of the *Pachucos* has left a lasting imprint in American schools and in the annals of American crime. Whenever the gang appears stamped out in one city, it upsurges in another urban area—or in the same old place under the camouflage of a new name like *Poco* or *Tirili.*

The origin of the word *Pachuco* itself possesses some interest, as it long has been a topic of disagreement. Octavio Paz cast no light on the sobriquet or its source in *The Labyrinth of Solitude* (1950); instead, he discussed the psychology of the *Pachuco*. But in the *National Police Gazette* (December, 1954) George McGrath connected the *Pachuco* terrorists with the Mexican town of Pachuca. "The word Pachuco . . . stemmed from the Mexican silver mining town of Pachuca, capital of the state of Hidalgo and 68 miles northeast of Mexico City. . . ." He added that "The town was notorious for bandit gangs, thieves, murderers and rapists in the early 1900's." Mr. McGrath also called attention to the large grouping at Juarez in 1933 of young farm workers who went to El Paso during the summer as *braceros.* These workers later migrated to Southern California, where they allegedly organized themselves into a gang under a "criminal charter." But to derive the word from the Mexican town leaves much unexplained. The behavior of the miners in the town of Pachuca was not uncommon in the 1900's, and that historical city had nothing to do with these juveniles and was in no way responsible for them. In fact, Mexicans frown upon the excesses of these and other youthful American gangs. It should be clear that Pachuca, the capital of Hidalgo, never served as the Mecca of these young hoodlums. A different derivation seems indicated, and such a one may easily be found.

In the *Diccionario General de Americanismos* (II, 370), Francisco J. Santamaría, its famous compiler, identified the noun *pachuca* in 1942 with a poker game played with a Spanish five-suited deck. The definition of *pachuca* is a poker hand of five cards, all of different suits, different figures, and different values.

> PACHUCA. f. En el juego del pócar, cinco cartas en mano, todas de distinto palo, de distinta figura y de distinto valor.

The *pachuca* hand, then, is worthless,[5] and players cannot use it to win money. It is a losing hand, a flop, a failure; it resembles a "sport" in biology or, in everyday vernacular, a "queer one."

That precisely describes the *Pachuco*. He certainly belongs to what society regards as an offensive class. The connotation of "queer" would be designated in his homoerotic behavior. The *o* in the spelling of the name would replace the original *a* to denote masculinity. Perhaps the word *poker hand* may also be connected with *Pachuco,* for the boys habitually decorate their hands with homoerotic signs, as when "I" on the thumb is followed by "L O V E" on the other four fingers. This suggestion would appear far-fetched were it not for the fact that puns appear frequently in the *caló* of the Border delinquents. For example, a *jorobado* (hunchback) means a marihuana cigarette crudely rolled; a *cristalero* (breaker of crystals), a thief who shatters auto windshields; and especially a *Del Toro* (a pun on Bull (*Toro*) Durham), a dealer in marihuana. Anyway, the *Pachuco* has consistently and thoroughly resisted all attempts at his Americanization, and so he is a failure in society.

It is well to ask if the Border delinquents have made any positive contributions to culture. Their revolt against the law has had little value as a protest movement. The influence of their dress on men's fashions, on "cool clothes." has also been rather temporary. It is their speech coinages which comprise a real contribution. Their inventiveness in building words and phrases, though relatively unstudied except by George C. Barker in a bulletin of the University of Arizona in 1950,[6] displays considerable imagination and intelligence. The words in their *caló* derive mainly from Spanish, with here and there a sprinkling from English.

Since peddling drugs affords him his livelihood, words related to narcotics figure most prominently in the *Pachuco's* vocabulary. The *agujeta* (hairpin) stands for the hypodermic needle. *Andar sonámbulo* (to walk in one's sleep) refers to the behavior of a person under the effects of alcohol and nembutal. *Birria* (lamb stew) means beer, the word being adopted because of its sound rather than its sense. A *cacahuate* (peanut) designates a red barbiturate pill because of the similarity in color. A *Camello* (from Camel cigarette) means a marihuana cigarette. A *cargo blanco* (white cargo) refers to a shipment of cocaine or morphine. A *chamuco* (devil) is a nembutal in a red capsule. A *chaquetero* (seller or maker of jackets) means a dealer in "yellow jackets" (barbiturate pills). *Mastuerzo* (nasturtium) signifies opium; *mota* (corn tassel), the marihuana plant; *perrero* (dog catcher), a seller of poppy opium; *racha* (short for *cucaracha*, cockroach), a butt from a marihuana cigarette; *submarino*, a yellow barbiturate pill; and *las tres* (three), puffs from smoking marihuana, as in *"Páseme las tres"*: "Give me some drags."

Phrases from smuggling likewise appear in the *caló*. A *Chuco*, short for *Pachuco*, may work with *vainilleros* (heroin dealers) who sell *vainilla* (heroin) to *tuerzos* who hide their *visagra* (cache). A man *al alba* (at dawn) is clever, alert; a *píldoro* is a smuggler of pills; and his female counterpart is a *pilota* (pilot). The criminal who informs against his associates is a *trompeta* (trumpet). A *cuño* (wedge) is an influential person who can help the criminal. *Estaba torcido* (I was twisted) means I was put in jail. *Lana* (wool) stands for money.

Other words may be associated with life in the brothels. *Ese de agua* (that one of water) refers to a homosexual. *Echar al león* (to throw to the lion) means to give someone the cold shoulder. A Negro is called a *tinto*. *Wilfredo* stands for boy; *heina*, girl; and *sardo*, soldier. A variant of *heina* is *jaina*. *Zura* may mean smart, as in *Mi jaina se cree muy zura*: My girl thinks she's smart. A *querona* is a pretty girl.

A few of their expressions have been built out of American words. *Ay te huacho* (watch) means I'll be seeing you. *Bute alerta ese* (a Spanish imitation of better alert yourself) is a warning. *Juila* (wheel), meaning bicycle, better illustrates the American influence; and so also does *vaisa* (from a vice), a word for hand. *Carrucha* (pulley) seems to pun on the English word "car" and then add an onomatopoetic suffix; it means hot-rod. *Bunche,* meaning a lot, obviously developed from bunch; and *calamasu,* a railroad, from handcars stenciled Kalamazoo, Michigan, where they are made. The *Chuco* labels a policeman a *chota,* using the word as a play on the phrase "big shot."

Clever as he was at coining words, the *Pachuco's* main interests centered in pushing illegal drugs. His culture was similar to that of the Asiatic assassins, who pushed hashish (*cannabis Indica*). In fact, at the end of the nineteenth century Chinamen had operated opium dens in both El Paso and Juarez. Later on, peddlers from the Near East replaced these Chinamen and entered into an unlawful trade in narcotics. A popular label on boxes of heroin featured a white Arabian steed. Another well-known brand of heroin likewise declared its Eastern origin, namely Hadji Ala Baba. The *Pachucos* from El Paso and their fellows in Los Angeles, way out in man's Westward migration, through their addiction to the Orient's narcotics, had returned to the East again.

The following illustrations of the *Pachuco* argot are characteristic of his current speech. The present list represents only about a half of the words studied. The collection was collated with the words garnered by Gilberto Cerda, Berta Cabaza, and Julieta Farias, *Vocabulario Español de Texas,* Austin, University of Texas Press, 1953. The entries with their definitions that appear below are thought to be more or less fresh examples of the argot.

A DONDE LA LLEVAS? Where are you going? (Literally, Where are you taking her?)

AFILORIAR (from *filo* and *afilar*), *v.* To knife someone.

AGUJETA, *n.* A hypodermic needle.

AHUEVAR (from *huevos,* a euphemism for testicles), *v.* To be frightened; to refuse to budge.

A LA BRAVA (from *bravo*), *p. phr.,* Straight-forward.

ALIVIANAR (from *aliviar*), *v.* To help somebody financially.

AL RECLE (from *reclinar*), *p. phr.* After a while.

AMACHINAR (from *amachetear,* or *machucar*), *v.* To beat, to help, to neck.

AMACIZAR (from *macizar*), *v.* To get hold of, to secure for oneself.

AMARRAR, *v.* To marry.

AMARRÓ CON UNA WISA, *v.phr.* He made a hit with a girl.

ANDA CANICA, *v.phr.* He or she is in love.

ANDA LOCO, *v.phr.* He is high under narcotics.

ANDAR SONÁMBULO, *v.phr.* A person under the effects of alcohol and nembutal.

ANFORA (from *ánfora*), *n.* A container with intoxicating beverages.

ARTA (from *harto, a*), *adv.* A lot, much.

ATORAR, *v.* To take advantage of the situation.

AVENTAR, *v.* To do something extraordinary.

AY TE WATCHO (from *ahí* and English 'watch'). I'll be seeing you.

BACHA, *n.* A cigarette butt.

BAIZA (from *vice*), *n.* Hand.

BALCONEAR, *v.* To betray, to talk against.

BANQUETEAR (from *banquet*), *v.* To have a good time.

BARAJEAR, *v.* To hang around.

BASCULAR, v. To mooch, to search.

BASIL (from *vacilar*), *n.* Fun.

BATO QUE NO TIENE CASA, *n.phr.* One who gets around.

BOFO, *n.* A weakling.

BOLA (perhaps from *dólar*), *n.* A dollar, a peso.

BOLANDO BAJO, *v.phr.* Flying low.

BONQUIAR (from *bunk*), *v.* To sleep.

BRECAS (from *brakes*), *n.* Car brakes.

BROCA (from *buck*), *n.* A dollar.

BUTI SUAVE, *adv.* Really swell.

CABALLO, *n.* Heroin.

CACAHUATE (from the Mex. word for peanut), *n.* Barbiturates, yellow jackets.

CACHIRULEAR, *v.* To fool, to deceive.

CAE DE AQUELLA, a*dv. phr.* How fine.

"CALIFA," *n.* California.

CALMANTE (from *calmar*), *n.* A red pill.

CALZETAS (from *calcetines*), *n.* Socks.

CAMIAR, *v.* To work.

CANICA, *n.* Love.

CANTAR, *v.* To make talk.

CAPEAR, v. To understand, to grasp.

CARGA, *n.* A shipment of dope.

CARGO BLANCO, *n.* A shipment of cocaine or morphine.

CARLANGO, *n.* A coat.

CARRILLAR (from *encarronar*), *v.* To molest, to bother, also to beat up constantly.

CARRUCHA (*ucha* is a common suffix) *n.,* A car.

CARRUCHAR, *v.* To be picked up by the police.

CARTA-MUERTA, *n.* Someone not liked.

CHABETA, *n.* A head.

CHAMUCO, n. A nembutal in a red capsule; colloquially devil.

CHANATE (from the word for crow; hence black), *n.* Coffee.

CHANTARSE (from *shanty* and *casarse*), *v.* To get married.

CHAQUIRA, *n.* A jacket.

CHAQUITO, *n.* A decent guy.

CHISQUEAR, *v.* To mess up, to blunder.

CHISQUAIDO (from *chisquear*), *adj.* Someone who is crazy.

CHIVA, *n.* Anything. *adj.* Afraid, shy.

CHIVEAR, *v.* To be afraid.

CHOLEAR, *v.* To shut up.

CHOLO, *n.* A scornful term for one of mixed blood, dark-skinned Mexican.

CHUTIANDO, *pres. part.* Shooting off your mouth.

CISCAR, *v.* To scare off, to frighten.

CLAVADO (from a coin of the same name), *n.* A person with illegal goods.

CLEMOS, *n.* Pennies.

CÓCONO, *n.* To be turkey; that is, to be under narcotic drugs, whereas, to take cold turkey is to take the cure.

COLECTAR, *v.* To collect dope.

CONTROL, *n.* The leader of a gang.

CORRE, *n.* A correctional institute.

CREPA, *n.* A restroom.

CRISTALERO, *n.* A thief who shatters auto windshields.

CUBRIR, *v.* To be afraid of.

CURADAS, *n.* Kicks.

CURANDERA, *n.* A witch, a healer.

DA-COLOR (from *to give color*), *v.* To find out, to be aware of.

DE-AQUELLA (variant of CAE DE AQUELLA).

DE-ALITA (from *ala*), *adv.* On the side, easily.

DE CINCHO, *p.phr.* For sure.

DESATONARTE (from *desatolondrar*), *v.* To get out of jail.

DESCUENTE (from *descontar*), *v.* Get out.

DESTRAMPADO, *adj.* Crazy.

DE-VOLE (from *volar*), *adv.* In a hurry.

DOMPE, *v.* Get off the car.

ECHEME UN TELEFONAZO. Call me on the telephone.

EL FUERTÓN, *n.* The head man in peddling dope.

EMPACHO, *n.* Severe indigestion.

ENGANCHADO, *adj.* Americanized.

ENGABACHADO, *ibid.*

ENGANCHOS, *n.* Men who hook or deceive peons into working in the United States.

ENJAULAR, *v.* To fight for one's friends.

ENJAULE, *n.* A theft.

ENTACUCHARSE (from *tacuche*), *v.* To dress up.

ENYODADO (exposed to *yodo,* iodine), *adj.* 'High' on Marihuana.

ES DE AGUA, *n.* A homo-sexual.

ESCAMAR, *v.* To terrorize.

ESCARCHA (literally frost), *n.* Cold.

ESE, *interj,* Hello.

ESTÁ PASODINA, *v.phr.* It is all right.

ESTABA TORCIDO, *v.phr.* I was in jail.

ESTAMPA (from stamp), *n.* A photo.

ESTAMPAR, *v.* To hit.

ESTUDIAR, *v.* To stare at.

ESTULIAR, *v.* To stool; to tell on.

FACHASO, *n.* A drink.

FALLÓN, *n.* To act up; to act wise.

FERIA, *n.* Money, small change.

FICHERA (from *ficha*), *n.* A prostitute.

FORJAR, *v.* To hit.

FORJE, *n.* Referring to a girl's figure.

FRAJEAR, *v.* To smoke.

FREGAL, *adj., adv.* Many, much.

FUSCA, *n.* A gun.

GABACHO, *n.* American (contemptuously). Also used for Spaniards or any light-haired people.

GACHO (from French *gauche,* left-sided, or wrong), *n.* Bad.

GATO, *n.* A hep cat.

GORILEANDO, *pres. part.* Trying to be brave while drunk.

GLOBAS, *n.* Yellow jackets.

GREÑA LOCA, *n.phr.* A zoot-suiter's haircut.

GRINGO (same as *gabacho*), *n.* A contemptuous term for an American.

HACER CHEAR, *v.phr.* To make boring.

HASPÍA, *n.* A hunger, craving for narcotics.

HÓRALE, *interj.* Watch out, there! Sometimes it means "all right."

HÓRALE, CARNAL. Hi, pal.

HÓRALE, ESE. Hi, guy.

HÓRALE, GATO. Hi, guy.

HAUCHAR, *v.* To see; to watch.

JAINAR (from *honey*), *v.* To make love.

JAIPO, *n.* One who uses morphine.

JALE, *n.* A job; also to cheat.

JAMBO (from *jambar*), *n.* The bad men in the picture show; one who steals.

JAULA, *n.* A jail.

JODER, *v.* To mess around; marital relations.

JOROBADO (meaning hunchback), *n.* A marihuana cigarette crudely rolled.

JURA (from *jurado*), *n.* The police.

KOKOMO (variant of Sp. *cócono*).

KOKONO (variant of Sp. *cócono*).

LA CORRE (from *correccional*), *n.* A correctional school.

LAMBIÓN (from *lamer*), *n.* An informer.

LAS-TRES, *n.phr.* Three puffs of marihuana or from a cigarette.

LEÑA, *n.* A cigarette.

LENO, *n.* A guy who takes dope.

LOCO, *n.* a dollar.

LOS, *n.* Los Angeles.

LOSCA, *n.* Los Angeles, California.

LLANTÓN, *n.* A Negro.

MACHIN, *n.* Someone who is outstanding, a gang leader; a husband, wife, or sweetheart.

MADERISTA, *adj.* A liar.

MALLATE, *n.* A Negro.

MANITO, *n.* A gangster from New Mexico.

MASTUERZO (because a dark *mastuerzo,* nasturtium, suggests the color of poppy opium), *n.* Opium.

ME APAÑÓ LA JURA. The police arrested me.

ME CAE DE AQUELLA. I think she is fine.

ME CAE PESETA. I don't like her.

ME CAE SURA. I don't like her.

ME ENJAULARON. They put me in jail.

ME GUSTA SER VAGO. I like to be a bum.

ME LA RAYÓ. He cussed my mother.

ME VAGUIARON. I got picked up on vagrancy.

MELENA, *n*. A hairdo.

MELENA DE PADROTE, *adj.phr*. A pimp's haircut.

MI PUEBLO ME MANTIENE. My folks support me.

MOQUETASO (from *moquete*, blow on the face), *n*. A blow in the nose.

MOTEADA (from *mota*), *adj*. Ready for smoking.

MULA, *n*. A guy who peddles dope.

NAIFA, *n*. A knife.

NEGREROS, *n*. Slave drivers.

NO TE FALLES. Don't get wise.

PACHUCA, *n*. A female juvenile delinquent.

PALOMAS, *n*. Jailbirds.

PANDO, *n*. A drunk.

PARAR, *v*. To buy.

PARLEAR, *v*. To talk.

PASA LA LUMBRE. Pass the dope (the fire).

PASIENTE, *n*. A gangster from El Paso.

PERRERO, *n*. A seller of poppy opium.

PESUÑAS, *n*. Feet.

PÍLDORO, *n*. Someone drunk with aspirins and coke.

PIMPO (from *pimp*), *n*. A person who sells prostitutes.

PINCEL, *adv*. Afoot.

PIRUJA, *n*. A cheap girl, but not a prostitute.

PISTO, *n*. A drinking spree.

PISTEAR, *v*. To drink.

PLANCHAR OREJA, *v.phr*. To go to sleep.

QUÉ CHICLOSO (another name for *caramel*, or chewing gum), *adj. phr*. How sharp, good.

QUÉ GACHO, *adv.phr*. How terrible.

QUÉ RELAJO, *n.phr*. What a dirty trick.

QUÉ SUAVE, *adv. phr*. How nice.

QUÉ SURA, *adv. phr*. How cheap.

QUEBRADA, *n*. A break, an opportunity, an opening.

QUEMÓN (from *quemar*), *v*. To try.

QUIERES UNOS KIKIS? Do you want some drags of the marihuana? (i.e., Kicks?)

REBOTE, *n*. A game.

REFINAR, *v*. To eat.

RELISAR, *v*. To release.

RESTA, *n*. A restaurant.

RIFA (from *grifa*), *n*. Marihuana.

ROLAS, *n*. Playing records.

RUCO, A, *n*. The husband, an old man; also an old woman, or anyone in authority.

RUMER, *n*. A smuggler.

SABLAZO, *n*. A loan.

SAFO. The same to you.

SANTO NIÑO, *n.phr.* A blackjack.

SE CREE MUY CASTI. He thinks he's a real lover.

SE FILEREA, SE SUENA. He takes dope by needle.

SE LAS TRUENA (from *trueno*). He takes it.

SE PONE AVIADOR. He gets intoxicated.

SONADO, *adj*. To be under the influence of drugs.

SON COSAS DE LA VIDA. That's life.

SORIAS, *n*. Tortillas.

SPIG (variant of the coinage *spic*), *n*. A contemptuous term for Mexicans.

SUBMARINO, *n*. A yellow barbiturate pill.

SUROTA, *n*. A louse.

TALLA, *n*. A tie.

TANQUE, *n*. The jail.

TAPITA (from *tapa*), *n*. A hat.

TE TORCIERON. They took you in.

TEA, *n*. Marihuana.

TEKARO, *n*. A guy who uses the needle.

TIENDA DE RAYA, *n.phr.* A credit store.

TIRAR CHANCLA, *v.phr.* To dance; literally to let your slippers go.

TÍRILI, *n*. A hoodlum.

TOLIDO, *n*. The toilet.

TOQUES, *n*. Shocks.

TORCER, *v*. To be put in jail.

TOREARLA, *v*. To defy the law.

TORNILLO DE MENTE, *n*. A brain screw.

TOSTA (abbreviation of *tostón*), *n*. Fifty cents.

TRAFICAR, *v*. To walk.

TRAGO, *n*. A nip.

TRAMOS, *n.* Trousers.

TRES GALLASOS (derived from *gallo* meaning rooster and *azo* meaning large), *n.phr.* Drags.

TRUCHA. Be smart.

VACHA (variant of *bacha*).

VACILÓN, *n.* A flirt; someone who is funny.

VAINILLEROS, *n.* Heroin dealers.

VAISA (variant of *baiza*).

VAMOS A JAINAR. Let's go make love.

VAMOS AL TRINCHE. Let's get some marihuana.

VASCULAR, *v.* To stool; to tell.

VIROL (corruption of *frijol*), *n.* Beans.

WATCHO. I look.

YA ESTUVO. That's all; it's all over.

YEDO, PODO, YESCA, *n.* Marihuana.

YO SOY BANDOLERO. I am a bandit.

NOTES

[1] *Southern Folklore Quarterly* (September, 1958), XXII, 129-138.

[2] Professor Muñoz is the editor of the newspaper *El Sol de Hidalgo* and author of the book *Memorias de un Adolescente,* Pachuca, Hidalgo, 1955. I also interviewed Lic. José M. Sepulveda y S., of the research department of the state of Hidalgo, who gave me valuable notes on Pachoa-can (or Pachu-can), a verbal word of native Mexican origin, in which he said that the first part means place of residence of the chief and the second part indicates the action of the verb (sic); see Presbítero Canuto E. Anaya, *Bosquejo Geográfico-Histórico,* Guadalupe Hidalgo, D.F., 1918, p. 1. On the other hand, I talked with numerous Mexicans who thought the word simply meant a "grassy place." In this connection, I now may note that the Nahuatl word *Pachtli* (derived from *pachoa*) refers to a grass-like hay (*heno*) that grows in trees parasitically; see Dr. Cecilio A. Robelo, *Diccionario de Mitologia Nahuatl,* Mexico, D.F., 1951 (sec. ed.), p. 209, col. 1; and *ca* (from *can*) means "place of"; see Davila Garibi, *Toponimias Nahuas,* Mexico, D.F., 1942, p. 25. Certainly this folk etymology is most illuminating, because the American *pachucos,* like all criminals, are actually nothing more than parasites on the social body. Miss Nina Keeler, formerly my student, suggests that the noun *pachuco* is a corruption or euphonious abbreviation of the adjective *pachucho* (*a*), meaning "over-ripe, weak, stumbling."

[3] The Narcotic Control Act of 1956 (Public Law 728, 84th Congress, Chapter 629, 2d Session, H.R. 11619) included marihuana with other narcotic drugs and provided the same severe penalties for violation (a seller of illegal drugs to a juvenile minor less than eighteen may be fined not more than $20,000, and shall be imprisoned for life, or for not less than ten years, except that the offender shall suffer death if the jury in its discretion shall so direct"). For this reference, I am indebted to my friend Mr. Robert S. O'Brien, of the Federal Bureau of Narcotics, Los Angeles, California, whom I consulted in August, 1960.

[4] A *pachuca,* a girl from Albuquerque, New Mexico, is the heroine of Joseph Foster's novel *Stephana,* New York, 1959.

[5] The same idea of worthlessness appears in the use of the word *pachuco* for a small bill of many colors but only in the value of a *peso;* see Francisco J. Santamaría, *Diccionario de Mejicanismos,* Mexico, D.F. 1959, p. 781, col. 1.

[6] Reissued with important additions in 1958 as *"Pachuco:* An American-Spanish Argot and Its Social Functions in Tucson, Arizona," *Social Science Bulletin,* University of Arizona, December, 1958, No. 18, p. 46. This fine essay states the word *"pachuco"* is a colloquial way of saying El Paso (but see my note 2), that the argot originated in the El Paso-Juárez underworld among marihuana smokers of the 7-x gang in the neighborhood of Florence and Eighth Streets (his informant being Gabriel Cordova, Jr., formerly associated with the El Paso police department), and that from about 1942 to 1945 Los Angeles became the capital of the *Pachuco* world. The argot shades rapidly into jargon, and for further examples of the vocabulary, see Miss Okla Markham McKee, *Five-Hundred Non-Dictionary Words Found in the El Paso-Juárez Press,* Texas Western College, Master of Arts Thesis, August, 1955, p. 82. For help in completing my study, I want to thank Professor Alton C. Morris, of the University of Florida, and Professors Fred Brewer, Joseph L. Leach, and E. T. Ruff, of Texas Western.

9

Big Talk of the Big Bend

There is an old story that western people are reticent by nature, utilize precious few words, and hate a lot of blown-up talk. They say, for illustration, that a cowboy and a greenhorn once moved together to a lonely spot. At the end of the day the greenhorn saw the cowboy packing his poke for traveling and said to him "Are you packing up your duds?"

"Yep," the cowboy replied.

Since it looked like he was taking everything with him, the greenhorn said, "Are you pulling up stakes?"

"Yep," came the same terse reply.

"Well, what's wrong?" the greenhorn wanted to know. "Why are you leaving?"

"Too damned much conversation," replied the westerner.

Whoever told this yarn about westerners being the silent type was not referring to Texans. He must have been referring to some other part of the country, perhaps California, for all Texans are prone to tall talk, particularly so out west of the Pecos River. Way out in West Texas there is silence, but it is a characteristic of the wide-open spaces, not of its inhabitants. The tallest talk in Texas is heard in the fabulous Big Bend region— a vast and colorful expanse of nature's wonders. Here big talk is the right medium, the only kind of language suitable for a big country.

The gateway to the Big Bend country is Alpine, Brewster

County. Of it a marvel must be related: Alpine is the largest city in the largest county in the largest state in these United States. The fact is attested by both the local chamber of commerce and the fame of believe-it-or-not Ripley. With an area of about six thousand square miles and a population of about six thousand Texans, this region of the Trans-Pecos abounds in almost everything, picturesque scenery, frontier customs, old legends, marvelous hunting and fishing feats, and in particular a mighty lot of tall talk.

Since there is one square mile to every person, maybe a fellow has to talk loud and proud to be heard by his neighbor. The miles are so long out in the Trans-Pecos that visitors sometimes complain they are incorrectly measured. This is the opening the westerner has been looking for. Now he can give the greenhorn a little of the big talk of the Big Bend. The native thereupon collars the visitor and explains to him that the miles were measured "by cowhides with the tails thrown in."

In the Trans-Pecos to this good day "cattle-raising" is without question the main occupation of everybody, so that cowboys and horses, boots and saddles, are everyday sights. The lingo of the people therefore springs naturally from the colorful conditions surrounding ranch life. For example, cowboys living a rough and hardy existence often develop into "tough hombres." The special phrase used to describe this "customer" is that he is "tough as a boot and twice as high." If he has committed all the vices, they say "he has gone the gaits." If he is an unreliable character, they say "he won't do to tie to."

On the other hand, if he is trustworthy, the westerner may continue to use "horseology" by remarking that "he'll do to ride the river with." Of course the river is the Rio Grande, not Jordan, and the expression is one that goes the limit. It means the "cow-waddie" could be relied on even for rustling contraband from Mexico to Texas.

If a Big Bender wants to give strong assurance about anything, he may repeat that "I'll take a paralyzed oath." If a rancher will take a paralyzed oath that a "wrangler" will do to "ride the river with," you can place one hundred percent confidence on his recommendation. A rancher or a "pusher" (foreman) may talk big, but he will not talk idly and dishonestly. In West

Texas people get vexed easily with a fellow who is always "showing out" (bragging).

In the free, open, and democratic Big Bend country, picturesque lingo or folk say is by no means restricted to the "men folks." Ranch women have their special phrases too. The West is the place where men are men—and women are glad of it.

Nonetheless a "tenderfoot" wife, sometimes proves unable to cope with ranch life. When she does, her neighbors say that "she don't know beef from bull's foot," implying that she lacks taste if she does not enjoy western life. If the "new" lady has been previously married, her neighbors may say that "she's been on the carpet before." Or they may say that "she jumped the broomstick before," this athletic stunt being a reference to an early marriage ceremony in pioneer Texas. If the lady tries to wear city clothes on the ranch, the people may say something like this: "Out here you've got no more use for them than a hog has for a side saddle." If people like the "new" lady, they will say that "she can count ties" (repair a barbed-wire fence).

But "between me and you and the gate post," if the "tenderfoot" lady remains "standoffish" or dresses "fit to kill," there are a few "plain speakers" who will come mighty close to "cussing" —for lady folks, that is—when they "vow and declare" that she is nothing short of a "son of a so-and-which."

In the wide open spaces of the Big Bend life can become dull and monotonous, especially in "slack" time when there is nothing much to do about the ranch. At times like these the boys "unlimber for a little stud and draw." Anybody who intends to play poker way out west had better "come full handed" (with plenty of money), not "half shod" (with little money), as some dumb optimists do. If you think you are not getting a "square deal," why speak right up, "pardner," and "don't be clabber-mouthed (silent) about it."

However, if you talk too much—that is, if you have "a busy lip"—somebody may "cut your water off," "take your meter out," or "comb your head with a six-shooter." The best thing to do, in any case, is to "take it standing up" (bravely) and "don't die with your heels up" (be shot in the back). If you have to, tell your partners "just how the wind's a-blowing and the dust's a-flying"; but in playing poker, it is far wiser not to "get a shuck in your snoot" (angry).

There is plenty of whiskey in most of West Texas. Although the ranch wife may be "dead set" and "tooth and toe nail against it," there are times when her husband may drink so much that he "gets quite a hearing" and reaches home, vows his spouse, "a-seeing elephants and a-hearing owls." The stuff he drinks is called, in the Big Bend particularly, "Wild Mare's Milk" or, in other parts of the West, simply "panther juice."

Love is not exactly the same everywhere, and out West courting is different from other places. When a cowboy prepares for the weekly dance on Saturday night, he "gets dressed up like a sore toe." Then he selects his favorite "taw" (dancing partner), who may be a "satchel" (honky-tonk employee), a "smooth hide" (city dame), or the "old stand-by" (usual escort). Above all he avoids the "slab-sided" (fat) girl, to whom he even prefers the "scantling" (thin girl). This gay young man is usually faithful to one sweetheart, it not being in the cards for him to "roach," "short pot," or "cabbage" on her.

The southern Trans-Pecos is a wide border territory where smuggling and the like occur. At all events, if cattle "stray" from Chihuahua or Coahuila into Texas, they are said to be "wet." In rough terrain the "chili chasers" (border patrolmen) use horses to give chase across "biyookies" (arroyos, from bayous used ironically) or to "rim up a gunyon" (ride up a canyon). The pursuers attempt to "double team" (encircle) the pursued. They are bound to catch him if his horse "turns a wildcat" (falls). But if the horse is not a "dead head" (inferior), he may save his rider. To escape the vigilant border rangers, the horse will have to "lay his belly in the sand" (travel with much speed).

A number of the expressions appearing here may be found in other sections of the country and reflect the broad field of folk say. Most of them belong to the region of the Big Bend. They are native English expressions, words which are often of Anglo-Saxon origin. The epic boast of the celebrated Anglo-Saxon hero Beowulf is, it is clear, pretty closely related to the big talk of the Big Bend people. Since they have a common ancestry, this is a natural result.

The true Texan is no braggart. The only thing to remember about him is that if and when he has something to say, he will say it in a lively, virile way. In America today much of the argot of jazz and crime is unpleasant and neither meaningful nor instructive. The tall talk of the Texas Trans-Pecos is something far different. It is a language of men, a big talk that gets up on its hind legs and says something loud and proud, right out where you can hear it.

III

PLACES

1

Out Where the West Is

In all seasons and at all times in the Big Bend country of Texas[1] there is the wind, and in the summers there are intermittent and widely-separated thunder showers. It is this wind, together with the occasional rain, which has created a territory of unsightly bad lands yet picturesque mountains, desert areas with oasis-like springs. The Big Bend, too, is a land at once dead yet alive: here is a government-maintained highway and there, a vanished Apache trail. It is a country both forbidding and appealing—a mighty contradiction of mountains and arroyos. Nothing in this whole vast area of proverbial West Texas seems permanent or abiding or inevitable except the wind erosion, and the progress of unpredictable old time. Here, in the past, are the bleached bones of Confederate soliders,[2] the black stone image of an Indian god,[3] the sandy trail of a camel caravan[4]—all lost and gone and forgotten in dead time. Yet here too, in this moment that is today, is a busy mining camp,[5] a gasoline station with free air, and—wonder of wonders—a twentieth-century hermit on government relief![6] Only great distances and the long silence can explain this: the virile, unvocal people inhabiting the changing, soundless land.

Under the physical conditions here obtaining, man is often subjected to the most severe experiences. For one thing, there are seasons when he can expect no rainfall, when he must rely on his own strength and native ingenuity to hoard what water he possesses or to take advantage of occasional thunder showers occurring nearby. The existence of these drouths is, of course, a subject for lamentation, but the hardihood of the true Westerner is not conquered by outrageous fortune. Moreover, since he is one hundred per cent American, he is able to extract humor from an altogether tragic situation. He tells no sad tales of the death of kings—but racy stories that invigorate the imagination.

Illustrating the length of one notorious drouth, natives tell the story of the father and his eighteen-year-old son who visited in New Orleans, where it rained almost every day. On the occasion of the first downpour, this father was heard to remark that he was "mighty glad it was a-raining; not for himself so much—because he had seen rain—but for the boy's sake!" Similarly, there is the account of the man who placed his children outside the door and threw pitchers of water through the screen in order to show them how rain looked and felt.[7] To say the least, in the land "West of the Pecos," the rain it raineth differently. The precipitation in West Texas is at best a desperately local affair: sometimes it falls in the mountains but not in the valleys; sometimes at the ranch house but not in the corral; and sometimes, claims an "old timer," on one side of the road but not on the other![8]

In any event, once upon a time there was a "regular cloudburst" in the north-central and no rain whatsoever in the south-central Big Bend. On this special occasion it was very likely no other personage than Pecos Bill himself who had gone to sleep under a cactus bush with his double-barrelled shotgun propped up beside him, for when he awoke, he discovered that the "north barrel of that double-barrelled shotgun was plump full of water and that the south barrel was as dry as a powder keg."[9]

Rain in the Big Bend is indeed fabulous. But when it comes to telling when it is going to rain, then that, as a "Big Bender" might say, is "a pig of a different bristle." However, if you are really interested, take careful note of these phenomena: a cloudy sunset, an absence of whirlwinds, dead snakes that do not turn their stomachs up, rings about the moon, and prairie dogs that seek their holes. These signs clearly portend a change in the weather.

For another thing, in studying this wild, bewitching, and altogether incomprehensible country,[10] one is always impressed with the remarkable vocabulary of the natives. Nothing so cultivates the acreage of one's imagination as to hear the lingo of the "Big

Bender." This cowboy entitles a gulley full of cat-claw "Rattle-snake Draw," a rough section near good terrain "Hell's Half Acre."[11] He calls hard liquor "Wild Mare's Milk," an extended inebriation "a ring-tailed tooter," and a skirmish with *delirium tremens* "a-seeing elephants and a-hearing owls." These are the men who tell the *cocinero* busy with a steak "to just cripple the steer and run him through." This Westerner is the man who says when he is in a hurry that "I'm heading for water," who will be your friend "from now on," "give you the shirt off his back," and who will claim when you die that "your spur has rung its knell." These are indeed those "Big Benders" who at times are as reticent as claimed, who at others will "talk your arm off," who can tell "John D. gollywhoppers," who know the difference "between beef and bull's foot," and who finally and above all and "on all hands" and "forever and three days" are precisely, and nothing short of, nor more nor less than, just about exactly the "best doggone square shooters" anywhere at all.[12]

It is not unnatural that the "Big Bender" should be inspired to recount stories to suit the Gargantuan geography of his habitat.[13] However, it must be understood that it is not a love of lying, attractive as this may be, which impels the narrator. It is rather the love of romance and pride in the native soil. The typical tall tale of the Big Bend country may be easily illustrated.

Once upon a time—and it was when Pancho Villa raided Ojinaga[14]—a group of Texans living in Presidio, just across the Rio Bravo from Ojinaga, were obliged to flee for their lives. Packing wives and children, and harnessing horses and mules, they set out at once for Marfa. Now it chanced *en route* that a matron—doubtless somewhat stimulated by the unusual excitement—gave premature birth to a bouncing baby boy. By the oddest coincidence or haphazard stroke of fate, a fine mare almost simultaneously delivered a fine male colt. Since Pancho was "whooping it up thereabouts," the party was in a pretty big hurry; so they decided to leave the baby and the colt on the road and to return for them later. But fortunately this proved entirely unnecessary. For long about sundown, when the Texans were preparing to return for the deserted child and colt, a swiftly moving dust whirlwind was seen approaching. A few minutes later everybody was greatly relieved to see a young lad, with a rattlesnake for a quirt and the umbilical cord for a hackamore, come tearing down the big middle of Marfa's main street astride that fine young pony.[15]

Now no one will be surprised to hear, next, that, after this young man rejoined his parents, he shortly developed into a most excellent huntsman. For example, one day he sighted, at a great distance, a splendid buck standing almost entirely hidden between two large boulders. To say the least, it was a difficult angle for a shot. Taking dead aim at a certain special spot hardly visible, he let fire one volley. Immediately after the shot, the buck was seen to rock from side to side several times and then fall heavily. Upon reaching the boulders, this fancy shooter discerned that although he had fired only once, there were by actual count no less than seven bullet holes in the deer. He had aimed so that the bullet struck the far boulder, split up or ricocheted, and mortally wounded the animal in seven different places.

Meanwhile the colt had developed into a splendid but somewhat skittish stallion. It was high time to "break" the bronco. One time our hero was walking through a "draw" when he saw his stallion's luxuriant tail hanging directly down from the top of a cliff. Immediately he clambered up, grabbed this long tail, wrapped it three times about his right arm, braced his legs, and then pulled that great big stallion clean back down off that cliff. He did this in order to tie the tail to a sturdy Juniper tree. Now this stallion also had a very long mane, mind you; so the cowboy just cut a portion of it off for a hackamore. After all this, he mounted the horse, cut the tail from the tree, and "lit a shuck outa there." It took him about three days and nights to "break" that bronco. But about three days later he rode him into the corral. Only then did he observe that six wild mares, three to the side, had become entangled in what remained of the stallion's incredibly long mane.

It is a distinct pleasure to report that this skittish stallion became an altogether satisfactory mount. Some people say he was the smartest horse ever to roam the ranges of the Texas Big Bend. Persons holding to this opinion point to the adventure involving a wild Brahma steer. It happened this way. Our hero and the celebrated stallion were one time chasing the steer. They went up, down, and across many a gulley and ravine; but finally the steer jumped a tremendous ravine. The stallion hardly knew what to do, but he made a gigantic effort. The jump, however, did not quite carry him to the opposite side; so when he was about half way across, that stallion simply showed his intelligence by turning right square-dab around and jumping back to safety.

The story[16] of the fabulous cowboy of the Big Bend and his matchless steed goes on indefinitely, but it is sufficient to say that all ended happily and, furthermore, in prosperity. Why, even the year of the great drouth, when there was no end of cattle rustling, every heifer on that cowboy's ranch had twin calves.[17]

There is one disease fairly prevalent among the natives of the Big Bend country. Like Cortes and the Conquistadores,[18] the Big Bend people "suffer of a disease in the heart that only gold can cure." Conditions being what they are, it is a wonder now that these prospectors survive their illness. But gold hunting must certainly be a form of romanticism. The dyed-in-the-wool prospector lives for the most part in the undiscovered country along the borders of the mind, the land of the chimera. Yet one must add the phrase "for the most part," because there really are gold producing mines in the Big Bend area. Today in Presidio County gold is being mined on a paying basis for shipment to Newark, New Jersey.[19] This fact, however, by no means accounts for such remarkable stories as the famous "Nigger Mine" of the Big Bend.[20] As most of the significant tales of this country have already been ably recounted elsewhere,[21] only a few fresh episodes in these "floating" legends need be told.

In the year 1916 or the year 1917, as a former banker will swear up and down, a certain *señor* was accustomed to bring various quantities of raw gold into Alpine. Sometimes the quantity was quite surprisingly large. These were always duly measured and subsequently sold at the local bank. For some twelve months this *señor* regulary traded in Alpine authentic gold for unequivocal greenback. But when someone began troubling this *señor* with questions, he decided never again to return.

It was only a year or two following this Alpinian episode that a Mexican of uncertain origin appeared in Marathon, a town about thirty miles from Alpine. This Mexican walked right into the middle of the leading drugstore of Marathon, as proud as you please. Moreover, he walked right up to the proprietor and he clearly said: "What acid do you use for testing gold?" "Nitric," replied the proprietor, and sold this *señor* two or three bottles of this nitric acid. That is about all there was to the story for quite a time, because that Mexican just walked out of the drug-store and quietly, unobtrusively, vanished into the canyons and arroyos down Mexico way. The "boys" talked about the episode for quite a spell, but before long its proportions were growing.

Then one day, when least expected, that Mexican showed up in Marathon again. But he was certainly a changed man! He had on store-bought clothes for one thing. What is still more impor-tant, even his wife and children had on new clothes! Moreover, he was driving a "spanking new Chevvy." And, what seems most incredible of all, he went all around town and paid up his bills. Some people say that he even paid up the bills of some of his friends. In any case, he walked right over to the leading drugstore, stepped up to the proprietor, bought three more bottles of the acid, and was overheard to remark: "Well, that sure was gold, all right." The whole affair caused quite a stir. But the only drawback—the inevitable drawback—is that this happened quite a spell ago; that is, in the year so-and-so, or so-and-so, and that at exactly this same time this Mexican and his family and all his friends moved permanently away from Marathon. He has not since been heard from.[22]

So far as can be determined,[23] it appears that the prospectors who know most about gold in the Big Bend are "Niggers." Do not be fooled by the term "Niggers," as these personages invari-ably turn out to be Indians, or, more usually, one third *Negroid* and two thirds *Indio*. These individuals not only know precisely where the mines are, but they also will sell for a dollar a map or "way bill" to the mine. When these maps are studied,[24] it is not infrequently determined that the significant directions have been torn away, burned off, or materially defaced.

Yet there is gold in the Big Bend country. Gold, to repeat, is being mined on a paying basis by the Cibolo Mining Company of Presidio County. The "Lost Nigger Mine" has not been found, but men to this good day are hunting it.[25] The stories will go on. At this very moment there is a "Nigger" living in Fort Davis who could take you to the exact location of the mine itself, but there are reasons why he will not. First, he will have you remem-ber that he is a "Nigger" and that he is accordingly afraid. Sec-ondly, since he is also a superstitious Indian, he will confess that he is the father of sixteen children and that if he tells where the gold is, everyone of his sixteen children will immediately die.

Of course there are people in the Big Bend who live a life highly civilized, but the important thing in the present connection is that in the Big Bend, not in the metropolis, there is also the primitive life of the Indian and the "wet" Mexican,[26] a Mexican who has crossed the Rio Grande without passport. And these people have a story to tell that is worth the hearing, and a life to live very much worth the living. They know the wind and the rain, the canyons and the arroyos, and they know how to live under privation. Where there are no signs on trees, no moss to give directions, no rivers to follow, they yet know the precious secret of making a livelihood. They know, too, what various herbs and plants may be used for; and modern science confirms their ancient knowledge, which should satisfy the most materialistic modern.

For a long, long time the Indians have known that the Strawberry Cactus or Pitaya (*Echinocereus stramineus*) is good to eat, and modern science employs the fruit in the treatment of diabetes. Tea may be boiled from the leaves of the Ephedra plant (*Ephedra antisyphylitica*) for treatment of venereal diseases. For hardening gums one may use the Leather plant (*Jatropha spathulata*). Ocotilla (*Fouguieria splendens*) trunks are used to make fences. Roots of small Mesquite (*Prosopis glandulosa*) trees whiten the teeth. Maguey (*Agave*) may be eaten when roasted. The berries of Silverleaf Nightshade (*Solanum elaseagnifolium*) mixed with goat's milk are the ingredients of *Hasaderos* (white cheese). Bear grass (*Nolina texana* or *Nolian erumpens*) can be employed to make shoes. And it is generally known that the Mexican Agave (*Agave wislezeni*) is responsible for such intoxicants as *aguamiel, pulque, tequila, et al.*[27]

Outside the cities and towns there flourishes a land rich in story, breathing romance; a land strong in rugged flavor, inspiring in magnitude; and, unless, and even after, you have visited it, learned something about it, a land somehow awesome and incredible.[28]

Winging after nightfall from the *Sierra Mojada* (wet mountain) in the interior of Mexico, the *brujas* (flying witches) are nocturnal visitants of the superstitious aborigines who live along the borders of the Rio Grande del Norte. These "flying witches," who may assume the most tempting forms, are, perhaps, descendants of the ancient Aztec demons. Translated by the Indians into pseudo-Christian forms and variegated by their sex-obsessed imaginations, these flying, eternally feminine witches are of that stuff which in the far-away and long ago created *Quetzalcotl,* the flying serpent. Nonetheless these *brujas* exercise over the superstitious mind the most terrifying and often pernicious influence. Goat herders dwelling all alone for long periods of time are most especially affected, the *brujas* not infrequently inducing them to suicide or madness.[29]

Happily there is one efficacious way to combat the flying witch. What you do is to take off your shirt, cross the sleeves, and then place in the opposite direction a pair of opened scissors. This cunningly designed charm guarantees the death of the *bruja,* for when she flies past this "crisscross" she finds her wings cut.

Plummet-like she hurdles to the moonlit, dead, cactus land, over which Caro de Alicate, the Apache God,[30] looks down from the Chisos mountains, inscrutably, upon the preposterous, and yet—since it is the Big Bend country—the not impossible scene.

NOTES

[1] Beginning near Fabens on the west and ending near Boquillas on the east, the Rio Grande (or Rio Bravo) del Norte meanders in a long semicircle before straightening its course for the Gulf of Mexico. The Rio Grande on the south and the Pecos to the north thus make natural boundaries for the Trans-Pecos area, that portion of which below the Southern Pacific Railroad is called the Texas Big Bend (D. M. Bennett and Barry Scobee, "Mountain Peeks," Alpine (Tex.) *Avalanche,* XLVIII, Nos. 34 (July 14) and 36 (July 28, 1939); but see P. J. R. MacIntosh, "In Farthest Texas," *Texas Monthly,* III (1929), 671; *Lure of the Southwest,* Dallas, Magnolia Petroleum Co., 1934, p. 118; Nevin O. Winter, *Texas, the Marvellous,* Boston, 1916, p. 147; H. Smith and D. Walker, *The Geography of Texas,* New York, 1923, p. 52).

[2] E. E. Townsend, *Publications of the West Texas Historical and Scientific Society* (Alpine, 1933), XLVIII, 29 ff.

[3] Specimens are in the Pioneer Museum, Sul Ross College, Alpine.

[4] Report of the Secretary of War, S. Ex. Doc., No. 2, 36th Congress, 1 Session, Serial No. 1024, pp. 422 ff.; O. W. Williams, "The Camels Come to the Big Bend," *Voice of the Mexican Border* (Marfa, December, 1933); and Lewis B. Lesley, "The Purchase and Importation of Camels . . . ," *Southwestern Historical Quarterly,* XXXIII (1929), 18 ff.

[5] Deposits of all the better known ores are known to exist in the Big Bend. The oldest producing silver mines in the United States are located in Shafter, Presidio County; see P. J. R. MacIntosh, "The Big Bend Country," *Bunker's Monthly,* I (1928), 370 ff.

[6] "Coyote" Carter, as the elderly man is called. If there is anybody who can assemble a good "stake," Carter stands prepared to lead him to the lost mines of the Chisos area.

[7] For these two anecdotes, I am indebted to Mr. Paul Preston Prichard, Moorehead School, El Paso.

[8] On characteristics of Western jokes in general, see Eric Howard, "Out Where the Jest Begins," *Esquire* (Feb., 1940), pp. 73 ff.

[9] This story was told to me many years ago by my lately deceased uncle, Mr. Alf Madden, then a resident of Colorado, Texas. On Pecos Bill, see Edward O'Reilly, "Saga of Pecos Bill," *Century Magazine,* CVI (1923), 827 ff.; Mody C. Boatright, *Tall Tales from Texas Cow Camps,* Dallas, 1934, pp. 68 ff.; Carl Carmer, *The Hurricane's Children,* New York, 1937, pp. 59 ff.; James C. Bowman, *Pecos Bill,* Chicago, 1937; and Irving Fiske, "Pecos Bill, Cyclone Buster," *American Mercury* (Dec., 1939), XLVIII, 403 ff.

[10] For descriptions of the Big Bend, see P. J. Ross, "A Rambler in Picturesque Texas," *Bunker's Monthly,* I (1928), 78 ff.; Frederick Simpich, "Down the Rio Grande," *National Geographic,* LXXVI (1939), 415 ff.

[11] On a celebrated place name in the Big Bend, see Victor J. Smith, "How Dead Horse Canyon Got Its Name," *Texas Folk-Lore Society,* III (1924), 209.

[12] On limited aspects of the language of this country, see my articles, "Some Southwestern Cowboy Lingo," *American Speech,* XII (1937), 153; "Cowboy Lingo of the Texas Big Bend," *Dialect Notes,* VI (1937), 617 ff.

[13] See esp. Mody C. Boatright, *Tall Tales from Texas Cow Camps,* Dallas, 1934.

[14] See J. E. Gregg, "The History of Presidio County," *Voice of the Mexican Border* (Marfa, Centennial Edition, 1936), pp. 10 ff.; my article, "Pancho Villa, Man and Hero," *Southwest Review,* XXII (1937), 338 ff.; and I. J. Bush, *Gringo Doctor,* Caldwell, Idaho, 1939.

[15] A considerably elaborated version of this story is told by J. Frank Dobie in Chapter X of his book, *Tongues of the Monte,* Garden City, New York, 1935.

[16] The authority for this narrative is Bryan Cartwright, of Marfa.

[17] For an account of verified historical events of portions of the Big Bend area, see Barry Scobee, *The Story of Fort Davis,* Fort Davis, 1936.

[18] Anita Brenner, *Idols Behind Altars,* New York, 1929, p. 61.

[19] Mrs. O. L. and Jack Shipman, "The Savage Saga," *Voice of the Mexican Border* (Marfa, 1938), p. 15.

[20] J. Frank Dobie, "The Nigger Gold Mine of the Big Bend," *Texas Folk-Lore Society,* No. III (1924), pp. 64 ff.; also, with extensions, in *Coronado's Children,* by the same author.

[21] Victor J. Smith, "The Lost Mines of the Chisos Mountains" and "The Lost Gold of Death Hole," *Publications of the West Texas Historical and Scientific Society,* No. I (1920), pp. 30 ff., 33 ff., and esp. J. Frank Dobie, *Coronado's Children,* Dallas, 1930, pp. 158 ff.

[22] For the two foregoing accounts, I am indebted to Mr. John Fortner, Superintendent of Public Schools, Presidio.

[23] This seemed to be the observation of Mr. Charley Livingston, of Alpine, who has more than once kindly assisted me in tracking down yarns.

[24] In studying maps, I was fortunate to have the assistance of Professor Xavier Gonzales, artist, of Tulane University.

[25] See, for example, an editorial of the Associated Press: "Lost Nigger Mine Still Is Sought for Its Gold Riches in the Big Bend Country of West Texas," San Angelo *Standard-Times* (Thursday, August 17, 1939), p. 9; and Mrs. Eugenia H. Chandley, "Old 'Lost Nigger Mine' in the Big Bend Area," *Sul Ross Skyline* (Alpine, March 22, 1939).

[26] On the folklore of the Mexicans, see Mrs. Eugenia H. Chandley, "Mexican Superstitions and Remedies" and "Manners and Customs of the Border Mexicans," *Publications of the West Texas Historical and Scientific Society,* No. I (1920), pp. 26, 27 ff.

27 For these data, I am indebted to Dr. Omer E. Sperry, of Sul Ross College, Alpine, an authority on botany and an indefatigable investigator of the flora of the Chisos mountain area.

28 For a description of the wonders of the Big Bend, see Charles McLean, "A Playspot for Two Nations," New York *Times* (Sunday, Nov. 15, 1936), Sec. 12, Pt. I, p. I; see also Mrs. O. L. Shipman, *Taming the Big Bend,* Marfa, 1926.

29 My informant is Mr. Ben Avant, rancher, of Marfa. For an account of these herdsmen, see C. M. Wilson, "American Pastoral," *Harper's Monthly* (Feb., 1936), p. 379.

30 The superstition is that Caro de Alicate (whose name is variously spelled), the Apache chieftain, entered the Chisos mountains after his death in a spiritual or astral form, so that it is perhaps not inappropriate to refer to him as a deity, especially since he seems by some so to be regarded.

2

The Rain Dance of Old San Vicente

In the arid wastes of *el estado de Coahuila,* down Mexico way, there lolls upon the banks of the Rio del Norte the little town of San Vicente. A small, colony-like pueblo upon the face of the timeless and desert earth, San Vicente, sometimes called Old Presidio Fort, is located in the shadowland of the Texas and Mexico boundary. Here the feeble wind blows corkscrew flurries of dust amid the desert plants, dull mesquite and flamboyant cactus; here everywhere vulnerable to the burnished sun lie the brilliant sands of earth, impoverished, dehydrated. To the north there looms the ghostly radiance of the Chisos Mountains, which at twilight mingle with the pink silhouettes of the Sierra del Carmen into a panorama bizarre and incredible. Meanwhile, from the upper sky great clouds have mirrored all day upon the earth beneath battalions of moving shadows. Great waves of shadows have coursed the land from the seminal sky. Thus, in the dry, dead, unmoving, incredibly dehydrated world, San Vicente looks upward for the unseen and as yet unheard high winging of the Thunder Bird.

The rain dance of San Vicente, with its mixed pagan and Christian forms, is of annual occurrence, and the period of prayer lasts some fourteen days, usually from June 2 through June 16. The procedure is somewhat as follows.

The *Jefe* of the village summons the people for a community ceremony of prayers. Two men carry a niche which is decorated

173

with pink paper-roses, silver Christmas tinsel, pretty leaves, and
other gaudy ornaments. In the center of the decorated niche there
is a picture ot the Virgin Mary and of Jesus Christ. Accompanied
by their fellow-worshippers, the two men now go to the fields,
kneel with their faces in the dust, set up the niche in the ground,
and by various sounds and gesticulations pray to their respective
saints. When the niche is afterwards placed in a tree, the *Jefe*
fires six shots from his revolver into the air as a token of faith,
love, loyalty, and, more importantly, also as a charm for frightening the Devil away.

After ten or twelve days of prayer, there remain two days of
dancing and feasting. To preserve a devout atmosphere, an altar
is constructed against the side of the *Jefe's* house under the porch.
This altar is decorated with net curtains, paper flowers, Christmas bells and tinsel, a clock, pages from an old magazine, wild
flowers, and a portrait of Christ. Now this device may be en-
visaged as a final means of banning whatever persisting devils
may remain after the ritual of the pistol shots.

The dancers and related personages next enter the setting. The
costumes of the dancers, flamingly provocative, are of red cotton
cloth. The skirts of these costumes have small tubes of river cane
sewn in at the hems, so that when the dancers perform there is
always a great fanfare of both movement and sound. The head-
dresses are composed of pieces of broken mirror, tinfoil, and
any other appropriate adornment at hand. The headgear of the
Capitanes, however, are more impressive, being composed of bits
of mirror and of radiant feathers. These *Capitanes* carry large
gourds embellished with crepe paper of divers hues. Moreover,
they carry bows measuring from two to three feet in length. The
bow has a hole bored in its center. The purpose of this contri-
vance is not to discharge the arrow but to make a noise, for when
the bow is placed in readiness, the arrow is not discharged but
is caught and thus emits a loud twanging sound.

The *Capitana* begins the ceremony, and she together with *la
Jovencita* dances to the altar, where they stop, snap their fingered
bows, and turn to dance again. The steps are uniformly short,
and the dance is a kind of one-two, one-two-three step—hops up
and down—varied only by side swings from the hips.

It is now that *el Viejo* comes down from the hills to capture
la Jovencita. El Viejo is wicked and aged; his beard is of *lechu-*

guilla fiber; he flourishes a snaky whip; and he very probably represents the Devil. *La Jovencita* is youthful and jocundly beautiful; her face is tinted by the desert dawns; she exhibits a decorative bow; and she is altogether probably both Our Lady and the Life-Force. The impotent wicked would debase the virginal fecund!

But as one body the dancers turn upon *el Viejo*. They weave a circle round him thrice and otherwise discomfit him with raucous noise of rattling gourds. The *Capitan* pretends to shoot *el Viejo* with his bow and arrow. *El Viejo* falls, and the dancers throw their bows and gourds at him. Thus is the Devil exorcised; thus is *la Jovencita* saved. Amid the mingled music of violin, guitar, and tambourine, the performers now jog into the magic ring and reclaim their bows and gourds which they have symbolically smeared with the blood of the Old Man. As a nearby drum joins the approaching crescendo, the dancers with mincing steps triumphantly install *la Jovencita* upon the symbolic altar.

Throughout the following night there is the sound of revelry, of festival with merriment and feasting. The feast consists of *frijoles, tortillas,* and *fritada;* the merriment is also of the carnal kind.

Thus the rain dance of San Vicente is a mixture of Indian and Christian rites. The occasion roughly corresponds with the honoring of *el Día de Corpus Christi,* and such figures as the altar and especially Jesus and Mary display an obvious Christian influence. On the other hand, the dance, the bow-and-arrow ritual, the rain prayers, and the decorative niche suggest an origin earlier and more native. It remains to be noted that the niche resides in the tree until it rains, and when there is rainfall, it is returned to the *Jefe's* custody. Following the dancing here described, it rained on the afternoon of June 16!

There almost seem prescient omens in the dark, serious faces of the dancers. For as the gathering clouds now stampede the earth with shadows, old San Vicente—"tee-tiny" waif of the desert—looks up expectantly and, as the incantations begin, hears already—from howsoever afar—the mighty winging of the Thunder Bird.

A Legend of the Lost Nigger Gold Mine

The Big Bend region of Texas—the last frontier of the United States—has always figured prominently as a rich locale among tales of gold mines in the great Southwest. Both gold and quicksilver are, indeed, mined on a paying basis along the borders of the Rio Grande, and this fact has naturally encouraged the inveterate prospector to continue searches long ago forsaken as fruitless by earlier hunters and also has invested even the most fantastic yarn with that small tinge of possibility requisite for its perpetuation and for the garbled contradictions inevitable in its many retellings. Thus in the Big Bend area there are many legendary or unfound mines; for example, Lost Peak Mine, Phantom Silver Mine, the Lost Gold of Death Hole, and the Gold Cairns of the Chisos Mountains.[1] Surely one of the most famous treasuries of the entire West is, however, the fabled Lost Nigger Gold Mine.

To trace the earliest accounts of the site of the Lost Nigger Gold Mine down to the narratives of the present day concerning its whereabouts is eventually to enter the realms of romance, the nowhere of fantasy. For the Lost Nigger Gold Mine, at first unquestionably located in old Mexico, some decades ago was placed anew on the Texas side of the Rio Grande, and—more recently still—has been located nearer the upper section of the vast stretches of the Big Bend country. The migrations of this

176

mine, the contradictory explanations of its origin and site, all come within the orbit of serious folklore as romantic fantasy, a phantasmagoria shifting and unsubstantial as mirage, an arrestingly incredible parcel of preposterous yarns, and yet a tale so fabulous with possibility that something more must, perhaps, always remain to be told about its strange developments.

South of the Rio Grande (sometimes called Rio Bravo), opposite the pale Chisos (Phantom) Mountains, there is a range of Mexican mountains called the Ladrones (Robber);[2] and it is this rocky Mexican bad-land that "the odds," to use J. Frank Dobie's phrase, favor as the true location of the Lost Nigger Mine.[3] As the story goes, the Reagan brothers (Frank, Jim, John, and Lee) in 1887 hired at Dryden, Texas, an illiterate Seminole "nigger" named Bill to help with ranch work. One night Nigger Bill stated that he had that day located a gold mine. None of the Reagan boys believed the Negro, and so they refused to go with Bill to the mine. When the Negro returned to Dryden, he immediately got in touch with a white man he knew in San Antonio; and, some short time later on, the Reagans received a letter addressed to Bill Kelley, the Negro in question, which stated that the ore sent by Bill had proved very rich when assayed. According to one account, the Reagan boys then killed the "nigger," the name "nigger" in the Big Bend being applicable usually to a half-breed, and then dumped or "pecosed" him into the Rio Grande. What seems more likely, however, is that the Negro ran away when the Reagans refused to believe that he had actually found a rich gold deposit.

There are, in fact, several differing accounts of what the Negro did as well as of subsequent hunts for the mine. The most serious early search was undertaken by a railroad conductor named Lock Campbell, the white man in San Antonio who had known of Bill's find. Now Lock Campbell had prospected for gold in Nevada, Alaska, and California; and it was he who inspired the Reagan brothers to make an arduous and concerted search for both the lost mine and the lost Negro discoverer. These cattlemen, who of course knew absolutely nothing at all about gold, vainly scouted both the north and south sides of the Rio Grande, finding neither the mine nor any definite trace of Nigger Bill. Later on, Campbell grubstaked several other prospectors who were more experienced at this sort of thing, but there were again no results.

On July 19, 1899, Campbell and four other men signed an agreement to hunt for and develop the lost mine, and one of these men later claimed that he discovered the mine in the Ladrones (sometimes Lothorone) Mountains. His story, in any case, was never verified, some persons thinking that, if he had found any sort of gold deposit in Old Mexico it certainly was not the lost mine of Nigger Bill. In 1909 an Oklahoman, Wattenberg by name, brought with him to Alpine, Texas, a map of a gold mine in Mexico opposite the mouth of Reagan Canyon. John Young, citizen and pioneer of Alpine, examined Wattenberg's map, entered into partnership with the Oklahoman, traveled to Mexico City, secured personally from President Díaz a permit to operate a gold mine in northern Mexico, and then wasted years of time, energy, and money, in fruitless expeditions.

This, then, is the substance of the story as it was recorded in 1931 by J. Frank Dobie, who then said: "There will be other stories of the Lost Nigger Mine."[4] In 1935-1936 and again in the summer of 1939 I lived in Alpine, Texas, and at different times listened to the "old-timers," including Mr. John Young, talk about the lost mine of Nigger Bill. It was at this time that I first began to assemble notes on and to travel over some of the territory so fruitlessly explored by early prospectors. In 1940 in Forth Worth I had the good fortune to talk about this mine with Mr. Dobie, who with typical enthusiasm and generosity encouraged me to write what I now record about what I saw, read, heard, and surmised concerning the lost Negro's unfound mine.

John Young, the most serious and ambitious of the many prospectors, died at Alpine, Texas, in 1938. On August 17, 1939, the San Angelo (Texas) *Standard-Times* printed from the Associated Press a report containing Mr. Young's final statement on the famous gold deposit, as follows:

> There is no doubt in my mind but that the Seminole Negro found the spew, or chimney, and that the others who found it probably erased or concealed it so other searchers could not locate the gold. If it was a lead, it could be traced, but a spew is just pushed up from the bowels of the earth. All who searched for the gold, except perhaps some of the Reagan boys, now are dead. There is a superstition that all who locate the gold are under a spell—are struck with tragedy or death before they can remove it.

Why is it that John Young, who apparently had more reason for disillusionment than previous prospectors on the basis of his many wasted years of vain searches, believed so firmly in the existence of this mine until his death? One of the factors supporting Young's belief, as also explained in the same newspaper account, is that Jack Haggard, of Musquiz, Mexico, wrote him a letter explaining that about 1901 "a Seminole Negro working for me at a mine at Los Espeya" told a "tale about the wonderful gold mine he had found in the Big Bend country." In point of fact, Haggard later came to Alpine and begged Young's son to go with him to the mine. Haggard's foreman, Harvey Turner, firmly believed in the Negro's story and claimed that he visited the very scene, which he identified by a sketch drawn from the Seminole Negro's description of the terrain. Upon returning, Turner told Haggard that he had found the gold lode.

There is one important datum in Turner's explanation which must be noted; namely, his claim that the gold lode was, not in Mexico, but in the Texas Big Bend. The student of folklore will here observe a phenomenon which in literature is termed a variant of the first story. Of course it is not impossible that this new detail might have immediately solved the riddle of this famous mine; but, in accordance with the tradition that ill fortune always befalls searchers for the Negro's gold, Turner was shortly thereafter killed, along with several other miners, in an explosion. Jack Haggard said that he found among Turner's papers what he believed was a description of the mine; but, unluckily again, it was in a cipher which he could not unravel!

In connection with the view that the lode is on the Texas side of the Rio Bravo, I have to report that one of my former students at Alpine—Mrs. Eugenia H. Chandley—who for many years taught school in the border territory—discovered that practically all of the people she talked with were convinced that the Lost Nigger Mine was hidden somewhere in the Texas Big Bend.

Another story I ran across in Alpine concerns a Mexican named Benito Ordones. In assemblying reports on this lost mine, I count Benito's recital as highly significant, since he claimed the truth of the matter to be that there is no lost Negro's mine but rather a lost treasure of pure gold. Benito said that he once wandered into a sort of "box" canyon in the Big Bend where he found a treasure of countless gold bars. As he was then heavily loaded, all he could do was to chip off a piece or two of the gold to return with as evidence of his discovery. What Benito wants now, as he explained to me, is an *amigo* who will spend a little time and money aiding him to re-identify the "box" canyon. Several persons have briefly explored sections of the Big Bend with Benito, but to no avail. Benito stated that he seldom had any difficulty in finding the treasure when traveling alone, but that when someone accompanied him, his *bruja* (from *embrujado,* "witch") seemed bent on misleading him; at least on these occasions he always lost the right trail. Moreover, Benito explained to me that he was simply too weak physically to bring from the canyon more than a few pieces of gold at a time and also that he was in no condition to manage alone a pack of burros for loading purposes. There was no question in Benito's mind, however, about the gold or the "box" canyon. This information may sound utterly fantastic, but Benito told me that the gold was abandoned there long ago by early Spanish explorers, and he offered as tantalizing proof the testimony of a rusty old *escopeta,* a sixteenth-century rifle, brought back from the very spot.

In the summer of 1939 I made my last trip to Alpine and the Big Bend. It was then that I heard the explanation which to me is the most amazing of them all, and yet even this tale is not in every way completely incredible. In point of fact, it may actually offer a practical solution to the riddle of this whole question of lost gold, refined or otherwise, in the Texas Big Bend. Charley Livingston, a businessman of Alpine, and I secured a map or "waybill" to a depository of huge quantities of gold from Professor Xavier Gonzales, now of Tulane University. Gonzales told me that he had secured the map from a Mexican and had to return it, but I was permitted to photograph the map. This particular "waybill" defines the site of the gold as near Paisano Pass, a point almost exactly midway between Marfa and Alpine, and even contains a designation with the explanatory phrase *"Aquí el oro"* (Here the gold). However, the scale of measurement used in this map is not clear, and in tramping over the terrain about Paisano Pass on, I most shamefacedly admit, more than two or three occasions, I was unfortunately unable to find any of the landmarks named in the map or to find the trail of the *mulas* that had brought the gold.

Perhaps the correct explanation of the whole story is this:

some prospector lucky enough to have gold in his possession went into the Big Bend area and unluckily dropped or lost his gold nuggets or gold ore. This "lost" gold was later found by a superstitious and highly imaginative Negro whose subsequent stories to equally superstitious and imaginative white men gave currency to the fantastic yarns about a lost nigger gold mine.

Where is the mine? Is it in Old Mexico? Is it just across the border on the Texas side? Or is it more than a hundred miles away—say, up near Paisano Pass? Or is it, after all, actually somewhere close to the very center of fantasy, at the heart of nowhere at all?[5] Well, the Big Bend is strange country, fabulous, and fabulously contradictory. There is, moreover, another detail: Mr. Alonzo Hord, a citizen of Alpine, showed me a piece of gold which he claimed was brought from Paisano Pass by a Negro he hoped some day to find when he had time. If conditions do not improve and things in general pick up, it seems to me that we might as well organize and go and find Nigger Bill's mine. Where is the mine? Rather, where is the grubstake?

NOTES

[1] Victor J. Smith, "The Lost Mines of the Chisos Mountains," *West Texas Historical and Science Society* (Alpine, 1926). I, 32 ff.

[2] For a description of this country, see my paper on "Folklore of the Texas Big Bend," *Journal of American Folklore,* LIV (1941), 60 ff.

[3] J. Frank Dobie, *Coronado's Children* (New York, 1931), pp. 159 ff.

[4] *Ibid.,* p. 179.

[5] The most recent story to come to my attention concerning a lost mine discovered by a Negro has for its setting Grandview, Texas—a town not far from Dallas. Ed J. Patton, who resides in Dallas, claims that a Negro working for his grandfather found a lost Spanish treasure in the neighborhood; but Patton, although his searches continue, has been unable thus far to find the lode (Dallas *Morning News,* May 17, 1945).

4

East Texas Hunting Windies

The tall tale is a distinctive type of folklore. Ordinarily anecdotal in form, it may be a piece of pure fiction or an exaggeration of an actual happening. With respect to subject and locale, the "windy" is less limited: its plot may involve any kind of topic either realistic or imaginary, its setting may be anywhere at all. The "windies" narrated below have East Texas for their scene and hunters and hunting for their subject. If they possess any special importance, it is that the incidents compose a sequence, inasmuch as a principal character, the hunter, is concerned throughout.

1. THE BIG BLOW

Once upon a time in the early spring a cyclone struck near the little town of Omaha, in a region that is definitely deep East Texas. A farmer who lived there on a very hilly and rocky farm was a hunter of sorts and owner of a trusty rifle. He said that one night a wind blew up that was as hot as seven hundred Indians and that by morning the cyclone had turned into a blue black blizzard. He and his family started for the storm house in the morning but stumbled off the porch and thus fell off the farm —the terrain being that hilly. By night they made it back to the storm house; by next morning they made it back home. This Texas cyclone, he discovered, had blown so hard that it had driven the nail in to the wall which supported the rifle but had left the rifle hanging there!

2. The Deluded Ducks

Sometimes, when hunting, this farmer used his rifle; sometimes he did not. A newcomer to East Texas was much surprised to learn this when he first went duck hunting with this hunter. One rainy morning the two men set out for the country when the wild ducks were flying high. The newcomer carried a rifle, the hunter, nothing at all. As the rain abated and the sun came out, the newcomer was all for firing away. The hunter, however, told him simply to save his ammunition and to walk over close to the paved highway. Pretty soon the sun came out full blast, creating a mirage effect similar to the phenomenon so often seen in West Texas. The ducks which were flying over thought they saw a river below and commenced to dive for it. Fifteen minutes later the men were loaded with ducks that in diving had broken their necks as pretty as you please.

3. The Ace Ice Hole

Now this hunter also had a young dog, at this time really a pup, which he was interested in training from the bottom up, as it were; for he did not wish to start the pup too early with difficult hunting assignments. Since there was still ice on Omaha Lake early in the spring mornings, he decided to introduce the pup to a special way of fishing. First, he cut a round hole in the ice; second, he coated the dog's tail with honey; third, he put the dog's tail in the ice hole. Shortly thereafter the pup began to scramble and then pulled out a big bass. Until the weather became too hot for ice to form, the hunter and his dog caught many fish in this way. Out of one hole they once pulled ten big bass, and accordingly this hole became known locally as the ace ice hole.

4. The Smart Hunter

When summer came, the hunter commenced to think of new tricks to teach his growing dog. But he had some difficulty in teaching the dog to retrieve squirrels. Often the hunter lost squirrels which fell from trees into the water, since a squirrel, as is well known, will go to the bottom and drown. Now as for hunting there is one point which must always be remembered: hunting cannot be a success unless the hunter is himself smarter than his dog. At last the hunter solved the problem. One day the dog treed a squirrel. This time the hunter with one hand took dead aim with his ever trusty rifle; with the other hand he more slowly cast a stick towards the river. The prompt dog immediately jumped for the water, arriving just in time to clamp his jaws firmly about the falling squirrel.

5. THE SMART BIRD DOG

It is said that you cannot teach an old dog new tricks; sometimes you need not teach a young dog too many before he catches on. That year autumn followed summer according to schedule, and so bird season came along. The dog proved a veritable genius at pointing birds; the hunter had the best season of his life. In fact, one time he set a record by shooting every bird in the covey. The only oddity is that after the dog had gone into the sparse bushes about Omaha Lake to flush the covey, the birds on this occasion did not all fly up simultaneously but one by one —at proper intervals of time indeed to allow the hunter to reload his old but storm-weathered rifle. Finally, when the gun barrel was hot and all the birds dead, the hunter walked over to the bushes. There he found that the dog had run the entire covey into a hole, had placed his paw over the opening, and then nonchalantly had let the birds fly out one by one.

5

The Spook of Sulphur Springs, Texas

On the outskirts of the region known as deep East Texas lies the flourishing little town of Sulphur Springs, center of a rich agricultural area, with a fairly large population of Whites and Negroes—the scene, late in the summer of 1945, of repeated and strange visitations by a mysterious spirit. The adventures involved in the appearance of this spirit compose an arresting story; but before attempting to explain the occurrences at Sulphur Springs, one must, first of all, briefly discuss certain terminology to distinguish one phantom from another.

The two terms—ghost and spook—are on closest examination not at all synonymous, since a ghost has to do with the return of a deceased person and since a spook is never similarly identified as a particular individual. Moreover, the ghost customarily makes a visitation at a definitely appointed hour (say, midnight), whereas the spook operates nocturnally upon a schedule not likewise limited to a special time. Furthermore, the ghost usually appears at a specific location (at the crossroads, in a haunted house, etc.), whereas the spook may be encountered in any number of unsuspected places. Finally, among other differences between the two words, spook stands out as a term quite properly regarded as humorous.

The point is that the night visits at Sulphur Springs were made, not by a ghost, but by a spook—a kind of phantom never successfully identified as any returning spirit of a person known to

be deceased, although later fully defined as an apparition of the
male sex. His appearances were never circumscribed to one definite spot; for he visited both the Negro population and the Whites
as well, and, in addition, was detected both in the country and
in the town. In none of his manifestations did he, in accordance
with the traditional behavior of the vengeful ghost, perform injury to the living or pronounce a fearful, lasting curse. The visitant at Sulphur Springs was thus no horrendous representative
from the supernatural world; instead, he was simply a wayward,
capricious spook whose initial appearances were not pernicious,
though towards the last his visitations became a very serious matter indeed.

To follow more or less the chronological order of the nocturnal
occurrences, the story commences in Negro Hollow—the section
of Sulphur Springs occupied by the Negroes. Early in the summer of 1945 rumors had circulated that all of the people in the
"hollow" were much exercised over the appearance of a spook,
so much so indeed that they stayed off the streets after dark, and
nightly locked their doors and windows. When inquiry was made
by the local police upon the request of the Negroes, it was
learned that the spook seemed to be a man; in any case, the spook
had a male voice and masculine laughter. The report was that
once the spook appeared to be cornered, but that when a body of
Negroes made a concerted assault the same apparition was suddenly behind them laughing a full, masculine laughter. The spook
was neither black nor white but rather similar to an albino, to
all appearances being completely covered in a misty white substance, out of which loomed two fiery red eyes about the size of
marbles. This latter datum was gleaned from a Negro man who
one night abruptly found himself facing the spook against the
kitchen wall when going for a drink of water. On this particular
occasion neither the spook nor the Negro spoke; but the apparition quickly faded through the kitchen wall without, strangely
enough, injuring the wall so much as to cause even one splinter
in the woodwork.

Upon yet another occasion, a beautiful young White woman
was early one evening confronted by the spook near a moldy
old haystack. Immediately she bent to her knees, praying in hys-
terical tones that he do her no harm, either to spirit or to body.
Before promptly vanishing, the spook is said to have replied to

this plea that he at no time, past or present, planned injury toward any woman. In all these early accounts, it is evident that in his initial appearances the spook of Sulphur Springs ostensibly was nothing more than a prankster. Certainly his visitations were not motivated by such practical purposes as revenge or transmission of messages to the living. Clearly in his behavior towards the pretty Texas girl he behaved as a gentleman should.

Despite the harmlessness of these visitations and although traditionally regarded as an affable personality with only a happy destiny, the spook eventually became in the affair at Sulphur Springs the instigator, presumably unwittingly, of near tragedy. One cloudy summer night a Negro shot off the nose of his sister-in-law. First, the police were summoned to take care of the Negro; secondly, an ambulance came to convey the Negro woman to the hospital. The only explanation offered was that the Negro mistook his sister-in-law for the spook: she was spending the night with her relatives, and at the time of the shooting, robed to the feet in a white gown, she was bent on some necessary midnight function. At any rate, this was the explanation tendered; it was accepted; it was probably a true avowal down to the last detail. Nor should this explanation appear in any way surprising, inasmuch as by this date everybody in Sulphur Springs had become leery of any untoward nocturnal sight. The Negro's account of the shooting thus appears far from incredible.

Although it seems impossible for a real person to have masqueraded as the spook, the next happening is not easy to explain. At the local Court House one day shortly thereafter someone found the following note: "I have been here three weeks, will be three more, then will clear." The evidence afforded by the discovery of this note would seem to point strikingly towards the handiwork of a local prankster wishing to have a little fun at the expense of superstitious Negroes. Bue since gunfire had now been introduced to combat the spook, it is obvious that a person would have been foolish indeed to take chances on this type of masquer-expense of superstitious Negroes. But since gunfire had now been to see. Perhaps the explanation is that mob fear now dominated the community. All that can be said, in any case, is that rumors did not cease to flourish; and even though the spook was thereafter never again encountered face to face, bands of spook-hunters continued to roam through the summer nights. If the deviltry which followed is to be traced directly to the spook, he quite evidently had abandoned his former affable air.

According to city officials (as noted in the Sulphur Springs News Telegram), one night in August, 1945, a man's milk goat, valued at twenty-five dollars, was shot and killed; and his horse, being frightened, jumped the fence and ran away. In point of fact, shooting became so wild among the hunters themselves that the police were obliged to instruct them to lay aside their weapons. Among later reports about the spook, the Sulphur Springs News Telegram, after stating that the spook would appear to be bullet-proof, printed early in September the following account:

> The spectral apparition has been seen ranging all the way from City Park over to the East End of town—sometimes among the white population and sometimes among the elite of the city's colored residents.
> Local officers have been called, neighbors have been yelled for, gunshots have resounded, and running feet have disturbed the slumber of Sulphur Springs—all to no avail.

The close of summer, however, brought with it a cessation of the nightly visits of the spook of Sulphur Springs. Whether he will appear again and become an annual summertime phenomenon, it is hard to say. The ugliest rumor circulated about this whole affair is to the effect that a White man desiring to own certain property in the Hollow masqueraded as a spook to frighten away the Negroes owning the coveted property. But this report appears to bear every ear-mark of unsubstantiated hearsay, to be only a belated rationalization of the events.

For something did happen in Sulphur Springs! Whatever was first seen—be it animal, human, or spectral—does not, after all, really matter one iota. Once a tale is started, the folk can minimize it or build it into as large proportions as they please. The importance to students of folklore of the recent phenomenon at Sulphur Springs is—in some ways—difficult to exaggerate: here in the United States, in the middle of the twentieth century, is a folk tale in the making, a story with all the appurtenances of communal origins, mob psychology, deep superstition, and fluid hearsay. It is a tale tinctured with those very contradictions inherent in man's own conflicting, mysterious nature; for even if all the folk had looked at one and the same time, some of them would have seen the spook, some would not have, and some would not have known what they saw.

An East Texas "Neck" Riddle

When I was a child, my father, John Winfield Braddy, used to
tell me a story about an East Texas outlaw who saved his neck
by confounding his captors with a riddle which they could not
solve. As I remember the tale, told about 1915, the outlaw rode
his horse into the woods and was set upon and captured by a
posse of the sheriff's men. These men were about to string up
the outlaw to a tree when, according to the custom in early Texas,
they told him he could win his freedom if he recited a riddle
which they could not unriddle. The noose was already around
the outlaw's neck and looped over the branch of a tree when his
chance to save himself came. The outlaw was so frightened that
he was hard put to think of anything, but after fidgeting about
nervously for a while, he finally thought of something just as the
sheriff's men were tightening the noose to pull him off the ground
and swing him in the air. Turning to the posse, the outlaw recited
the following rhymed riddle:

> A horn ate a horn
> Up a high oak tree;
> If you can unriddle this,
> You can kill me.

The sheriff's men were completely mystified by the verses and
pressed the outlaw for an explanation. When they gave up guess-

ing, this is the story he told them, and it won him his release. He said that his name was Mr. Horne and that he once climbed into a tree to protect himself from his pursuers and that he there would have died of hunger had he not eaten a soft cow horn which he carried in his belt to use as a trumpet. (On this genre, see further Herbert Halpert, "The Cante Fable in Decay," *SFQ* (1941), V, 197-200.)

7

Running Contraband On The Rio Grande

One summer night an automobile sped rapidly down the Texas highway out of Sierra Blanca toward El Paso. Its driver, Mrs. Grace W., did not at first notice that a government car had trailed her when she turned north from the Rio Grande to intersect Highway 80. After she headed west for the Pass, her pursuer turned on the speed, quickly overtaking her outside of Fabens.

"What's the hurry?" the border patrolman asked.

"No hurry," Mrs. W. replied.

"What's that you got in the back?" the officer questioned.

"Nothing," Mrs. W. replied. "Just empty gunny sacks. I carried some grain for the stock down to the farm and was just on the way home. What's up?"

"We are looking for a woman. A lot of wet Mexicans are coming in right now to gather the crops or work as maids."

"Oh, yeah!" Mrs. W. said, irritated. "Well, I can tell you there's nobody with me. I got a maid, all right, but she has a pass and goes home to Juarez every night. You don't catch me hauling her all around the country or out of the state, much less bringing her across the river. I'm not breaking any law, you know."

"Pardon me, madam. We have to check, you know. You're O.K. Go on home now, but watch your speed," the patrolman said, climbing back in his car and watching her start away somewhat less precipitately than before.

192

That is how it happens some of the time, but not how it happens much of the time. Border rangers stay forever on the alert along the Rio Grande. They do not annoy innocent citizens, but these citizens often are not as cooperative as they should be. Over the years women "runners" have outnumbered male smugglers, so that the policeman's interest in Mrs. W. had a basis in experience to support it. Generally, border officials seldom question river crossers without reason, or "make a strike" without effect. Their eyes, however, must be everywhere at once: on aliens, ammunition, cowhides, guns, horses, jewelry, metals, narcotics, parrots, perfume, spies, undesirables, watches, and yearlings prone to stray—in a word, on everything. The cause for this is of course close at hand. "Importing" ranks as a very old business on the Texas-Mexico line.

2

During the Mexican Revolution and indeed until his death in 1923, the rebel Pancho Villa virtually hypnotized most of his countrymen with fear. When he rampaged up and down the Rio Grande at the outbreak of hostilities, he frightened many Mexicans into smuggling their cattle and anything else they had, including prostitutes, across the border into Texas. In *Them Was the Days* (1925) Owen P. White told how whoremasters brought "wet" totsies across the river, setting up business on the Texas side, first at Presidio, then at Shafter, and finally at El Paso. The Mexicans, scared within an inch of their lives by the bloody tales of the murderous Villa, sold everything they had or could lay their hands on. They sold this produce, chattels or women, cheap. They knew Pancho would confiscate whatever he ran into.

That was the era of "Chink runners" and "yellow goodsmen." Pancho Villa so mistreated the Chinese in Chihuahua that they hired smugglers to convey them to the United States. Numbers of them reached the northern banks of the Rio safely, but most of the Chinese had to leave their possessions in Mexico, in the clutch of the rebels.

"Chink running" was brisk around 1909 until smugglers killed an American border patrolman. It seemed impossible to discover the identity of his murderer. The head of the ring in Juarez was a wealthy Chinaman who sported a big diamond ring. He took great pride in the ring. American agents induced a pretty young *gringa* woman to become the Chinaman's girl and steal the ring from him. She did so. The American agents then traded the diamond back to the Chinaman in exchange for information that led to the arrest and execution of the smuggler who had killed one of their respected immigration agents.

Needing munitions in 1913 to carry on his revolution, Villa himself smuggled an unknown but large amount of valuable ore out of Mexico to trade for war supplies in Texas. In *The Brites of Capote* (1950) Noel L. Keith recorded how Villa took over the fabulous riches of General Louis Terrazas, in his epoch "the undisputed dictator of Chihuahua," and smuggled the Terrazas gold into the Big Bend country. According to Keith, Villa also rushed silver out of Mexico in those days: "J. Y. Basking and A. H. Burke were bringing out two heavily loaded mule trains with more than a half-million dollars in silver bars from the Alvarado Mining Company of Parral and the Inde Mining Company. The two mule trains crossed to the Texas side of the Rio Grande into Presidio at the same time."

Much more of this kind of business went on during that era in the Big Bend and all along the Rio Grande. Most of the Big Benders want to forget the smuggling as well as the later raids by the Mexican rebels at Ojinaga and the Brite ranch. Repeated inquiries in that area about a "wet embargo" have gleaned the fact that other instances of large-scale "border running" then occurred; but the details must be omitted. Too many people in places too high were involved "hand in glove" with Villa in the Big Bend.

About 1918 Pancho Villa tried his luck elsewhere, attempting to sell Mr. Vince Andreas, a well-known citizen of El Paso, several wagonloads of silver ingots. Mr. Andreas made him an offer, twenty cents on the dollar valuation, if Villa would make lawful delivery on the Texas side, but the bandit wanted more money and declined. Some say Villa buried this silver in Mexico near the town of Villa Ahumada; others believe that he crossed the river and buried it on Texas soil between Fabens and Ysleta. At that time a price had been placed on Villa's head. In order to encourage his men to betray him, the Mexican government offered a reward of one thousand dollars for his capture, dead or alive. Always leery of everybody, including his own treacherous gang,

Villa may have regarded Texas as a safer place than Mexico for hiding his treasures.

Of treasures, Pancho Villa had an abundance. He got money from kidnapping *gringos* and holding them for ransom, from butchering the Chinese and rifling their pockets, from forcibly entering Mexican homes or offices and ransacking them of money or heirlooms, and from putting the bite, *la mordida,* on everybody he could.

Mr. Jimmie Caldwell, now of Santa Fe, New Mexico, qualifies as the best possible eye-witness to the opulence of Pancho Villa. Once the bandit's foreman at Canutillo, Mr. Caldwell supplied the ranch with American tractors and threshing combines, in return for which he always received payment in gold. On one order of $17,000 Villa delayed payment so long that Mr. Caldwell was obliged to screw his courage to the sticking place and ask for the money. When he made his request, Villa told him that he would be paid in a day or two, as soon as he got back from a trip into the Sierra Madre. True to his promise, Villa returned to the ranch two days later and had his men unload a heavy trunk from a wagon bed into the house. There Caldwell counted out the amount due him from a trunk filled with twenty dollar gold pieces. After counting out his $17,000, he started to show Villa how much he had taken, but the bandit dismissed him: "O.K.; *es nada."*

All the gold stories—those cited and those hinted at by informers afraid to have them printed—underline one impression on the reader indelibly: Villa smuggled more gold out of Mexico than any living person now knows or is willing to say. In a confession made in Mexico City in 1912 Villa said himself that he had buried silver in Santa Barbara and that he knew where another treasure lay in the basement of a house in Parral. For this reason, more credence should have been given, in 1955, to Dolores Vasquez than she received. On August 6, 1955, Dolores Vasquez, a purported nurse with Villa's army, told the United Press that Pancho buried smuggled gold at "Cinenia" (possibly the King Ranch), Corpus Christi, Robstown, Roma, and San Antonio. However that may be, he certainly cached some of it in the Big Bend and in or around El Paso.

The days of Pancho Villa, now past, constitute an incomplete history. His daredevil tactics set the tempo for all future "border

running," and his ghost still walks the Rio Grande today, threaten-
ing and big as life. He galvanized everybody he met with fright,
with an ineradicable fear. Many of his doings therefore remain a
mystery, a closed door one does not venture to open.

3

During Prohibition El Pasoans went over to Juarez, not only to
drink, but to bring home large supplies of contraband liquor. For
a while it was sold in Juarez on the streets to customers in the
traffic lines bound for the Texas side. When Mexican authorities
tightened down in 1930, "rum runners" came into the picture,
engaging the police in pitched gun battles while smuggling their
merchandise over the river. Nineteen federal officers were killed
between 1919 and 1932 in gunfights with "rummers." The dead
smugglers never were totalled up.

The talk of the border in the era of Prohibition centered on a
place called "The Hole in the Wall." The original "Hole in the
Wall"—all such places were later so named—had its location
southeast of El Paso on a spot of Mexican earth near the town
of San Elizario. A nondescript building set in a kind of garden,
this "Hole in the Wall" contained two or three long narrow tables,
plenty of plain chairs, and two stuffed camels of life-size, one at
each long side of its only otherwise unadorned room. Here the
Paseños of yesterday foregathered to drink their *copitas,* to swig
their *tequila* with salt and lemon. Here they also purchased a few
spare bottles of drinking whiskey and tried to return unappre-
hended to the Texas side. The appropriateness of its name derived
from the fact that "The Hole in the Wall" became the easiest
place to penetrate the barrier created by the United States government to prevent the illegal transportation of liquor into Texas.

The one near San Elizario became, then, the first "Hole in the
Wall." Its patrons included rich and influential men of that area
who did not welcome interference from the customs men. Those
patrons did not smuggle liquor to sell it for a profit but to allay
their own recurring thirst. According to one customs agent, who
prefers to remain anonymous, it was not a smart move to arrest
a patron who brought only a bottle or two across the river for his
own use. In those days such an action carried the law too far,
arousing the animosity of the local citizens and sometimes incur-

ring the criticism of the agency itself. The anonymous informant said that one wealthy farmer whom he apprehended made it so "hot" for him that he almost lost his job. Custom agents were supposed to concentrate on criminal "rum runners" and leave respectable parties alone.

Vanished glories of Prohibition included a Hole in the Wall on Cordova Island at the foot of Eucalyptus Street. Cordova Island came into being as a result of the flood in July, 1897. According to Mr. O. C. Coles, a veteran El Paso realtor, the flood on the Texas side extended from the International Bridge to Washington Park, backing up water to the downtown districts, so that Mayor Magoffin arranged for the digging of a channel which created Cordova Island when the Rio Grande then straightened its course. This Hole stood about three hundred feet from the boundary line, in easy reach of thirsty international travelers brave enough to recross to Texas after a "wetting" and face the Border Patrol, Customs Service, and City Police who kept a close watch there.

In that period Mr. Alfonso Mendez, Senior, worked as a cab driver for the old City Service Company. On April 8, 1956, Mr. Mendez described in the El Paso *Times* how during Prohibition he often drove fares to the foot of Eucalyptus Street, where they walked across the international line to refresh themselves.

> On Saturday night and all day Sunday where there was a big crowd of crossers, the City Police used to park the Black Maria there; and if you came back *muy borracho,* they would put you in it. When they got a full load, they would take you to jail.

In the same issue of the *Times* a former federal officer, who declined to have his name used, also remembered well the various "holes," especially one on Fabens Island. He declared there was little smuggling at these points, not nearly so much as at the bridges.

> Sometimes we'd catch some guy with a pint, but most of the patrons were content to bring their liquor back inside them. We kept a pretty close eye on them. I've seen men and women in evening dress going and coming to them, but those were special events like New Year's Eve when somebody would be having a party and run out of liquor.

Officials certainly had plenty of trouble enforcing the law during Prohibition. Female informers, "squawk women," might give them a reliable clue, a "third rail"; but "rummers" became specialists at illegally importing prohibited liquors and grew rich enough to bribe judges, or "rum beaks," who set them free. A crafty smuggler of the day, called "Nellie the Booze Queen," became adept at eluding the law and grew rich from fat profits.

The Repeal Amendment in 1933 rendered the smuggling of liquor obsolete, its illegal flow dying down to a trickle. Today smugglers of pure grain alcohol are now and again arrested. Evidently there are still people who prefer "white whiskey" to "store-boughten" stuff. In the magazine *Cavalier* (May, 1956) Mickey Spillane described how he rode with hot-rod "Moon-shiners" in North Carolina. On the Mexican border it is best to stay clear of "white" liquids. Odorless, colorless, and tasteless, such liquids contain the equivalent of deadly hashish. After a drinker swallows a glass of the stuff, he suddenly goes boi-ing! There is a much bigger business than "rum running" in El Paso today.

4

Recent smuggling at the Pass has centered on five significant commodities. These five comprise, in ascending order of impor-tance, aliens, watches or their springs, war materials, jewelry, and narcotics. Facts about running these contraband goods ap-peared in *American Speech* (May, 1956); these now may be reviewed together with newer evidence.

Attmpts to bring aliens and enemy spies into Texas have now sharply declined, due to the efficiency of the F.B.I. Occasionally visitors from out of town still try to smuggle *"perdidas"* (prosti-tutes) across the river. There continue to be a few housemaids unlawfully entering Texas, not from the new Cordova Bridge, but from Cordova Island, a Mexican area north of the Rio Grande. These rather harmless crossings, effected by "amusers," or accomplices, have always occurred throughout the Texas-Mexico country and constitute no serious menace to America.

As for watches, the premium is on those of Swiss manufacture, and the probability is that these rarely come into the Southwest in "bundles," or large quantities. There exists some traffic, how-ever, in "buttons," or small amounts. An exception occurred in

1956, when a Mexican national was captured with close to $40,000 in contraband watches. A different condition holds true for jewelry, particularly precious diamonds, which usually do not come to El Paso overland from Mexico, but go to New York City, the diamond center, by sea or air routes from Belgium or Brazil.

Instruments of war, on the other hand, pose another question and return the focus, importantly, to the Southwest. Importations into Mexico from the United States, happening as they do with some regularity, were particularly serious during the recent emergency of the Korean conflict. Today, in a time of peace, war munitions continue to be passed illegally across the International line, throughout the Southwest as well as at Tijuana, Baja California, so that "gun running" appears a steady phenomenon of the borderland.

Corruption among erring policemen of both El Paso and Juarez has not helped matters. Late in 1954 two gun-packing Mexican officers crossed to El Paso from Juarez in a stolen automobile and created a disturbance, on the Texas side at the juncture of Copia and Pershing Streets. When apprehended, the "hopped-up" Mexican policemen, or "arms," were found to have hidden their contraband *marijuana* cigarettes in their car where it had stalled. In April of 1955 a top newspaper reporter exposed the mad narcotic orgies then regularly occurring at the city jail in El Paso itself. Soon afterwards, on June 19, three thieves broke into Shain's Jewelry Store, or "ice palace," in downtown El Paso and stole $1700 worth of valuables, or "collat" (*i.e.,* collateral). Upon his capture, one of them confessed that he smuggled the loot to Juarez and there traded it for heroin to a Mexican dope ring.

Yet later, pregnant Pat Arthur, in the Juarez jail on the charge of murdering Mr. Arreola, issued from her prison cell on the arm of a Juarez police official (theoretically to help him and others "finger" men in the drug racket, but actually to dine, dance, and disport themselves). This American girl had given Mr. Arreola a photograph of herself and had written thereon the salutation to my "Silver King," or "Silver Ring." Whatever the key word was, her nocturnal sortie has never been satisfactorily explained. Did "aureole" refer to ring? Was she an unwitting "leg" in this aureole, or dope ring?

5

Smuggling, centrum of many ills corroding border culture, may appear in some instances as relatively inoffensive. Anyone who sneaks by the busy customs men at rush hours without paying duty on a taxable product becomes guilty of a crime thereby. Such petty "border running" is termed "jam." Minor offenders comprise men of the type who cheat on their income taxes or women of the sort who can not resist a bargain or a sale. Women are rumored to be talented at selecting "annexations," quantities of merchandise to be taken over the border, and at concealing "candy," small pieces of jewelry. When a female acts as a criminal lookout, customs men refer to her as "bright eyes," whereas a male spotter may be called almost anything from an *"aguador"* (water bag) to a "soldier" (one who stands guard). Petty offenders often graduate to professional smuggling, entering thereby a criminal class which speaks an underworld argot. Well equipped and ably organized, professionals do a sizable volume of illegal trafficking each year all along the Mexican border in taxable or prohibited goods.

To "run" merchandise successfully, the "sneaker" (smuggler) needs an "Adam," or partner, one who is an "ace" or a "major"; that is, a man who can be depended on. He further needs a "lagger," or contact man, and, to avoid detection, may hire the services of a "jigger moll," a female lookout. Sometimes he utilizes a "jacker," an expert at camouflage. Men who wade the river with contraband goods strapped to their backs are identified as *"burros"* or *"mulas,"* both being Spanish words for donkeys or mules. If they sleep in the open overnight, they used "Mexican *zarapes,"* actually newspapers spread out like a blanket. A "stop" is a place to "fence goods," and a "swagman," the fellow who receives illicit materials. The "pullers" may be handling "milk ropes," pearl necklaces; "muggles," an impure or poor quality of sap that comes from a marihuana bush; or "the queer," counterfeit money. The place where prohibited goods are assembled before being taken "under the bridge" is designated the "dump." Mail and contraband are received at a "drop."

If the smuggler has any doubts about his operations, he will look for "eels," or spies, in his "ring." He also will seek out the opinion of his "hawks," lookouts. He then may station at a dangerous spot a "walking tree," a watchman. If he still remains worried, he may make a "dry run," a test to discover the whereabouts of his "family men," the sellers of smuggled articles. The really careful operator will send forward a "doaker," a man to draw attention away from the actual smuggling, or, better yet, carry with him a *"prégon"* (proclamation), a pretty girl who draws the eyes of everybody to her own person. What he fears most is a "finger louse," a person who informs for government agents only; or a "red shirt," a man who refuses to obey orders. The phrase to describe a Negro stool-pigeon is "faded bogey." If the operator becomes frightened, he will return to his side of the border in a "bootlegger turn," or in a hurry; for he has respect both for *"chotas"* (suckling lambs), the police, and for *"Los Panchores"* (fat border patrolmen).

Southwestern operators fall into all shades, forms, and descriptions. They will do practically anything to cheat the United States of its import duty—from "planting" a package on the automobile of an innocent party to lining the casket of a dead man with drugs. If they are dope addicts as well as smugglers, as often they are, they may camouflage their own person from top to bottom by hiding *"cachuchos"* (caps or capsules) either under their wigs or in a "rectum stash." A thrill-seeking young Anglo in 1956 hid fourteen marihuana cigarettes under the dash of his car. Still another Anglo lad hid five types of narcotics on his person before crossing the Bridge. Both were caught. They usually are caught— if not by either Border Patrolmen or Customs Inspectors, then by officers of the Bureau of Narcotics. Agents frequently secure information from clues furnished by "bat carriers" or "belchers." Agents also sometimes hire a decoy, whose name is "Conny." The Federal government maintains a well-conducted prison to correct "boneheads," or lawbreakers, at nearby La Tuna, Texas, once they are tried and convicted. This "hutch," with its inmates, or "geezos," is familiarly known on the border as "La Tuna Tech."

The lure of easy cash brings "rum runners" from everywhere to the fabulous Rio Grande. At an early date they used only horses, and some of them still do. In the rough terrain of the southern Trans-Pecos, a wide territory, livestock "stray" from Chihuahua and Coahuila. The "chili chasers," border patrolmen, ride horses when chasing "wet" cattle across arroyos or "biyookies" (bayu + bayuco) and also when "rimming up a gunyon," riding up a canyon. The pursuers attempt to "double team" the pursued. They are bound to catch him if his mount "turns a wildcat," stumbles and falls. But if the horse is not a "dead head," he may save his rider. To escape the vigilant border rangers, a smuggler's horse must travel fast and "lay his belly in the sand." Animal figures of speech evoke more color than symbols for machines. The fast automobiles of present-day smugglers are known, jocosely, as "mule trains."

Thus far, bird symbols for airplanes have apparently not developed; at least none have come to public attention. Airways are, however, the newest routes to be explored by smugglers. In 1954 two violaters of the International Boundary landed with "wet" merchandise at an airfield in their twin-engine Cessna near the Arizona-Mexico border. When arrested, they admitted several other earlier unlawful flights. Testifying before a Senate subcommittee at San Antonio in 1955, Grady Avant, head customs agent at El Paso, said that the border was virtually unprotected from big-time dope importers who fly their drugs across the line for distribution in the United States as well as in Canada. In 1956 General Swing of the Border Patrol, reported sixteen planes apprehended in the act of international smuggling. Shortly after that, six men were arrested in a conspiracy to fly two million dollars in smuggled gold out of Mexico across the Rio Grande.

Why do drugs rank next only to Communism as a threat to America? They poison the manpower of the armies of tomorrow. They kill off the brains of brilliant men that Communists can not reach for washing in the Orient. Since the dope habit spreads like a contagious disease, it tends to enslave, not the few, but the many. Everywhere prostitution flourishes and where night life runs rampant, there lodges the breeding place of the dismantlers of Americanism. The battle today, as Averill Harriman once said, is a struggle for man's mind. For winning this struggle, the healthy body stands out as a primary prerequisite. Horror drugs like the Oriental "hiropon," an ephedrine-hydrochloride compound, inactivate the minds of men.

6

Among elements of society firmly aligned against traffic in dope, law enforcement agencies, newspapers, and church organi-

zations opposed the criminal importers on every side. Border
Patrol inspectors recently arrested a woman at the railway station
in El Paso. She had in her trunk and suitcase fifty-seven one
pound cellophane bags of highly "manicured" marihuana, with
a wholesale value of $22,800 and worth five times as much
when made into cigarettes for delivery in major United States
cities.

At Laredo and its twin city of Nuevo Laredo, the illegal traffic
had for its "head" the dread personage known as the Black
Angel (*El Angel Prieto*). He did a "heavy" business in contraband drugs. In December, 1957, there occurred a seizure at
Menosha, Wisconsin, of $700,000 of marihuana (in twenty three
sugar sacks of thirty pounds each) that originated in Nuevo
Laredo, Mexico. A number of years ago El Pablote Gonzalez
ruled the narcotics roost in Juarez. When a secret agent killed
Gonzalez some years back, his drug ring fell into the grip of his
widow, Ignacia Jasso. A nonpareil of the netherworld, she is
known around the globe by the diminutive of her Christian name,
La Nacha. In her own devious ways La Nacha is as infamous
on the Border today as Pancho Villa was in his epoch.

Yet more recently and back at El Paso again, a border dope
ring led by a Negro smuggler was punctured through the undercover work of an exceptionally able policeman, Mr. Bill Risley,
formerly a Juarez night-club entertainer. This ring had long been
feeding a band of high school students. The constant parade of
those as well as other narcotic violaters at the Federal court
drew this comment from United States District Judge R. E.
Thomason: "From the cases moving through the courts here,
at Eagle Pass, Del Rio, and other places, we don't seem to be
making much progress against the narcotics traffic."

Newspapers continued to assail what Judge Thomason designated as the number one problem on the border. El Paso area
churches also co-operated fully with the group. So did the Texas
Alcohol-Narcotic Education Incorporation. One of its members,
Dr. Walter R. Willis, remarked that the problem was no longer
personal, but national. Statistics show, he said, that it had entered
the family and influenced the economic life of America.

The most elusive smuggler was the elite criminal who used an
airplane. One point stood out clear about solving the narcotics
problem: The Old Man had to be brought down from the Mountain. Border fences did not stop him. Senatorial belittling of the

situation helped him. This bold robber of the government meant business. His trafficking in drugs aided the enemies of the United States, for he poisoned the sap of future generations in striking down the young.

8

The Birth of the Buscadero

"Tio" Sam Myres was a good man with a gun himself, and he knew well many of the most celebrated gunmen of his day, outlaws and lawmen alike. One of the most famous of these was Captain John R. Hughes of the Texas Rangers, man-hunter extraordinary and a frequent visitor to Myres' shop. It was Hughes, in fact, who provided the inspiration for the name of Myres' most famous product—the "Buscadero" Belt.

"Tio" means "uncle," and "Tio" Sam Myres had become by the time of his death in 1953 at the age of 81, not only one of the Southwest's most famous saddlemakers and leather craftsmen but also the beloved "uncle" of all Western gun-fanciers. Born in Clebourne, Texas, moving later to Sweetwater and thence to El Paso, Tio Sam was the image of Buffalo Bill Cody. Like Cody, he was the visual embodiment of the romantic Western Hero. To the very end he walked proudly erect and straight, grey mustache spreading above his firm lips, grey goatee flowing full on his aggressive chin, fine white hair sweeping to muscular shoulders. A-foot or a-horseback, Tio Sam in his buckskin coat never failed to bring the past into the present for all who beheld him in his Wild West regalia.

Tio Sam spent many hours worming secrets from ambitious bullet-slingers on both sides of the law, and then designing belts and holsters which they (or he) thought might improve their speed "on the draw."

Two leather-maker sons, Bill and Dale, survived the pioneering S. D. Myres, Sr., and recently each had a bit to say about their father's association with the renowned Ranger, Captain Hughes, and something to add also about the origin of the celebrated "buscadero" belt.

According to Bill Myres, his father first met Captain Hughes during the epoch when Hughes served as a hired investigator in the panoramic Big Bend. At that time, Captain Hughes was a left-handed gun-flagger, because a Choctaw Indian had permanently incapacitated his right hand when Hughes was only 15 years old. The Indian's rifle shot (as explained by Mac Martin in *Border Boss*) crippled the future Ranger's right arm for life. Forced thereafter to draw from the left side, Hughes developed into a sure-fire shooter, but he always remained interested in improving his draw.

In those days Hughes had a learned friend, the distinguished author, Eugene Cunningham. It was Cunningham who suggested that the Ranger talk over his problem with "Tio" Sam Myres. Together, the saddlemaker and saddleduster evolved a remarkable belt and holster, a rigging at once pleasing to the most critical eye and quick to reach with a drop of the hand. Hughes had become lightning fast through constant practice; and since his right hand remained unusable for a safe draw, his left hand compensated for the defect by a speedier and speedier leftward swoop. The first outfit won the name of "Myres' Quick Draw." At this juncture the writer Cunningham stepped in and, according to Bill Myres, christened the revolutionary new design the "Buscadero Belt."

In his book *Triggernometry, A Gallery of Gunfighters* (1941), dedicated to Captain Hughes, Cunningham wrote that Captain John R. Hughes was "directly responsible" for what Myres called the buscadero belt. Myres took the idea from Hughes' gun harness. Hughes conceived the design for his own harness to make the quick draw quicker still. Author Cunningham viewed the new belt as a revolutionary step forward in speeding the gunman's draw. He noted that the studied horizontal position in the close-fitting belt canted Hughes' pistol butt forward and his holster toe backward, permitting what he depicted as an unusually "quick disengagement of the weapon."

In his matchless tome, *Fast and Fancy Revolver Shooting,* the gun expert, Ed McGivern, gave full credit to Cunningham for explaining the source of Myres' buscadero belt. McGivern added, "The word 'buscadero' is of Spanish origin. *Buscar* is the verb to search or hunt. The suffix *dero* means 'he who is' or 'he who does.' Buscadero, then, could be translated as either *the one who hunted* or *the one who was hunted*. In the last mentioned sense, it became current from Utah to Cananea (of the State of Sonora, Mexico) in the days of Butch Cassidy and the Wild Bunch (probably in use long before this; it spread particularly in Butch's day) as the general name for the outlaws—the men who were hunted."

Was Captain Hughes, Tio Sam, or Eugene Cunningham the originator? The name of the person who first applied the coined word "buscadero" to the rigging does not appear as a certain, incontestable fact. Moreover, neither Tio Sam nor his sons, Bill and Dale, ever secured a patent for the historical belt.

Nonetheless, it was the fate of the buscadero belt to fare exceptionally well. It contains so many fine, mechanical features that it has become the favorite of gun experts everywhere.

Earlier designs strapped the gun holster up high on the hip. The buscadero style incorporated three radical improvements: it lowered the holster, made the gun easier to draw, and was curved to fit the body. Two billets loop onto the buscadero, one entering the hole in the belt strap, the other fastening down over it. The single buscadero of the Hughes' type supports one gun; the double, two. The loops in the buscadero belts allow various types of holsters to be fitted to them, or to be interchanged at will. It was Ranger Hughes who rounded up the last of the bad outlaws in the Big Bend country and put the *quietus* on them permanently. Thus the six-shooter won the West, but the buscadero belt helped to tame it.

Born in 1855, John R. Hughes hailed from Cambridge, Illinois, where the word "buscadero" was unknown. Later, when he had run-ins with Butch Cassidy in deep South Texas, Hughes no doubt heard the word often. Why? Because Butch Cassidy's Wild Bunch, whose members included the gun-flagging Kid Curry and the Sundance Kid, were known far and wide as buscaderos. Cassidy came to Texas out of Utah and spent years in the mining regions of Mexico. According to George A. Brown, retired U. S. deputy marshal, Butch reappeared in El Paso about 1912 under an alias. He then acted as an agent for Pancho Villa, rebel leader of Mexico, and there bought from Brown a splendid horse, Prince Tyrant, a striking bay gelding with a star in his forehead. All along the Rio Grande, Butch Cassidy (alias George Leroy Parker, Jim Lowe, etc.) bore the name of buscadero.

It is probably a bit more respectable to associate the word with the law officer Hughes than with the outlaw Cassidy. One must remember, though, that bandits like Billy the Kid, Butch Cassidy, Pancho Villa, and a raft of others, had a hand too, or both hands, in the making and molding of the West.

The invented word buscadero, though ultimately of Spanish derivation, drew its meaning from the speech of Mexico. Frequently the two Latin languages differ as much as the two Anglo tongues, British and American. A "subway" in England may designate an alternative thoroughfare, but in the United States it signifies an underground railroad. Similarly "buscadero" would stand for one thing in a Spanish sense and quite another in the New World along the southern Rio Grande. In the eminent Francisco J. Santamaría's *Diccionario General de Americanismos,* the verb *buscar* means *"irritar, provocar."* According to Soledad Perez, notable folklorist who lived long in Mexico, the coinage "buscadero" is familiar about mining camps in Chihuahua as a term for a bully or a trouble-maker—one who irritates or provokes. It is never synonymous, Miss Perez said, with a hired gunslinger, whom Mexicans call a *pistolero.*

The Mexican people south of the Rio Grande who dubbed Hughes a buscadero probably never thought of him at all as a hunter but rather as an official who made bothersome inquiries. Certainly they did not think of him as a cold-blooded killer, although Hughes had the reputation for shooting down his man when conditions made a killing necessary. The sight of Captain Hughes simply spelled trouble to them. Mexicans in the Big Bend would be provoked but not murderously enraged if Hughes, or one of his deputies, interfered with their smuggling or stealing when the Texas Rangers made their usual patrols up and down the Border. Unquestionably, the actions of Hughes irritated the Mexicans, for they knew him to be a man bent on straightening out such embarrassing Border incidents as stealing cattle and horses. As a buscadero, Captain Hughes acted in the lawful but informal office of what everybody now calls a trouble-shooter. He "stole" the Mexicans' "strays" in order to return them to their proper Texan cattlemen owners.

Buscaderos also gained notoriety in the days of the Wild Bunch as dangerous two-gun flaggers. Butch Cassidy winning a firm infamy for his unique type of ambush, which the biographer Jack Martin described as "his usual course." Those buscaderos lived in the wastes near cow towns and mining sites. They robbed, they fought, they itched for trouble. But rowdy Butch Cassidy, Boss of the Buscaderos, was no killer! In fact, he alone among outlaws performed his daring robberies without having to kill.

On the other side, Captain Hughes had fewer qualifications as a dyed-in-the-wool buscadero. He could fire only one gun, and he shot to kill. But this left-handed Texas Ranger provided the inspiration and name for the oldtime saddlemaker's design of a harness for a faster, easier draw that has become the favorite of fast draw experts everywhere.

9

The Pan-American Race

Though some say next May, the sixth *Carrera Panamericana* looks farther off than that. The Central Highway to Mexico City from El Paso, Texas, is in better than fair condition, but it is too rough for the high speeds of road racing.

For lovers of automobile racing, it is disappointing that the Pan-American Race will be delayed, if not discontinued. Sportsmen all over the world have come to view it as an annual event. The first contest—in May, 1950 (from Juarez to the northern border of Guatemala)—created racing history. Covering 2,178 miles, it was the longest such race ever run. Since then, the distance was shortened to around 2,000 miles, the date changed from May to November, and the route reversed. In the last four contests Tuxtla Gutierrez marked the starting point and Juarez the finishing line. In 1950 the road south of Mexico City was largely unpaved, but now the whole course is paved. Nonetheless the *Carrera Panamericana* remains the most dangerous in the world. For this reason, Robert M. Barsky described it in *True's Automobile Yearbook*, 1954, as "The Race of Death." In 1954, as is well known, a number of contestants crashed and killed themselves in order to avoid hitting careless spectators who had run into their paths. Today in Mexico the hottest political question is this long, arduous road test.

Some inkling of the great distance involved in the race may be drawn from a description of the route of the Central Highway. All main traffic in the Republic travels either on or across this grand *camino*. The first large city within the interior is Chihuahua City, Chihuahua. This *cuidad* is a rich mining point, containing numerous Spanish colonial monuments worth visiting. Chihuahua is the largest state in Mexico. The next romantic site southwards is Parral, in the same *estado*. It is prized for its minerals and ores. In the country near Parral, Pancho Villa built his *Rancho Grande del Canutillo* in 1920. Rock fences, picturesque but hard to construct, decorate the Chihuahua countryside.

Other major cities on the Central Highway are Durango, Zacatecas, Aguascalientes, Leon, Queretaro, and Mexico City. Durango, capital of the state of the same name, is noted for its thick forests and fine lumber. Its impressive cathedral with a cupola adjoining dates from 1695. Zacatecas, to the south and in a valuable mining area, boasts an aqueduct with a Spanish arch, the work of *conquistadores* of long ago. Aguascalientes, celebrated for fiestas held every April and May, is a typical colonial city. Leon, named after a metropolis in Spain, is the center of wealthy leather industries. Anywhere along this highway the traveler may turn off the chief route to visit such fascinating *pueblos* as Torreon, Guadalajara, or Guanajuato. Back on the Central Route, Queretaro comes next, with its Hill of Bells. Here Emperor Maximilian was executed. Yet farther on lies Mexico City, a distance of 1,340 miles below Juarez. The renown of Mexico City is worldwide. Within its immediate environs are pyramids and floating gardens; a short span away tower two extinct volcanoes and a much farther space away the live crater of awesome Paracutin.

South of Mexico City, still on the Central Highway, are such historical landmarks as Puebla, Oaxaca, and Tuxtla Gutierrez. Constructed in 1531 after the pattern of its namesake in Spain, Puebla is memorable in Mexican annals. Here French ambitions met their Waterloo in 1862, and here the Revolution to overthrow President Diaz began on November 18, 1910. Because of its splendid churches, Puebla is called "The Rome of Mexico." Oaxaca, described as the "Green City" after the green rock used in its edifices, was founded by the Aztecs in 1533. The architectural thrill of Oaxaca is its Church of Santa Domingo. The "Millionaire" trees that grow so profusely there are said to live a million years. Finally, in a rich and fertile terrain, comes the smaller town of Tuxtla Gutierrez, touted in recent years as the starting place of Mexico's epic *Carrera Panamericana.*

To date there have been five races. To start the ball rolling, the El Pasoan Bill Sterling, driving a Cadillac, set a lap record in 1950 between Juarez and Chihuahua of 98.4 m.p.h. That year 132 cars entered the *Carrera.* In 1951 the number fell to 105. In 1952 the entries totalled only 91, the sum of two categories, 27 Sport and 64 Standard cars. In 1953 the figure reached 197, the largest of all five races, and comprised four classes: Heavy Sport, Heavy Stock, Small Sport, and Medium Stock. In 1954 the entries fell to 155, even though a fifth category, Light European Stock, was added. Each year the race went faster and faster. The taker of the first race, over bad country south of Mexico City, won with an average of 77.88 m.p.h.; the winner of the last race, over solid pavement all the way, averaged an incredible 108.56 m.p.h.

Winning pilots and their cars from 1950 through 1954 represented both the New World and the Old.

1950—Hershell McGriff, of the U.S.A., in an Oldsmobile 88.

1951—Piero Taruffi, of Italy, in a Ferrari.

1952—1. (Sport) Karl Kling, of Germany, in a Mercedes.
　　　2. (Standard) Chuck Stevenson, of the U.S.A., in a Lincoln.

1953—1. (Heavy Sport) Juan Fangio, of Argentina, in an Italian Lancia.
　　　2. (Heavy Stock) Chuck Stevenson, of the U.S.A., in a Lincoln.
　　　3. (Small Sport) Jose Herrarte, of Guatemala, in a German Porsche.
　　　4. (Medium Stock) C. D. Evans, of the U.S.A., in a Chevrolet.

1954—1. (Heavy Sport) Umberto Maglioli, of Italy, in a Ferrari.
　　　2. (Heavy Stock) Roy Crawford, of the U.S.A., in a Lincoln.
　　　3. (Small Sport) Hans Hermann, of Germany, in a Porsche.

4. (Medium Stock) C. D. Evans, of the U.S.A., in a Dodge.
5. (Light European Stock) M. D. Favera, of Italy, in an Alfa-Romeo.

This chart brings the *Carrera* up to the year of 1955, when no race occurred. Why not? Well, let it be understood clearly that today the Central Highway is safe for tourist travel but not for road racing. Between El Paso and Mexico City there are, however, only one or two rough places. Quite recently Professor Howard J. Sherman, of Texas Western College, found the road bad south of Parral for a stretch of 25 or 30 miles, where the pavement was broken and full of holes. Repairs were then being made. The professor said that no place was impassable but that the tourist should exercise care and drive slowly. A second rough stretch of about the same length was met near the city of Durango itself. The Honorable George Rodriguez, a well-known lawyer of El Paso, has made 8 or 10 trips to Mexico City in the past 10 years. His statements about the road agree with those of Professor Sherman. Another recent traveler of the highway was Mr. Ed Pooley, distinguished editor of the El Paso *Herald Post*. In the opinion of Mr. Pooley, the Central Route is the best road to Mexico City and by far the most interesting highway into Mexico from the States.

Today many people in the border country are concerned about the future of the contest—automobile dealers, car pilots, and experts like Tony Oliveto, who handles speed equipment. Since nobody scheduled a race for 1955, will there be one in 1956? Yes, answers the authoritative Mr. Charles J. Amador, Director of United States Racing Headquarters in El Paso. Mr. Amador says that "due to the tragedies in world sports events, as at Le Mans where a car exploded to kill 78 spectators, and the lack of safety for pedestrians and spectators, officials have decided to tighten up on safety conditions for fast racing, and President Ruiz Cortines has requested a postponement of one year." Addicts of the *Carrera* have their fingers crossed, hopefully.

10

Revolution: Agony South of the Border

The facts about the Mexican Revolution which erupted in 1910 have often been told. But for Americans, the Latin civil struggle comes into sharper focus if it is presented in terms of the Mexican leaders who fomented its early stages, particularly in connection with the political machinations of the United States south of the border.

American financiers became involved in modern Mexico through investment. One Yankee lady bought over a million acres in the southwestern Isthmus of Tehuantepec. Other Yankee investors bought more land—and whatever else they could—and President Porfirio Diaz sold it to them. By 1910 the total American investment exceeded the total capital owned by the Mexicans themselves.

The seeds of revolution, long suppressed, burst forth. Mexico became the scene of political upheavals, a succession of leaders who came to power by violence and died by violence. In 1916, on the eve of World War I, the peace-loving but harassed American President finally sent General John J. Pershing on his celebrated Punitive Expedition. Our purpose here is to set forth, leader by leader, the highlights of Mexico's agonizing political life during those violent years.

DIAZ THE DICTATOR

For over thirty years (1876-1911), Porfirio Diaz held Mexico in the shackles of his tyranny. The country had endured three centuries of iron rule, from the invasion of the Spaniards in 1519 until the native people, mostly Indians, won their independence in 1822. The people were well steeped in cruelty by the time Diaz the Dictator deposed incumbent President Lerdo, who fled to New York City.

Diaz, now known as the Strong Man of Mexico, was a Mixtec Indian with a little Spanish blood, who ascended to his high position without benefit of a full education. Stockily built, with full chest and fine head, he stood only five feet eight inches tall. He sought to conceal his relative smallness by an unusually erect posture and a penchant for riding big horses.

On December 23, 1876, Diaz became President, proclaiming his primary objective was peace. To achieve it, he resorted to harsh measures, enforcing them with an army in the cities and a strong police in the provinces. He succeeded in putting a stop to banditry, theft, murder, and rapine, and Mexico became, for the first time in many years, relatively safe for natives and travelers.

The President used his *pan o palo* (bread or the club) policy as a means of either recruiting or eliminating his enemies, the theory being that a dog with a bone in his mouth will not bite. To bandits who might unseat him, Diaz gave positions of authority, making them *rurales,* or state mounted police. Their cavalier-like costumes concealed "knights"—ruthless, cunning, daring, and often cruel. The loyalty of others came from gifts or concessions. Diaz would make a friend from an enemy by appointing him the governor of a state, and then sending a general to keep an eye on the governor. If newspapers behaved too critically, he either bought or suppressed them.

During the Diaz regime, a powerful group known as the *cientificos* arose. Composed of the ablest younger lawyers and intellectuals, this group advocated material development of the country, but regarded the natives as backward and barbarous, to be governed only by aristocrats. The peons hated and feared them.

The economic basis of the Diaz dictatorship rested on the sale of many concessions to foreigners. Thanks to his liberal policies, concessionaires flocked to Mexico. The French concentrated their interests in textile mills. The Spanish preferred retail trade, land, and tobacco fields. The English invested in oil, precious metals, public utilities, sugar, and coffee. The Americans, who held the largest concessions, owned three-quarters of the mines and more than half the oil fields, as well as large cattle ranches and sugar, coffee, cotton, rubber, orchilla, and maguey plantations.

The Diaz regime assuredly brought a measure of prosperity. Railway mileage increased from 400 to 15,000 and telegraph lines from 4,500 to 20,000 miles. New industrial plants flourished; the number of textile mills reached 146. Mining in gold and silver advanced, and the improvement of harbor facilities augmented exports and imports. The national income rose 500 per cent.

The price the commoners paid for these things, however, weighed heavily. Moreover, Dictator Diaz did comparatively nothing in the field of education. In 1900 illiteracy prevailed in Mexico. More than seventy per cent of the peons over ten years of age were unschooled. The masses lived in incredible squalor, brought on by low wages and high prices. Tax laws were loosely administered and the unbelievably low levies benefitted foreigners and the rich, not the peons. In the state of Guanajuato the land tax on all estates amounted to less than the few pesos in taxation paid by the street peddlers.

Probably the most disastrous blow to the peon, however, was the concentration of land in the hands of a few. Beginning in 1888, Diaz enforced the *Ley Lerdo,* providing for the sale of all church and corporation properties and Indian communal lands to tenants or individuals. Wealthy foreigners and Creoles who could pay the price took advantage of the law. Don Luis Terrazas of Chihuahua became the outstanding example when his estate reached a staggering 70,000,000 acres.

By the outbreak of the Revolution in 1910, almost half of Mexico's land belonged to less than three thousand families. There were, at the same time, ten million landless agricultural laborers. Land problems caused many workers to drift into industrial centers. Mexican labor, considered inferior, had its wages fixed accordingly. The accumulation of labor problems, the land policy, and the distribution of natural resources to foreign powers contributed to the collapse of the Diaz regime.

In 1908, in an interview with an American journalist, James Creelman, Diaz announced his willingness to retire, stating that he wanted the citizens to choose his successor in a free and honest election. Creelman's story appeared in Mexican newspapers, and opposition arose.

MADERO THE SAVIOR

The publication of the Creelman interview brought forth the diminutive figure of Francisco I. Madero. Five feet two inches tall, ill-shaped and delicate, with a high-pitched voice, high-domed forehead, and receding hairline, this little man hardly seemed a likely candidate to oppose the Strong Man of Mexico. Besides being a vegetarian, Madero cultivated the ouija board and communed with departed spirits. Even his wealthy Creole family considered him a bit odd. His humanitarian ideas probably resulted from his liberal education at the University of California and an engineering school in Paris.

In 1908 Madero's book, *The Presidential Succession in 1910,* was published. It called attention to evils in politics and advocated a single presidential term. Since its publication meant only the educated were informed of his ideals, Madero began making political speeches throughout Mexico. In January, 1910, in El Paso, Texas, he said to a few reporters: "Personally, we have not been harmed by Diaz, and we think that he has used his great power with much moderation, but we want full political liberty as guaranteed by the Constitution."

In April the anti-re-electionist party nominated Madero for the presidency after 30,000 of Madero's supporters demonstrated before the National Palace. Alarmed, Diaz imprisoned Madero at San Luis Potosi on a charge of plotting rebellion. With the announcement of election returns in October, Madero found that government tabulators had graciously allowed him 196 votes. He escaped from prison and disguised himself in blue overalls and straw sombrero, boarded a train and ended up in San Antonio, Texas.

There Madero published his *Plan of San Luis Potosi,* which demanded effective suffrage and a ban on re-election, the abolition of local bosses in the central government, and the restoration of lands to small owners. He further declared the recent election fraudulent, announced his provisional presidency, and called for a general insurrection on November 20, 1910.

Orozco and Villa

The revolution had an incongruous beginning. When he crossed into Mexico on November 20, Madero expected an army, but encountered only about twenty-five partisans, half of them unarmed. Disappointed, he decided to go to Europe, but stopped in New Orleans when he heard of the defeat of the state troops in Chihuahua by Pancho Villa and Pascual Orozco. In February, 1911, Madero re-entered Mexico to join the rebel forces.

Chihuahua, a northern state, had suffered acutely during the Diaz regime. The Terrazas family virtually owned and ruled the largest Mexican state.

From the poverty imposed by the Terrazas came a dark man from Durango allegedly named Doroteo Arango, alias Pancho Villa. Because his cattle-rustling and other outlaw activities made him a wanted man, he reportedly adopted the name Francisco Villa to conceal his true identity. He was called by the nickname Pancho, a variant of Francisco. His followers included lesser bandits, cow-punchers, and mule drivers.

From the southern part of Chihuahua came Pascual Orozco, a tall, gaunt mountaineer with blue eyes and a fair, freckled face. His occupation was a sometime storekeeper and a sometime muleskinner. He answered the call when the anti-re-electionist party recruited volunteers for the revolution.

The success of Orozco and Villa stimulated other uprisings throughout Mexico, but the capture of the border town of Ciudad Juarez on May 9 and 10, 1911, proved to be the decisive battle. Although Orozco and Villa had stationed their troops outside the city in preparation for battle, Madero, an eternal pacifist, had hoped to effect revolution without bloodshed. A meeting between the federals and revolutionaries ended in a deadlock when Diaz's agreement to resign carried a proviso that he would remain in office until peace returned. Madero refused to accept.

The battle of Ciudad Juarez commenced suddenly and without the knowledge of the federals or Madero. Totally disregarding Madero's orders, Orozco and Villa began to dynamite the city, which capitulated to the rebels on the second day. General Juan Navarro, commanding the federalist troops, surrendered with five hundred men.

While Villa and Orozco prepared for the execution of Navarro, Madero provided for his safe-conduct across the border to El Paso, Texas. This humanitarian act almost proved disastrous because Villa and Orozco descended upon Madero's headquarters and attempted to arrest him. By using his oratorical talents and hastily assembling his troops, Madero retained control.

Eleven days after the defeat at Juarez, Porfirio Diaz promised to resign. Commissioners from both sides prepared articles of peace. Francisco Leon de la Barra agreed to serve as provisional president until an election could be held.

Then, in November, 1911, Francisco Madero became president of Mexico. The people clamored for him to turn Mexico into Utopia. A popular verse of the day described how enthusiastic they were about having little work to do, plenty of money, and a cheap intoxicant to drink:

> Poco trabajo,
> Mucho dinero,
> Pulque barato—
> ¡Viva Madero!

When the battle of Juarez ended in victory for the rebels, Madero's father reportedly said: "I greatly fear this is the beginning of chaos for Mexico." Whether this remark reflected his knowledge of the Mexican people, or a lack of confidence in his own son, is not known.

The fact remains that the Madero regime brought no measure of peace. An idealist and a dreamer, Madero expected to lull the country into complacency by political reforms. The masses were disinterested in suffrage; they wanted land and social reforms. After Madero had been in office only a few months, Bernardo Reyes started the first rebellious uprising. When Reyes failed to win supporters, he surrendered to the authorities, who sent him to the penitentiary at Tlatelolco.

In March, 1912, Pascual Orozco launched a second serious uprising, leading a group called the Red Flaggers. He had become dissatisfied with the fifty thousand pesos and federal generalship awarded him by Madero. Reports say the glitter of Terrazas gold proved too much for him; when confronted by the Terrazas agent with a proposal to defect, he pronounced against Madero and asserted that the dreamer had betrayed his revolutionary aspirations. The president sent General Gonzales Salas to oppose Orozco, but Salas committed suicide after his decisive defeat at Rellano. General Victoriano Huerta succeeded Salas.

Pancho Villa, enjoying Madero's rewards of a meat market and a bullring in Chihuahua City, received a call to return to the federal army for service under General Huerta. The Orozco rebellion met a crushing defeat, and its originator more or less went into hiding. Orozco's former cohort, Villa, proved capable and popular during the battle.

Through jealousy and a personal quarrel over ownership of a stolen horse, Commanding General Huerta brought a trumped-up charge of defection against Pancho Villa. The intransigent Villa, though innocent of defecting from President Madero, was court-martialed and sentenced to be shot. The President's brother, Emilio Madero, intervened just in time; Villa's sentence was commuted to imprisonment in Mexico City. After a few months in prison, the wily bandit escaped and crossed into Texas at El Paso with one companion.

Zapata and Felix Diaz

From the southern state of Morelos came handsome Emiliano Zapata, a third revolutionary leader. His graceful figure, white teeth, and heavy moustache gave him a suave appearance which belied his peasant background and upbringing. His Indian blood could not tolerate the great landed proprietors who grew rich at the expense of the Indians. Organizing a band of peasants, he took back the land by burning haciendas and killing the overseers. These cruelties won him the title of the Attila of the South. His army, which included women soldiers and officers, had helped sweep away the last traces of Diaz's power. He expected Madero to supply land to his peons by immediate, direct action.

When Madero did not return the land immediately, Zapata lost confidence in him and did the only thing he knew: he started a guerrilla war, lighting a fire of revolution that would not be easily extinguished.

The fourth defector was Felix Diaz, nephew of exiled President Porfirio Diaz. His attempted revolt against Madero resulted in imprisonment at the capital along with Bernardo Reyes. The presence of these two leaders in Mexico City enabled other conspirators to plan another coup.

Persuaded by Rodolfo Reyes and Miguel Mondragon, officers in the Federal District decided to revolt. Soldiers of the Tacubaya barracks and the disaffected cadets from the military academy then released Felix Diaz and Bernardo Reyes from their prison. These two planned an attack on the National Palace for February 9, 1913. However, Gustavo Madero, brother of Francisco, heard about the plot and persuaded the palace guards to remain loyal. General Villar, who had not defected, remained in command of the Federal troops. When the rebels rode forward, expecting to take command as prearranged, they met a rain of bullets. General Reyes died, leaving Felix Diaz in full command. General Villar suffered a serious wound, necessitating his replacement by General Victoriano Huerta, a small, dark-skinned Indian, who longed for the presidency.

HUERTA AND HOMICIDE

Madero's decision to appoint Huerta as general proved disastrous, because he turned traitor by entering into a pact with Felix Diaz. History records that Henry Lane Wilson, the American ambassador, acted as a partner in this treachery. A battle was planned to cause as much damage as possible to the city, thus forcing the citizens to resort to desperate remedies for restoring peace. According to the plan, Huerta would assume the provisional presidency after Madero's elimination, until Diaz could be elected. By apparent prearrangement, ten days of battle resulted—the so-called *Decena Tragica*. According to reports, the civilian dead, too numerous to be buried, were piled together and the bodies burned.

On February 18, 1913, the triumphant Victoriano Huerta arrested President Madero and Vice President Pino Suarez. After receiving promises that they and their adherents would be allowed to retire into exile, they resigned. Señora Madero, wife of the president, called on Ambassador Wilson and begged for the life of her husband. Although Madero and Pino Suarez expected to be relased immediately, officers held them in confinement at Huerta's headquarters palace until February 22.

That evening, as they proceeded to the penitentiary, assassins removed the two from their carriage and shot them.

Many stories flourished about the exact circumstances of the killings. One version said they were shot while trying to escape. The official story maintained that in a fracas with their would-be rescuers, policemen accidentally killed the two notables. Later it was charged that only the bodies were shot to pieces because Madero and Pino Suarez had already been strangled by Huerta's hired assassins. Whatever the case, a shocked President Woodrow Wilson refused to recognize Huerta's "government by assassination."

Following Madero's death, curt telegraphic messages announced to Mexico and the world that Huerta had assumed the presidency. Mexico's self-appointed ruler, who wanted prestige and no work, was a half-blood Huichol Indian, who would tolerate no criticism. The affairs of state often had to be carried on in bars, where the nervous Huerta would be found downing his *copitas* in an effort to escape the boresome business of governing. In addition to alcohol, he was said to be addicted to narcotics.

Huerta shortly prepared to obtain the presidency legally by appointing Felix Diaz, who had been promised this office, to a military mission in Japan. He allowed the Felicistas to indulge in violent reprisals, so he could eliminate them on the pretext of re-establishing order. The elimination of the Felicistas became the least of his problems, because Huerta met with growing opposition, both inside and outside Mexico.

Great Britain, Spain, and Germany quickly recognized Huerta, but not the United States. Although Henry Lane Wilson reported to Washington that state and municipal authorities had accepted Huerta, Presiden Wilson refused to recognize him because of the questionable death of Madero, the fact that no election had been held, and Huerta's control of only the capital and a small portion of Mexico open toward the Gulf.

Huerta's relations inside Mexico caused him even more anxiety. On February 19, 1913, Venustiano Carranza, governor of Coahuila, announced that he would not recognize Huerta—this to avenge the death of Madero. Carranza's *Plan of Guadalupe,* issued in March, called for a national uprising to overthrow Huerta. Meanwhile, Governor Carranza assumed the pompous title of the First Chief of the Constitutionalist Army.

Moreover, Huerta had difficulty with Zapata, who wrenched Cuernavaca from his control. The city capitulated through the machinations of Helene Pontipirani, a beautiful Rumanian spy, who was liaison between Zapata and Villa. Zapata, who was to be assassinated by a Carranza henchman in 1919, now returned to the south.

Huerta remained to face a rebounding Villa, because Madero's demise relaunched his spectacular career. Following his escape from prison in Mexico City and his flight north, Villa watched Mexico from the border town of El Paso. On March 13, 1913, with a band of eight he crossed the Rio Grande into Mexico. By reckless bravery, he took town after town, collecting troops along the way. Villa's army soon rolled up a staggering number of victories over the Federals, making him the undisputed rebel leader of Chihuahua.

In April, 1913, the unfortunate incidents at Tampico and Veracruz occurred. At Tampico, Huerta's soldiers arrested some American Marines from the gunboat *Dolphin* for being in a restricted area. After one and a half hours, the Mexicans released them with an apology.

The Yankee commander demanded a twenty-one-gun salute; Huerta's refusal brought the American fleet into the Gulf of Mexico. On April 21, 1913, Woodrow Wilson ordered the seizure of Veracruz to prevent the delivery of machine guns and ammunition by the German merchant ship *Ypiranga*. This decision cost the lives of almost two hundred Mexicans and sixteen Americans.

Huerta tried in vain to use the incidents at Tampico and Veracruz to unite Mexico. Many revolutionaries hotly resented what they considered a violation of Mexico's sovereign rights; however, they continued to accept and fire the arms furnished by the United States. Then Pancho Villa won credit for the downfall of Huerta—by a victory at Zacatecas.

In July, with Villa, Carranza, and Zapata closing in, President Huerta deserted the capital and sailed for Spain. He returned in 1914, only to be arrested by immigration authorities for planning a revolt while on United States territory. He lived for a while under loose arrest at Fort Bliss, where he attracted the sympathy of several American officers, including General John J. Pershing. He died in El Paso in January, 1916, before he was brought to trial.

CARRANZA THE DUCK

Victoriano Huerta's exit brought Venustiano Carranza to the forefront of the Mexican scene. Like Madero, his ancestors were Spanish and owned extensive land. Unlike Madero, bespectacled Carranza had an imposing appearance—tall and strongly built, with side-whiskers and a flowing white beard. His stubborn determination and strong will brought him the sobriquet "Carranza the Duck."

Five days after the surrender of federal troops on August 10, 1914, General Alvaro Obregon occupied Mexico City for Carranza. This infuriated Pancho Villa, whose march toward the capital halted when Carranza cut off the coal supply. Thus the open break between Villa and Carranza began. Other revolutionaries in Sonora objected to Carranza's occupation of the federal seat. The only alternative was to call a convention to decide who should become President of Mexico.

Aguascalientes, midway between the Villa and Carranza camps, became the site of the convention, called in October. Deliberations quickly became deadlocked, after which Villa proposed to commit suicide if Carranza would do the same. When Carranza did not agree, the delegates compromised at last on General Eulalio Gutierrez. However, the Carrancista sympathizers turned from him to Carranza. This left Gutierrez with Villa and Zapata as his only important supporters. Obregon also returned very quickly to support "The Duck."

Villa and his army moved toward Mexico City as Carranza fell back to Veracruz. Before Villa reached the capital, his ally, Zapata, arrived from the south to take possession. Private citizens, terrified by Zapata's savage reputation, were pleasantly surprised when his occupation proved quiet and orderly. Villa arrived in December. As a result of a conference at Xochimilco, the two Indian chiefs made a double entry into Mexico City, parading their armies down a boulevard jammed with spectators.

While Villa and Zapata lolled around the capital, Carranza conducted his own government in Veracruz. He strongly resented any interference with his will, and his will was to become president. To counter the reforms demanded by Villa and Zapata, he announced a series of decrees, the major one dealing with land. For the first time, the Revolution took on real meaning for the people. The rebels might now fight for a better life instead of revolutionary glory and loot.

OBREGON AND CALLES

Carranza was not a miltary man. Credit for his military campaigns belonged to other men, the most prominent being stalwart, one-armed Alvaro Obregon. Heavy, muscular and of medium height, Obregon had a round, rather Irish-looking face. He was from a rural area near Alamos, Sonora. Before he entered the revolution, he worked as a factory mechanic. Although better qualified for leadership himself, Obregon chose to support Carranza. After assisting Carranza with political reforms at Veracruz, he returned to the battlefield, defeating rebel elements at Puebla while Villa remained in Mexico City. From Puebla, Obregon marched toward the great city, forcing Zapata to withdraw. No sooner had he re-entered the capital than Obregon set out to settle the score with Villa once and for all.

Obregon camped his army at Celaya. He had unbridled respect for the military talents of his audacious enemy and planned the battle with precision. He strung miles of barbed wire, dug trenches and stationed his Yaqui Indians in the front trenches with machine guns. There he awaited Villa's cavalry charge. In April, 1915, action began. Three times in three days, Villa charged his cavalry, but his brute force could not match Obregon's machine guns and barbed wire. Villa was forced to flee northward, his defeat marking the turning point in his turbulent life.

One of the most redoubtable figures of the Revolution, Alvaro Obregon won wide favor in the United States. General Pershing, for one, had a high personal regard for him; during the Punitive Expedition, Obregon cooperated with the Americans. He seemed to have a clearer understanding of the American mission than had Carranza. Moreover, he thoroughly detested Pancho Villa.

Another prominent figure in the Mexican Revolution was Plutarco Elias Calles, a large and rather fierce man who headed Carranza's army in Sonora. After the defeat at Celaya, Villa decided to attack northern Sonora. Although his army had been slightly weakened, he led a force about twice the size of the one assembled by Calles at Agua Prieta. Unknown to Villa,

Carranza had asked and secured permission from the Yankees to move his troops over American territory. These reinforcements enabled the lion-featured Calles to inflict a crushing defeat upon Villa at Agua Prieta, leading to the dispersement of the Villistas at Santa Isabel in December, 1915.

Earlier, in October, the United States had recognized Carranza as the head of Mexico. Villa now rallied against America for its interference, and there was some obvious justification for his resentment.

During the Revolution, occupants of the Mexican presidential chair changed frequently. Leaders were seated and unseated, no one appearing to be certain who should claim the right to remain there.

Villa had his picture taken in it, with Zapata sitting beside him, although these two Indians never obtained the political right to rule.

The following list of Mexico's deposed presidents from 1911 through 1928 leaves little doubt as to the aspirations of the other revolutionary chiefs. The roster extends as late as the term of the bolshevik Plutarco Elias Calles because his ascendancy to the office was implemented, in part, by his victory over Villa at Agua Prieta. Venustiano Carranza, in accordance with the "plan of Tuxtepec" which prevented him from succeeding himself, served two separate terms of varying length which were followed by interim office-holders who were his opponents.

1. Francisco Leon de la Barra (Interim President) resigned November 6, 1911.
2. Francisco I Madero (1911-1913) died by assassination February 19, 1913.
3. Pedro Lascurain (Interim President for 28 minutes) became president for one day only, February 19, 1913.
4. Victoriano Huerta (Interim President) sailed for Spain in July, 1913.
5. Francisco Carbajal (Interim President) resigned July 15, 1914.
6. Venustiano Carranza (First Chief) served until the following November.
7. Eulalio M. Gutierrez (Provisional President) received his appointment, November 10, 1914.
8. Roque Gonzalez (Provisional President) came into office January 16, 1915.

9. Francisco L. Chazaro (Provisional President) replaced his predecessor July 31, 1915.
10. Venustiano Carranza (Constitutional President) came again to power, serving officially until his assassination May 24, 1920.
11. Adolfo de la Huerta (Interim President) held office from 1920 to 1921.
12. Alvaro Obregon (President) won the election in 1921 and died by assassination in 1928.
13. Plutarco Elias Calles (President) governed from 1924 to 1928.

American interest in the revolution focused directly on the progress of Mexico and Pershing's Expedition into that country. During the Diaz regime, as previously noted, Yankees of wealth and influence had acquired multiple properties. The revolution threatened their continued ownership, and they applied political pressure for American intervention. President Wilson refused to recognize the murderer of Madero, sending his personal representative, John Lind, to Mexico City to arrange a free presidential election and receive Huerta's promise not to be a candidate.

At first Wilson resisted armed intervention, but he resorted to it when the threat from Huerta arose. Wilson's decision to favor Carranza meant the Americans denied arms to Villa. This rebel leader suffered an unexpected defeat when the United States permitted the Carranzistas to travel by American railway through New Mexico from Del Rio, Texas, to Douglas, Arizona, crossing from Piedras Negras in Coahuila all the way to Agua Prieta in Sonora. Villa further claimed that in his night attack the Yankees operated high-powered searchlights against him. He turned his wrath against the United States, culminating in the fateful attack on Columbus, New Mexico.

The earlier American seizure of Veracruz embittered all warring factions against the United States, even though President Wilson afterward lifted the embargo on munitions which had aided the Carranzistas. Carranza's attitude led to the encouragement of Villa by certain wealthy Yankee businessmen in Mexico. Wall Street energetically urged Villa's recognition by the United States.

Historically, among educated Mexicans, two attitudes prevailed toward the Yankee involvement in the agony across the southern border. One group contended the Americans should have ob-

served a strict hands-off policy. Another group believed the only
way Mexico could avoid further bloodshed and the assassination
of one president after another was for the Americans to intervene
and take a firm grip on internal policies.

The poorer elements had yet a different view. The success of
foreigners—especially Americans—in Mexico brought a violent
protest from the peons. Their rancor could be understood, since
foreigners seemed to own everything and even had a hand in the
government. Because of the closeness of America, the Mexicans
vented their anti-foreign sentiments principally against *gringos*.
The incidents at Veracruz and Tampico, especially, threatened
Mexico's national dignity.

At the same time, Mexicans feared the United States, remembering the defeat in the war of 1846-1848 and the further loss
of territory by the Gadsden Treaty of 1853. These factors, together with Porfirio Diaz's unending concessions to American
investors, lay at the base of Mexico's bitter resentment.

When President Wilson's agent, George C. Carothers, suggested to Carranza and Villa that the people hold an election in
1915 and vote for the candidate of their choice, Villa strenuously
protested. He denounced the proposal as interference. He bluntly
told Carothers that he would personally kill the next agent
Wilson sent to Mexico.

In March, 1916, General John J. Pershing led his Punitive
Expedition into Chihuahua state in pursuit of Villa in reprisal
for the attack on Columbus, New Mexico. While the Americans
never caught the leader of the New Mexican assault, Pershing's
long sojourn in Chihuahua state—eleven months—united the
whole country under Carranza.

The Mexican Revolution that began in 1910 continues to
influence the course of the Mexican Republic; its dominant
political body is still called "Revolutionary Institutional Party."
Looking back to those unstable years, Pershing's mission in
Mexico seems to have achieved salutary results. Although con-
temporarily resented by the Mexican people and their political
leaders, the Expedition had one prime—if temporary—attain-
ment. It was the establishment of a more orderly and less san-
guinary solution to the critical problems that had climaxed in
1910 to spawn the last grand revolution in history.

After a brief respite following Pershing's departure, the turmoil in Mexico soon commenced anew, though never again so bloodily as before. In the view of most experts, the Revolution lasted at least until 1920. Many writers on the subject contend that it still goes on—though in peaceful ways with the presidency being decided by legal popular elections. The agony of 1910-20 endures no more.

Strife between America and its southern neighbor has of course long since ended, with the agreement to return the hitherto disputed Chamizal land strip to Mexico in 1963 and the replacement of Project Intercept (on smuggling narcotics) by Project Cooperation in 1970. Our neighbor now is both a peaceful and a prosperous country. As old edifices and ancient institutions give way, new skyscrapers and modern technology replace them. The *Republica* today exhibits a benign visage, assuring her of a future of rich promise and continued achievement.